THE CORONA LIBRARY
FIJI

SUVA MARKET

FIJI

BY

SIR ALAN BURNS G.C.M.G.

A Fijian Island

LONDON

HER MAJESTY'S STATIONERY OFFICE

1963

First published 1963

© *Crown copyright* 1963
Published by
HER MAJESTY'S STATIONERY OFFICE
To be purchased from
York House, Kingsway, London w.c.2
423 Oxford Street, London w.1
13A Castle Street, Edinburgh 2
109 St. Mary Street, Cardiff
39 King Street, Manchester 2
50 Fairfax Street, Bristol 1
35 Smallbrook, Ringway, Birmingham 5
80 Chichester Street, Belfast 1
or through any bookseller

Price £1 10s. od. net

*Printed in England under the authority of Her Majesty's Stationery Office
by Butler and Tanner Ltd., Frome and London*

THE CORONA LIBRARY

A series of illustrated volumes under the sponsorship of the Colonial Office dealing with the United Kingdom's dependent territories, the way their peoples live, and how they are governed. The series has been designed to fill the place between official Blue Books on the one hand and the writings of occasional visitors on the other, to be authoritative and readable, and to give a vivid yet accurate picture. The books are being written by established authors whose qualifications include, where possible, experience of colonial administration and first-hand knowledge of the territory concerned. Neither Her Majesty's Government in the United Kingdom nor the Governments of the territories necessarily associate themselves with the personal views expressed by the authors. Each volume will contain maps and be fully illustrated.

FOREWORD TO THE CORONA LIBRARY

By the Rt. Hon. Sir Winston S. Churchill

K.G., O.M., C.H., M.P.

NOT since the days of the Roman Empire has a single nation carried so great a responsibility for the lives of men and women born outside her shores as Great Britain does today. Within her forty or so dependent territories dwell eighty million people for whose welfare and enlightenment Britain is, to a greater or lesser degree, answerable.

There has been no lack of critics, at home and abroad, to belittle Britain's colonial achievement and to impugn her motives. But the record confounds them. Look where you will, you will find that the British have ended wars, put a stop to savage customs, opened churches, schools and hospitals, built railways, roads and harbours, and developed the natural resources of the countries so as to mitigate the almost universal, desperate poverty. They have given freely in money and materials and in the services of a devoted band of Civil Servants; yet no tax is imposed upon any of the colonial peoples that is not spent by their own governments on projects for their own good.

I write 'their own governments' advisedly, for however much diverse conditions may necessitate different approaches, the British have for long had one goal in view for their overseas territories: their ultimate development into nations freely associated with the Commonwealth framework. The present state of the Commonwealth is the proof of the sincerity of this policy.

It is because I believe that Britain's colonial record is too little known and her policies too little understood that I welcome the books of the Corona Library. The aim of these books is to present a contemporary portrait, at once reliable and attractive, of each territory. I warmly commend the series to the attention of the public at home and abroad, for if these publications do even a little to clear away the clouds of misunderstanding and prejudice that have gathered round the very idea of colonial government, they will have been well worth while.

Winston S. Churchill

(*Chartwell, September 1956.*)

vii

CONTENTS

ILLUSTRATIONS

xi

DRAWINGS AND MAPS

JACKET by Liz Moore

DRAWINGS by Jane Coats

FOLDING MAP at the end of volume by Directorate of Overseas Surveys

DRAWINGS

A Fijian island (title page); Fijian *bure* (page 6); cannibal fork (page 27); double canoe (page 31); *tabua* (page 39); wooden head rest and cosmetic dish (page 42); toad (page 54); types of war club (page 69); Fijian village (page 74); Devil's thumb, Ovalau (page 123); two shells (page 148); bamboo raft (page 157); beating a *lali* (page 173); mangrove tree (page 193); reef heron (page 203); hibiscus (page 214).

MAPS

ENDPAPERS

Fijian bark-cloth from the collection of the Royal Commonwealth Institute.

ACKNOWLEDGEMENT

We are grateful to Mr. Rob Wright for his photographs.

PREFACE

IN 1950 I spent a few days in Fiji on my way to and from Western Samoa when, as chairman of a Visiting Mission of the United Nations, I went to the four Trust Territories in the Pacific. In 1959 I was in Fiji for three months as chairman of a Commission of Enquiry into Land and Population Problems in the colony. Unfortunately, I did not then know that I should be asked to write this book for the Corona Series, but, in the course of the investigations carried out by the Commission, I learnt something of conditions in Fiji and visited the more important centres.

I was however too fully engaged in taking evidence from witnesses and studying reports to be able to see much of life in the villages and the more remote parts of the islands. I am therefore glad that Mr. R. T. Sanders, an Administrative Officer in Fiji since 1950, most of whose service has been in the country districts, has agreed to contribute a chapter to this volume which fills what would otherwise have been a gap in the account.

In the other chapters, for which I alone am responsible, I have quoted and drawn freely from the Commission's report of which I was a part-author. Before and after my visit I read a great number of official reports and books dealing with the territory, and have had the advantage of help from several people who knew and know Fiji well.

First among these I place the late Mr. R. A. Derrick, the historian of Fiji, from whose works I was able to gain much information. Shortly before his death Mr. Derrick had sent me some useful answers to various questions I had asked and had promised further help, of which, alas, I have been deprived.

Secondly, I must thank Mr. Robert Strick, of the Fiji Administrative Service, for helping me to get information which otherwise I might have had difficulty in obtaining.

The Governor, Sir Kenneth Maddocks, and the Colonial Secretary, Mr. P. D. Macdonald, kindly put sundry reports and papers at my disposal, as did Mr. F. Mallam, the London representative of the Colonial Sugar Refining Company.

I am grateful also to the staff of the Colonial Office, especially Mr. B. Cheeseman and Miss B. H. Fricke of the Library; Mr. H. P. Hall and Miss M. Fairlie of the Pacific Department; and Mr. O. H. Morris and Miss M. E. J. Orna of the Information Department, for the great help they have given me. I am indebted for the same reason to Mr. D. Grant, Miss J. C. Lindeck and Mr. R. D. Binfield of the Central Office of Information.

ALAN BURNS

London, 23rd February, 1962.

INTRODUCTION TO FIJI

To those of us who live in England the colony of Fiji seems very far away, and it is, indeed, as far away in time as it is possible to be—twelve hours by the clock. So when it is five o'clock this afternoon in London it is five o'clock tomorrow morning in Suva, the capital of Fiji.

The 180th meridian of longitude passes through the colony, and although for most of its way this meridian forms the international date line, the date line deviates slightly to bring all the Fiji islands to the west of it. It is said that before this deviation was agreed upon an enterprising shopkeeper was able to evade Sunday closing, and do business for seven days a week, by maintaining that the meridian passed through his shop, so that when it was Sunday at one end of the shop it was Saturday or Monday at the other!

It was because the first information about Fiji was gathered from the Tongans that the name of the colony is spelt and pronounced as it is today, although the name of the largest island, Viti Levu, pronounced Vee-tee Lev-oo (Great Fiji), is still spelt and pronounced in the original local fashion. The Tongan pronunciation sounded like Feejee, and this was the spelling used by the explorer, Captain James Cook, who had heard about the Fijians at Tonga in 1774. Other writers followed his example, although the shorter form of Fiji was later adopted, and the inhabitants became known as Fijians. They, however, call themselves 'I Taukei', or 'owners of the land', a title which expresses the value they place on this ownership.

Apart from this, the spelling and pronunciation of most names in Fiji are difficult for the visitor, as the system of orthography adopted by the Wesleyan missionaries who reduced the Fijian language to writing in the middle of the nineteenth century used some of the letters of the Roman alphabet to express sounds common to the Fijian language which are quite different from the sounds of the same letters as used in English. For example, the letter *c* is pronounced as *th* in *that*, and *b* is given the combined sound of *mb*. The name of the famous chief Cakobau, who ceded Fiji to Queen Victoria in 1874, was originally spelt Thakombau, and it is still so pronounced, the last syllable rhyming with *now*. In the same way, *d* is given the sound of *nd* and *g* the sound of *ng*. Philatelists will remember that *Toga* is the form of the name appearing from 1896 to 1950 on the postage stamps of the Kingdom of Tonga, the nearest neighbour of Fiji. Most confusing of all is the use of the letter *q* to express the sound *ngg*.

The traveller arriving by air is told that his plane will alight at an airfield spelt on the maps, as it is pronounced, Nandi,

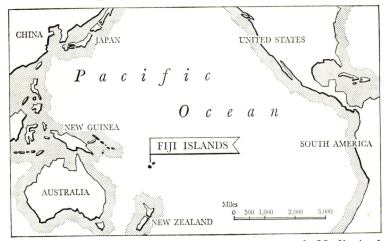

but will find that in Fiji the name is always spelt Nadi. And the visitor to Suva can see in the distance the island shown on the maps as Mbengga and is puzzled by the local spelling, which is Beqa. In old books and maps, and in the majority of modern ones, Fijian place names are spelt phonetically as in English; in the official annual report on Fiji for the year 1960 the airport is referred to in the text (prepared in Fiji) as Nadi but in the attached map as Nandi.

In this book the official standard spelling, as laid down by the Committee on Geographical Place Names for Official Use, is followed for all place names, which are pronounced as spelt (with the local spelling sometimes indicated in brackets to avoid confusion). Personal names, however, and Fijian words, are spelt in the local fashion, and although to the majority of those outside Fiji the correct pronunciation of words so spelt is perhaps of little importance, for those who wish to use it the following table will be a sufficient guide:

> *b* is pronounced as *mb* in *timber*
> *c*   as *th* in *thy* (not as in *thigh*)
> *d*   as *nd* in *band*
> *g*   as *ng* in *bang*
> *q*   as *ngg* in *younger*.

Another difficulty, and a fruitful trap for the unwary, is the similarity of Fijian names. For example, the small island of Mbau (locally spelt Bau), which is close to Viti Levu, can easily be confused by a hurried reader with Mbua (Bua), on Vanua Levu.

By those early navigators who sighted the islands from a distance, and even by later seamen who brought their ships to anchor close to land, there was little to be seen of Fiji but mountains and trees—on the low-lying coral islets nothing but coconut trees and on the higher islands a fringe of coconut trees along the beaches backed by thickly forested mountains. Only occasionally would the thatched roofs of houses in small villages be visible among the trees.

Today, in most cases, the view from seaward would be similar, but in the two main islands there is a change. On my first visit to Fiji, as the aircraft in which I was travelling approached the airport of Nandi (Nadi), I could see the sugar factory and other modern buildings in the town of Lautoka, and the light green of extensive sugar-cane fields which lie between the sea and the central massif of mountains. On a later visit, arriving by steamer at Suva, I was struck by the prosperous appearance of the city and a better acquaintance did not change the favourable first impressions, in spite of the tumble-down condition of the wharf at which the steamer moored. The earliest European visitors could not have expected such a change from the Viti Levu that they knew.

There has, however, been no change in the grandeur of the mountains, the greenness of the trees, and the beauty of the water within the reefs, calm and peaceful, in contrast to the rolling seas outside. As Professor G. C. Henderson, the Australian writer, has said, 'there is not one island in the Fijian archipelago that is not rich in scenes of surpassing loveliness: the rainbow colours that adorn the reefs or hover and quiver about the spray that dashes over them; sub-aqueous gardens in which multicoloured plants grow round patches of branching coral; flowering trees and shrubs gorgeous with the most vivid colours; mountain torrents with their sparkling waters rushing and swirling round dark grey boulders; dense forests where creepers hang like garlands from tree to tree whose branches are decked with orchids; limestone crags and hills through which subterranean streams cut their way past stalagmites and stalactites; places silent and aware—haunted with memories of crimes in days gone by—all or nearly all can be seen in every island of the archipelago. There is romance everywhere in Fiji, witchery and enchantment too.'

To me it was the glory of the sunsets and the colours of the water produced by passing clouds that were the most enchanting, together with the appearance of the people. Tall, strongly built Fijians in their national dress, many of them with great mops of hair; graceful Indian women in their saris; and Europeans in light tropical clothing; all seemed to fit into the scene and lend it colour.

The poet Rupert Brooke, who was in Fiji shortly before the first world war, wrote enthusiastically in his letters of the islands and the people: 'The sunsets here! the colour of the water over the reefs! the gloom and terror of those twisted mountains! and the extraordinary contrasts in the streets and the near country—for there are fifty thousand Hindoos, indentured labour, here, emaciated and proud, in Liberty-coloured garments, mournful, standing out among these gay, pathetic, sturdy children, the Fijians.' While staying in the mountainous interior he wrote: 'Fiji in moonlight is like nothing else in this world or the next. It's all dim colours and all scents. And here, where it's high up, the most fantastically shaped mountains in the world tower up all around, and little silver clouds and wisps of mist run bleating up and down the valleys and hillsides like lambs looking for their mother.' He spoke of the Fijians as 'these dear, good people, with their laughter and friendliness and crowns of flowers'.

*

From the point of view of the tourist Fiji has much to offer, and geographically and climatically is in an ideal position. It is sufficiently far north to attract Australians and New Zealanders who wish to escape the winter of the southern hemisphere and offers a tropical climate to those in the United States and Canada who seek to avoid the rigours of the northern winter. It is easily reached by sea or air. Passenger ships running from Australian and New Zealand ports to ports on the west coast of North America—Vancouver, San Francisco and Los Angeles—call regularly at Suva. Nandi airport can accommodate modern jet airliners and is a regular staging post on the route between Sydney and San Francisco via Honolulu. It is only about four hours by jet aircraft from Sydney and seven hours from Honolulu.

Within the colony the small aircraft of Fiji Airways run services from Nandi to Nausori airport, twelve miles from Suva, and to small runways on the islands of Vanua Levu and Taveuni. There is a motor road round Viti Levu which for most of the way follows the coast; it is narrow and dusty with numerous turns and twists, but to the visitor there are objects of interest to be seen all along the route.

Probably the first thing to be noticed by the tourist would be a small steam locomotive drawing a long line of trucks loaded with sugar-cane to the mill. On certain days he might see something unique, the same locomotive drawing a number of trucks almost over-loaded with humanity, people having a ride on what is probably the only free railway in the world. When the Colonial Sugar Refining Company obtained its concession to construct a railway line through the sugar-cane areas, one of the terms on which the concession was granted was that a train for the free conveyance of passengers should be run from end to end of the line once or twice a week, according to the season, on a schedule approved by the government, and this free service has been given for more than fifty years.

Along the road between Nandi and Suva might also be seen, at different times of the year, cane farmers ploughing their land with bullocks or cutting the cane and loading it into railway trucks. Even when no work was visible there would be the light green of the growing cane in the fields between the road and the mountains which seem to be thrusting their peaks up into the clouds. On the other side of the road would be perhaps a sandy or a rocky beach with a smooth sea between it and the offshore reefs.

In the small towns through which the road passes there are well-built modern houses and shops and at certain hours numbers of small boys and girls, Indian and Fijian, going to or returning from school, in neat uniforms and with bright cheerful faces. In the villages along the road there are typical Fijian houses, the *bure*, with thatched roofs and sides, the interiors in

Fijian *bure*

many cases decorated with bark-cloth strips in various designs. This bark-cloth is known as *masi* in Fiji and as *tapa* in other parts of the Pacific. Everywhere the first and most striking impression that one gets is of the friendliness of the people.

The visitor who is not prepared to face the long drive of 139 miles from Nandi to Suva can fly in a small aircraft to Nausori, over the mountains and plateaux that lie between, and if he is lucky enough to make the journey on a clear day is rewarded by magnificent views of the wild country beneath him and the distant sea, with other islands in the distance. In the short drive from Nausori airport to Suva, the visitor crosses the largest river, the Rewa, by a fine bridge, and passes the Agricultural Department station at Koronivia before entering the city, the streets of which seem to be full of more motor vehicles and pedestrians than one would expect.

Suva, which has a population of over 43,000, is the administrative headquarters, the largest town, and the busiest port of the colony. There are many fine churches, public buildings, business premises, and, particularly in the suburbs, well-built private residences. At one end of the city, standing on a hill in beautiful grounds, is Government House, which was completed in 1928 after the original Government House had been struck by lightning and burnt down some six years earlier. As a token of loyalty and sympathy for the homeless Governor, a large *bure*, in traditional style, was built by the Fijians for his use until the new house was erected. It was built entirely of local woods, with close and accurate thatching, the pillars and beams encircled with patterns of coir braid, and is said to have been a striking and beautiful example of Fijian house building.

Adjoining the Government House grounds, in the area where the original Suva village once stood, are the Botanical Gardens where many interesting tropical plants and trees are to be seen. Within the Gardens is the Fiji Museum which contains a valuable collection of specimens of Fijian culture, models of war canoes, and two of the actual huge steering oars of these craft.

Separated by a street from the Botanical Gardens, and immediately behind the Grand Pacific Hotel, is Albert Park, where at different seasons cricket, hockey, 'rugger' and 'soccer' games are played before large and enthusiastic audiences. The Fijians are very keen on games and generally very good players. Rugger was introduced after the first world war and quickly became popular with the Fijians, to whose temperament and physique it appears particularly well suited. Until they began to play against overseas teams the Fijian players seldom wore boots. I saw two interesting games in Suva in 1959 between Fijian players and a team from Tonga, both sides consisting of large and powerful men who tackled strongly and never seemed to lose their tempers. During one game the wind was blowing so strongly across the field that when the ball went into touch it had to be retrieved by a small boy from a long distance, while to save time another ball was brought into play at the line-out. Fijian 'rugger' teams have played in Australia and

New Zealand, and a visit to England by a Fijian side would certainly be a popular attraction.

At cricket also the physique of the Fijians stands them in good stead, particularly as hitters. Tall even by Fijian standards, *Ratu* K. K. T. Mara, an administrative officer, is said once in 1959 to have hit a towering six, the ball landing some 133 yards from the wicket. Another hitter, Nacanieli Uluiviti, during the same year scored 40 in one eight-ball over with 6 sixes and 1 four. Altogether in that innings he hit 8 sixes and 2 fours before being caught for 74. Nearly all Fijian cricketers are big hitters.

In a chapter by Philip Snow in *Cricket Heroes*, tribute is paid to a great Fijian hitter, generally known as 'Bula', who made more than 1,000 runs in 29 innings in New Zealand in 1948. The full name of this very popular batsman ran to sixty-two letters, but for convenience only the first two syllables of the name were entered in the score-book. In the same chapter is a reference to the impressions made on the New Zealand public by the Fijian players, 'figures in gleaming white shirts and skirts, with noble heads of hair, shiny bronze legs flashing in the sun, brilliant white teeth radiating natural good will in the dignified features of the Pacific islanders'.

The Indians do not play 'rugger' but play 'soccer' and hockey, while cricket is more or less multi-racial. There is, however, little mixing of the races in sport. Of the various clubs in Suva the most interesting is the Union which has members of all races who meet there on a very friendly basis. Although a large majority of the members are Indians, care is taken to see that the Fijians are well represented on the committee. Suva harbour offers good opportunities for yachting and at week-ends is gay with small sailing boats. There are golf-courses and tennis courts at the larger centres.

Since 1956 there has been held every year at Suva a Hibiscus Festival organized by a committee which includes all races and affords the opportunity (not too common in Fiji) for multi-racial co-operation and harmony. For a week the city is given over to the carnival spirit, and processions, games, and such special items as fire-walking entertain large crowds, including passengers from cruise ships. There is a beauty competition which differs from those in most other countries in that the competitors are not required to wear bathing dresses; the winners are chosen, according to the rules, 'for their physical beauty, personality, conversation and dress sense'.

One very interesting place in Viti Levu is Nandarivatu, where there is a Forestry Department station some 2,600 feet above sea level. It is reached by a steep and winding motor road and the view from the station is superb. At this elevation fruit and vegetables generally found in temperate zones flourish remarkably, besides mahoganies and other tropical trees.

In each of the main centres there is at least one hotel which offers reasonable comfort and in the larger towns the standard is naturally higher. In most of the hotels imported meat, poultry and vegetables are served at all meals, with tropical fruit and sometimes local dishes. At one hotel in which I stayed for several weeks curry was on the menu at every luncheon, the geographical description of the curry changing from day to day—Bengal curry, Madras curry, Singapore curry, etc. As they all seemed to me to be the same I once asked the old Indian waiter what difference there was between them all. After profound thought he pointed out that the names were different. It did not greatly matter as they were all good.

There is one charming hotel at Korolevu where the guests live in separate *bure* which externally are built in Fijian fashion with thatched roofs but inside are provided with 'all modern conveniences'. There is a central dining-room and lounge, also in Fijian style, and a sandy beach from which to swim. From the tourists' point of view the drawback of Suva is the absence of nearby beaches, but there is a good municipal swimming bath. At the hotels the *lali*, a drum made from a hollowed log, is often used instead of a gong to summon visitors to meals, and it has also been used instead of a church bell.

For the visitor who has time to visit other islands there is much to see. Flights to these offer different views from those seen on the Nandi–Nausori flight but they are no less spectacular as the aircraft passes over coral reefs and a sea which seems to be always changing its colour. In one flight, from Nausori to the northern end of Taveuni, the aircraft passes near to the eastern face of the high mountain range which forms the backbone of the island, with a peak of over 4,000 feet above sea level.

High in the mountains, its surface some 2,200 feet above the

9

sea, is a crater lake well worth seeing but difficult of access. Much of the lake surface is covered by floating sedges and the water near the shore is of a greenish hue, caused by submerged vegetation. This explanation, however, is very prosaic and less popular than the legend that the colour comes from the green fat of the turtles killed on Taveuni, which is taken to the lake by spirits. The lake is not visible from aircraft on their regular flights, but all along the face of the mountain range numerous streams, probably more than a hundred, can be seen rushing down the steep slopes or plunging over cliffs into the sea.

There is a road along the western shore of Taveuni, from the northern to the southern end of the island, passing over several streams and watercourses by means of paved causeways. The watercourses are sometimes quite dry but after heavy rain in the mountains may suddenly become roaring torrents which are impassable to traffic.

Along this road there are large well-equipped coconut plantations which are generally better managed than any others in Fiji. The soil of Taveuni is rich and deep and the island has long been known as the 'Garden of Fiji'. In the early days of European settlement cotton, and later sugar, were grown and tropical fruit grows easily. Cattle and poultry are also raised and on some estates cattle graze on the grass beneath the coconut trees and help to keep down the undergrowth. Some of the European familes living on Taveuni have been there for three or four generations, and it was in the hospitable house of one settler that I spent one of the most amusing and instructive evenings of my visit to Fiji.

Across a narrow sea channel from Taveuni is Vanua Levu, the second largest island of the group. The principal town is Lambasa (Labasa) on the northern coast, where there is a mill of the South Pacific Sugar Mills, Ltd., which processes the cane grown in the fields east and west of the town. Some of the cane is grown in areas which were formerly mangrove swamps and are now protected by sea-walls. There are good motor roads from Lambasa to various points on the island. At the western end of Vanua Levu, but not accessible by road, lies Mbua Bay, where British and American ships came early in the nineteenth century to obtain sandalwood, the beginning of overseas trade with and interest in Fiji.

Beyond the mountain ridge which lies between the northern and southern shores of Vanua Levu is the small town of Savu-savu, where the Hot Springs Hotel is only a few yards from the boiling springs which give it its name and provide it with hot water. Stepping rashly under the shower on the first morning there I received a shock which made my approach more cautious on the next occasion.

From Savusavu there is a good road, the so-called Hibiscus Highway, which passes through extensive coconut groves to the end of the curiously shaped Natewa peninsula. From the end of this road one can see, not far away, the two small islands of Rambi (Rabi) and Kioa.

Rambi, which was occupied by Tongans from 1855 to 1860, was then sold to Europeans and was for a time owned by Lever Brothers. In 1942 it was bought on behalf of the Banabans from overcrowded Ocean Island, but almost immediately afterwards Ocean Island was occupied by the Japanese and it was not until 1945 (after abominable treatment by the invaders) that the Banabans were able to move to their new home; they now number about 1,300. The Fijians, with their usual hospitality, were most helpful to the newcomers, assisting them with their house-building and showing them how to plant the local crops.

Kioa was acquired from its chief by a European shipmaster in 1853 in return for conveying a large number of passengers from Somosomo to Mbau, and, after passing through several hands, was bought with their own money in 1947 by the Polynesian people of the island of Vaitupu, in the Ellice Group, where the land was insufficient for the growing population.

One of the most interesting islands, which can easily be visited by ship, is Ovalau, which was the first Fijian island to be settled in any numbers by Europeans. Commodore Wilkes, in his account of Fiji written in 1845, said that 'each island had its own peculiar beauty, but the eye as well as mind felt more satisfaction in resting upon Ovalau'. The only town is Levuka, once the capital of the colony, most picturesquely crowded between the mountains and the sea; some of the houses can only be reached by long flights of steps up the steep mountain-side. In the town a monument stands on the spot where the Deed of Cession was signed in 1874. At the same place and hour on the 10th October 1924, fifty years later, the same *lali*, or native drum, was beaten by the old Fijian who had beaten it at the ceremony of Cession. In the tower of the Catholic church at Levuka there is a French clock which strikes each hour twice.

From Levuka there is a motor road which runs along the eastern and southern coasts of Ovalau, and from this road another leads to the crater valley in the centre of the island which is the home of the Lovoni tribe. These people long resisted attempts by other Fijian tribes to subdue them and they were a constant menace to the European inhabitants of Levuka, raiding their properties and burning their houses. They were conquered by Cakobau in 1871 and sold into virtual slavery to planters in other islands. After the Cession they were returned to their old home.

Only half a mile from the eastern shore of Viti Levu, and easily reached from Suva, lies the islet of Mbau which is joined to the main island by a reef which is partly dry at low water and fordable at half tide. The islet is only a little more than twenty acres in extent and some even of this small area was reclaimed, towards the end of the eighteenth century, from the mud flats and reefs which surrounded the islet. A stone wall was built to prevent erosion and docks to accommodate the large canoes which formed the naval and mercantile power of Mbau and brought food to the numerous inhabitants. In spite of its tiny size it is historically the most important place in Fiji and should certainly be visited. Today, instead of heathen temples there is a Methodist church, and colourful *meke* (pronounced *mek-kee*), ceremonial dances and songs, are performed where savage cannibal feasts were once the rule. Here can be seen the graves of the great Cakobau and of his father Tanoa.

In 1959, when *Ratu* George Cakobau was installed at Mbau as *Vunivalu* (Commander-in-Chief), the first full installation since that of *Ratu* Seru Cakobau, his great-grandfather, in 1853, there was an elaborate display of pageantry and well executed *meke*. Enormous quantities of food were brought from different places in Fiji which in the past had owed allegiance to the chiefs of Mbau—pigs and yams and *dalo*, the principal food crop, in profusion, and much *yaqona* (pronounced *yang-gona*), the popular drink. For days before the ceremony numerous canoes could be seen bringing to Mbau the tribute of food and those who were going to take part in the ceremony or merely to look on.

A little further from Viti Levu but within sight of Suva is the island of Mbengga (Beqa) where the people of one village perform at certain times the ceremony of fire-walking. In a large pit lined with stones a pile of logs is set alight and allowed to burn until the stones are very hot. The unburnt wood is then removed and the performers, dressed largely in leaves but with bare feet and legs, enter the pit and walk in a circle, in single file, on the hot stones. They then jump out and green leaves are thrown on to the stones, after which the performers again enter the pit to crouch for some minutes amid the clouds of steam rising from the heated leaves.

This fire-walking ceremony is occasionally performed at Suva, and in 1935 it was performed there before members of the British Medical Association who were passing through on their way to Australia. Tests were carried out upon the performers both before and after the ceremony, but no agreed explanation of their immunity from injury was arrived at.

It is, however, generally accepted that there is no trick about the ceremony. At the Hibiscus Festival at Suva in 1960, more than twenty men from Mbengga walked barefooted over white-hot stones and after the ceremony the spectators were given the opportunity of examining the feet of the performers; they were found to be quite unharmed and indeed unmarked. The Mbengga people themselves have a legend that explains it all; their ancestor, they say, captured a god and received the gift of immunity from fire in return for sparing the god's life.

A different fire-walking ceremony was performed by Indians in Suva while I was there. This had a religious significance and the performers were Fiji-born descendants of immigrants from southern India. After a ceremonial wash in the sea the devotees went in procession to the spot where a pit full of burning wood had been prepared. Many of them had needles or skewers thrust through their cheeks or lips, and walked several times from end to end of the pit over the glowing embers. They seemed dazed and appeared to feel no pain and the devotees were less excited and emotional than the Indian women who were present. After the ceremony I spoke to some of those who had undergone the ordeal; they seemed by then quite natural and at ease, and willingly posed for photographs.

Off the north-western coast of Viti Levu lie the Yasawa chain of small islands which can be visited by launch from Lautoka or Nandi. The islands are picturesque and interesting, and on one island there is a cave in the limestone formation which contains petroglyphs of uncertain age and origin.

Altogether, there is a great deal in Fiji to attract visitors but much remains to be done before the tourist industry can be fully developed as a money-earner for the colony and to ease the growing problem of unemployment. The first and most important need is for more and better hotels, both of the luxury and of the more moderate class. Additional hotels are now being built but it is doubtful whether the increasing accommodation is keeping pace with increasing demand. The number of tourists has been rising steadily year by year, and 14,722 visited Fiji in 1961. It is estimated that over £1,000,000 was spent in Fiji by tourists and visitors in cruise ships during the year. A number of these cruise ships visit Suva and moor alongside the wharf where they are entertained by the band of the Fiji Infantry Regiment in their picturesque uniforms or by Fijian choirs. The second need is for better roads along which visitors could travel in greater comfort than is now possible. It is essential that money should be spent on improving the main road between Nandi and Suva, and on other roads which, although chiefly necessary to facilitate agricultural development, would add to the pleasure of the visitor. Thirdly, and of great importance, is the need for an advertising campaign, especially in the United States, to make Fiji better known to potential visitors.

Some fears have been expressed that the development of tourism would commercialize Fiji and disrupt village life, to the detriment and perhaps the disruption of Fijian culture, the fate of Hawaii being mentioned as a horrid example of what might happen. There is, of course, a possibility that the traditional Fijian ceremonies might be cheapened in order to entertain the tourist, but this depends on the Fijian people themselves, and they are not likely to sacrifice their traditions for a mess of pottage. I have seen the *yaqona* ceremony and a *meke* performed before a crowd of visitors at an hotel, and in no way was the dignity of the occasion affected. A short explanation of what the ceremony stood for was sufficient to prevent any breach of good manners.

*

It may appear strange that a country with so many attractions should have remained for so long unknown to Europeans, although neighbouring islands in the Pacific were frequently visited at a much earlier date, but in fact there were two good reasons for this. In the first place there are numerous coral reefs around and between the islands which make navigation dangerous to sailing ships and for a long time no charts of these waters were available. The first approximately correct chart of a *part* of the group was only published in 1814. This was produced by Aaron Arrowsmith, and it was not until 1840 that the coasts of the principal islands were surveyed by the United States Exploring Expedition under Commodore Wilkes. It is said that this is 'one of the most reef-infested areas in the seven seas' and that reefs close all but a few of the approaches to the islands. The number of sailing ships wrecked on these reefs give proof of the danger.

Secondly, the Fijians had the reputation of being ferocious warriors and cannibals who murdered and ate all strangers who fell into their hands. When Captain Cook was in Tonga in 1777 he found that the Tongans were very much afraid of them because, they said, the men 'of Feejee are formidable on account of the dexterity with which they use their bows and slings; but much more so, on account of the savage practice to which they are addicted . . . of eating their enemies whom they kill in battle'. This unfavourable account, amply justified by later evidence, quickly spread among mariners in the Pacific, and probably lost nothing in the telling. The American Commodore Charles Wilkes, for example, who wrote in 1845 of his visit to the islands, considered their aspect so beautiful 'that I could scarcely bring my mind to the realizing sense of the well-known fact that they were the abode of a savage, ferocious, and treacherous race of cannibals'.

So even as late as the end of the eighteenth century only a few of the islands had even been seen by Europeans and no one had any idea how many there were or what they contained.

In fact Fiji is an archipelago which includes besides the two main islands, Viti Levu and Vanua Levu (Great Land), and the two of moderate size, Taveuni and Kandavu, about five hundred islets, of which about one hundred are permanently inhabited. The total land area is 7,040 square miles (nearly the size of Wales), the two largest islands comprising some 87 per cent of this total. Some of the islets are less than an acre in extent and the following table will show clearly the extremes of size between the islands of the group:

	Square Miles
Viti Levu	4,010
Vanua Levu	2,137
Tavenui	168
Kandavu (Kadavu)	158
500 other islands, on average not much more than one square mile each	567
Total area of Fiji	7,040

The islands are scattered over a large area of the Pacific Ocean. They extend from longitude 177° west to longitude 175° east, some 375 miles, and between south latitudes 15° and 20°, 300 miles. Suva is about 1,250 miles from the equator, 1,960 miles north-east of Sydney, Australia, and 1,317 miles north of Auckland, New Zealand.

In addition to the islands mentioned above, there are Ovalau (40 square miles) with the small town of Levuka; Lakemba (Lakeba), the largest of the Lau group, where the first missionaries to Fiji began their work; Mbau (Bau), historically of the greatest importance as the home of the most powerful pre-Cession tribe; and Makongai (Makogai), where there is a leper hospital to which patients come from many parts of the Pacific. Some 400 miles north of Viti Levu is the island of Rotuma, eighteen square miles in area, which became a dependency of Fiji in 1881. It was discovered in 1791 by Captain Edwards, of H.M.S. *Pandora*, when a search was being made for the *Bounty* mutineers.

The four larger islands and many of the smaller ones are of volcanic origin, while others, especially the eastern islands of the group, are of limestone or coral formation. All the volcanic islands are mountainous, with limited areas of low-lying land around the coasts, and these are often referred to as 'high'

Above: A landing party from the French corvette *Astrolabe* going ashore
to avenge the massacre of the crew of *L'Aimable Josephine*
Below: The *Astrolabe*, under the command of Captain Dumont D'Urville,
during the same voyage, 1838, and a Fijian canoe in foreground

Above, *left:* Seru Ebenezer Cakobau, who ceded Fiji to Britain. *Above*, *right:* Sir Arthur Gordon, first Governor. *Below*, *left:* The late *Ratu* Sir Lala Sukuna, first Fijian Speaker of the Legislative Council

Above, left: Corporal Sefanaia Sukanaivalu, who won a posthumous Victoria Cross. *Above, right: Ratu* Penaia Genilau, D.S.O. *Below:* The Legislative Council in session.　　　*Overleaf:* The interior of Viti Levu

Above: Nabui, one of the twenty-nine well defined peaks in the interior of Viti Levu. *Below:* The Rewa River 'about one hundred miles long . . . navigable by launches for over forty miles'

Above: Loading copra in the Lau Group of islands. Because of the coral reefs in the area, loading has to be done by ship's boat while the ship itself waits safely out at sea. *Below:* Cumming Street, Suva

Above, left: Fijian girl. Her life consists of 'finding food, fishing, fetching firewood, cooking, washing up', but she still finds time to play
Above, right: Fijian man   *Below:* Indian gathering

islands, in contrast to the 'low' islands of coral formation which rise only a few feet above sea level. The interior of the larger islands is extremely rugged, the rough, high lands being broken only by deep cut river courses and gorges. Even the so-called plateaux are so dissected by rivers that there is little flat land. The highest peak, Mount Victoria, 4,341 feet, and several others of more than 3,500 feet, are on Viti Levu. In the comparatively small island of Taveuni there is a height of 4,072 feet.

There is no record of volcanic eruptions in Fiji but numerous craters and volcanic 'plugs' can be seen as evidence of intense volcanic activity in the distant past. Several hot springs exist.

The principal mineral exports from Fiji are gold, silver and manganese. Copper, iron, coal and bauxite have also been found, with traces of other minerals. There are outcrops of limestone at many places and phosphates are found in some of the islands of the Lau group.

The windward slopes of the larger islands, where the rainfall is heaviest, are very thickly forested, many of the trees carrying valuable timber. On the drier leeward side of the mountains there are extensive *talasiga*, or 'sunburnt' areas, with only sparse vegetation and a general appearance of aridity. Fires and over-grazing, as well as irregular rainfall, have contributed to the ruin of this *talasiga* land. Guava bushes, which in many tropical countries are valued for their fruit, from which guava jelly and other preserves are made, grow like weeds in Fiji where they are regarded as a pest. Much of the eroded land and many of the badly cared for coconut groves are overgrown with guava bushes.

The largest rivers are found in Viti Levu, the most important being the Rewa and the Singatoka (Sigatoka). The former, which is about one hundred miles long and has large tributaries, is navigable by launches for over forty miles and much further by boats of shallow draught. All the rivers except the Singatoka, some seventy-five miles long, have built up deltas, the intricate channels of which are lined with mangrove forest. It is estimated that there are about 50,000 acres of mangrove around the coasts of the islands, but this is a small area compared with that covered by other trees as more than half of the land surface of Fiji is still covered with forest.

Considering the nearness of the islands to the equator the

climate is a pleasant one, the heat of the sun and the high humidity being tempered by the cool sea breezes which blow steadily from the east or south-east. At Suva, the temperature seldom rises above 90° or falls below 60°, the annual mean temperature being about 77°. Fiji being in the southern hemisphere, the warmest period is from December to March and the coolest from May to October. Fiji is fortunate in being free from most of the dangerous tropical diseases. Yellow-fever and malaria are unknown, but filaria is present. The major public health problem at present is tuberculosis. Like most peoples long insulated from outside contacts, the Fijians were, and perhaps still are, particularly susceptible to imported diseases, and the terrible epidemic of measles in 1875 was fatal to thousands.

There is a heavy annual rainfall in the windward areas. At Suva, for example, the average annual rainfall is over 120 inches, while on the leeward side of Viti Levu, sheltered by the high mountains, the average is only about 70 inches a year. The rainfall is heavier in (Southern) winter months and lighter between May and October, but in the windward areas there is little apparent difference and it is said that in Suva a month with less than one inch of rain would be regarded as a drought. I was in Suva for three so-called 'dry' months—July to September, 1959—and during that time it rained almost every day, often very heavily. Sir Arthur Gordon, afterwards Lord Stanmore, the first Governor of Fiji, arriving in the colony for the first time in June 1875, records that 'it has been raining all the morning and is now raining as hard as ever it can rain. If this is the weather in the *dry* season, what must it be in the wet'.

From mid-November to mid-April is the hurricane season, when tropical cyclones may occur in the South Pacific. Fiji is liable to hurricanes but, although small 'blows' are not infrequent, really serious and destructive hurricanes seldom occur. There was a particularly destructive one in March 1910, which did great damage in Suva, another in 1941, and yet another in January 1952, when gusts of over 150 miles an hour were recorded.

Of the crops now grown in Fiji most are probably indigenous, while a few have been introduced or at least harvested on a commercial scale by European enterprise. *Dalo*, known in other parts of the Pacific as *taro*, is the tuberous root which has been and still is the Fijian 'staff of life'. Other tubers grown are yams and sweet-potatoes. Bananas and sugar-cane have long been cultivated for food and in recent years commercially. Sugar is now the main export crop and bananas are shipped in fair quantities for sale in New Zealand and Japan.

The coconut palm has always been of enormous value to the Fijians. Its products, copra and coconut oil, together represent the second largest export crop, while the nuts provide food and drink for local consumption. The trunks and leaves of the tree are used for various purposes and the husk of the nut yields a fibre used for making cordage.

The breadfruit is another tree indigenous to the islands of the South Pacific, and several varieties are found in Fiji where it is valued as a food. It will be remembered that Captain William Bligh was sent to the Pacific in command of H.M.S. *Bounty* to collect breadfruit plants and transport them to the West Indies, where it was hoped they would provide a suitable food for the Negro slaves; in the famous boat voyage which he made after his ship's company had mutinied in 1789, he passed through the Fijian archipelago, the first European to do so. (Some relics of the mutiny in the *Bounty*, brought to Fiji at a much later date, are in the museum at Suva.)

Another tree which should be mentioned is the paper-mulberry, the bark of which is used for the preparation of bark-cloth. The root of the *yaqona* shrub provides a popular beverage, which will be referred to in the next chapter.

There were no large indigenous animals in the islands, but pigs, and probably dogs, were introduced at an early date, perhaps from Tonga. Cattle and horses were first brought to Fiji by European missionaries about the middle of last century and have increased in numbers to a considerable extent. A large number of horses have escaped from their owners and bred in the wild country of the interior of Viti Levu and it is said that there are now several thousands of them. Wild horses, wild cattle, wild pigs and wild dogs, as well as 'European' starlings, do a great deal of damage to crops and poultry, and receive the attention of the Vermin Control Officer of the Agricultural Department. In 1959, sixty wild cattle and several hundred starlings were destroyed. The number of other animals disposed of is not known, but the official report sounds a plaintive note when it states that 'the destruction of wild horses presents a number of problems, including the disposal of the carcases as, unlike wild cattle, they are not acceptable for food'. The Fijian name for cattle is *bulumakau* and a story, almost certainly apocryphal, is told of the origin of the word. It is said that when the first pair were landed the Fijians asked what they were and were told 'a bull and a cow'. They had, of course, never seen such animals before, nor had they seen horses, and at the first sight of these, in 1857, the people fled in fear.

Sheep were introduced by European settlers but have not been a success. The mongoose was brought to the large islands of Fiji about eighty years ago to deal with the rats which were damaging the sugar-cane plants; they have increased rapidly and have become a pest, being especially destructive of bird life. In the mountains of the large islands and in most of the smaller islands there is a large and varied indigenous bird fauna, which includes several varieties of parrots. The 4s. stamp of Fiji, issued in 1959, shows the brilliantly coloured parrot which is found on the island of Kandavu. More often seen, as they frequent the towns, are the mynahs and bulbuls imported from India which have increased at a prodigious rate.

Snakes are found in several of the islands but only one kind is known to be venomous and it is rarely seen. There are no crocodiles in the rivers but small sharks have been known in the Rewa more than forty miles from its mouth.

Whales are frequently found in Fijian waters and many of the early contacts with Fijians were made by the crews of whaling vessels. While I was in Fiji in 1959 the sight of a whale in Suva harbour caused much excitement.

There are quantities of fish and turtle in the sea around the Fijian islands and a certain amount of fishing is done by Fijians, especially in the sheltered waters within the reefs. Prawns are also obtained in large numbers in the rivers. The sea-slug, known as *bêche-de-mer* or *trepang*, is found in Fijian waters and was at one time exported to China.

At some places the inhabitants profess to be able to call up various creatures from the sea, and they are often successful in doing so for the benefit of visitors. Near the village of Koro-levu, on Viti Levu, large eels can be summoned, and at Kandavu, off a certain headland, turtle will rise in response to traditional songs and calls. Readers of Sir Arthur Grimble's book, *A Pattern of Islands*, will recall his account of porpoises being summoned to the beach of one of the Gilbert Islands.

Perhaps the most remarkable of the many remarkable things to be seen in Fiji is the annual *balolo* festival. The *balolo* is a small sea-worm which lives in the crevices of coral reefs and rises to the surface twice a year, for breeding purposes, with great punctuality, between the months of October and December, the exact date depending on the conjunction of moon and tide. The Fijians, who value them as food, aware of the *balolo's* cycle, and forecasting these dates with accuracy, are ready in their canoes when the worms rise. The surface of the sea then becomes covered by a dense mass of wriggling *balolo* which the Fijians scoop into their canoes with buckets and baskets, amid great laughter and shouting, and in lively competition with predatory fish.

Sir Basil Thomson, for some years an official in Fiji, points out, in his book, *The Fijians*, that 'the fact—and it is a fact —that an annelid should observe lunar time would not be very remarkable in itself, but it appears that the *Mbalolo* observes solar time as well. . . . The moon directs its choice of a day, and it follows that the creature cannot maintain regular intervals of either twelve or thirteen lunations without changing the calendar month of its reappearance. For two years it rises after a lapse of twelve lunations, and then it allows thirteen to pass, but since even this arrangement will gradually sunder solar and lunar time it must intercalate one lunation every twenty-eight years in order to keep to its dates. It has been under the observation of Europeans for more than sixty years, and it has not once disappointed the natives who are on the watch for it. What are the immediate impulses of tide or of season that impel it to rise on its appointed day no one has yet attempted to show. Consider for a moment how many centuries must have passed before the desultory native mind became impressed with its regularity.'

Before passing, in the next chapter, to a description of the aboriginal inhabitants of the islands, the Fijians, it is desirable to state quite briefly the number and racial origin of the total population, which was estimated to be, at the end of 1961:

Fijians	172,455
Rotumans	5,195
Other Pacific islanders	6,623
Indians	205,068
Europeans	10,417
Part-Europeans	8,958
Chinese	5,039
Others	117
Total population	413,872

The first Indians were brought to Fiji as indentured labourers in 1879, and from that date to 1916, when the indenture system was stopped, some 40,000 to 50,000 arrived. At least 92 per cent of the Indians now in Fiji were born in the colony. Of the Europeans, a few hundred are permanent settlers, some belonging to families which have been in the colony for three or four generations; the majority, however, are temporary residents employed as missionaries, business men and officials, and most of these come from Australia and New Zealand. The part-Europeans are for the most part descended from Fijian mothers and European fathers—the early traders at Levuka or the later settlers who established plantations in the various islands. Chinese have been coming to Fiji in small numbers since the date of Cession and in increasing numbers since the last war; they are principally engaged in trade and market gardening. Most of the Chinese in Fiji speak Cantonese.

The other Pacific islanders, from Tonga, Samoa, the Gilbert and Ellice Islands, and the Solomon Islands, have come to Fiji at various periods and to some extent are integrated with the Fijian people.

The Rotumans are racially different from the Fijians, and speak a different language. They are Polynesians with a Mongolian strain and some admixture of European blood, several escaped convicts from New South Wales having settled in Rotuma before it became part of the colony of Fiji. Some 2,000 Rotumans live in Viti Levu.

PART ONE

History

1. THE FIJIANS

IF European knowledge of Fiji was extremely limited up to the end of the eighteenth century, still less was known of its inhabitants, and even today little can be said with any confidence of the origins and early history of the Fijian people. It is probable that successive waves of immigrants of Melanesian stock were among the earliest to arrive in the islands. They probably came in their canoes from the westward in small groups, independent of and hostile to each other, without 'high' chiefs or tribal organization, and established themselves in various parts of Fiji. They have left no written records and little even of reliable oral legend. The present population is descended mainly from these dark-skinned, fuzzy-haired people.

There is, however, an important strain of Polynesian blood in the small eastern islands of the group and on the windward coasts of the larger islands, and Polynesian influence has had a considerable effect on the appearance and culture of the people in those areas. The fairer-skinned, straight-haired Polynesians from the east came mainly from Tonga and Samoa. Later, in historical times, there came another wave of Tongan immigration and influence, partly hostile and partly in search of trade. Fiji is, in fact, the meeting place of Melanesian and Polynesian peoples and culture, which, interacting on one another, have produced the present Fijian race.

It was due to Polynesian influence that chieftainship attained importance in Fiji, and that 'high' chiefs, with control or at least suzerainty over areas beyond their own home boundaries, came into prominence. *Ratu* is the title borne by chiefs and the ladies of chiefly families are styled *Adi* (pronounced *An-dee*). At the beginning of the nineteenth century the strongest political units were those in the eastern parts of the archipelago, where Polynesian influence was greatest. Lakemba, in the Lau group, was the nearest to Tonga and sometimes was under Tongan control. On Vanua Levu and Taveuni was the territory of Thakaundrove (Cakaudrove); Mathuata (Macuata) was on the

25

northern coast and Mbua (Bua) on the western coast of Vanua
Levu. On the eastern coast of Viti Levu was Verata, which also
controlled for a time the small island of Viwa. Rewa occupied
the delta country of the river of that name. Last, and later of
the greatest importance, was Mbau (Bau), a small island close

to the eastern shore of Viti Levu, so close indeed that it is
possible at low tide to wade across the channel which separates
it from the larger island. The remainder of Viti Levu was still
as it had been for a long while, the home of small isolated and
mutually hostile tribes, untouched as yet by the increasing
powers of the seven leading political units mentioned.

Except where family relationships through the marriages of
chiefs led to temporary friendships, there was little peaceful
contact between any of the tribes, great or small. Visitors were
not encouraged and the crews of canoes wrecked on the shores
occupied by the people of another tribe, who came 'with salt
water in their eyes', were liable to be killed and eaten, as shipwrecked persons were believed to have incurred the wrath of
the gods and to have been abandoned by them. (It has been
said, however, that the Fijian was hospitable to all strangers

26

whom he did not feel it necessary to eat.) Many European sailors from wrecked vessels shared the same fate. Cannibalism was a universal practice and prisoners taken in war, or even women seized while fishing, were invariably eaten. Most of the early European accounts of Fiji emphasized this trait to the exclusion of almost everything else, and at one time the group was referred to as 'The Cannibal Isles'.

Cannibalism among the Fijians was not a mere ritual nor was it only a form of vengeance on conquered enemies, though this was important, and there can be little doubt that human flesh was enjoyed by those who ate it. One chief on Viti Levu is said to have eaten nine hundred and ninety-nine persons and to have set up a line of stones to register his exploits; a Wesleyan minister was shown these stones by the son of this record-breaking cannibal. The leaves of a special vegetable (*Solanum*

Cannibal fork

anthropophagorum) were used to wrap around the human flesh and cooked with it on heated stones or in special ovens. Wooden forks, with handles richly carved, were used at cannibal feasts by men who for other food would have relied on their fingers, as it was considered improper to touch cooked human flesh.

The ordinary food of the Fijians included, as is largely the case today, pigs, fish, *dalo*, yams, sweet-potato, cassava, bananas and breadfruit. A quantity of breadfruit was sometimes stored as a useful stand-by when other food was short; it was buried under leaves weighted with stones in a pit, and in about two months it had formed a homogenous and smelly mass, the pit being opened and drawn on as required. Turtles and snakes were as a rule reserved for chiefs. The snakes were kept in pits and fattened for some special feast; they were then rolled in banana leaves and roasted, after which they were skinned and eaten like eels.

The casualties in the interminable tribal wars were not very heavy, partly because of the conventions which regulated the fighting and partly because of the ineffectiveness of the weapons available. Until Europeans introduced firearms, the principal weapons were bows and arrows, slings, spears and clubs, the last named being the most popular. These were of little use against strongholds perched on almost inaccessible crags or behind moats and walls made of tree-trunks and bamboos, in which the weaker side could take refuge. According to Sir Basil Thomson, 'every tribe had a natural stronghold, stored with food and water for many weeks, into which it could retire in times of danger. If they did not carry it at the first assault, by surprise, or by treachery from within, the besiegers went home to await a better opportunity, for the slow starvation of a garrison by organized siege had never occurred to any native leader.' The remains of many of these strongholds can be seen today.

The heroism of the warriors was, as a rule, tempered by military conventions, and indeed some writers have expressed the view that they were in general lacking in courage, a curious fact in view of the heroism displayed by Fijian soldiers during the last war. The Reverend J. Hunt, for instance, referring to an attempt to seize a trading vessel and the murder of her captain, thought that the Fijians were 'too great cowards to attempt taking (anything) by force as long as there is any danger in doing so. Their plan, therefore, is to pretend friendship towards their victim, then watch the moment he is off his guard and put him to death.' Another missionary, the Reverend Joseph Waterhouse, who thought the Fijians 'thoroughly two-faced', wrote that he found that they were not 'at all celebrated for courage, but quite the contrary; their way is to fall upon the defenceless and to overcome by numbers rather than by personal bravery'. Great importance was attached to the capture of villages or fortresses but it is said that the first care of a besieging army was to prepare for defeat by clearing paths by which it could escape from an enemy sortie. Much of the 'fighting' consisted of the cutting off of stragglers or attacks on helpless noncombatants. The Tongan missionary, Joel Bulu, describes some of the fighting that went on in the Rewa country during his time. They were, he says, 'always at war in those days. They lay in wait for one another in the paths: they hid themselves in the long reeds on the river banks, whence they fired their guns and threw their spears at the women as they came down with their water-pots or their fish-baskets, at the canoes as they passed by, and at the children at their play. Seldom could you pass their towns without hearing the death-drum booming forth from one bank or the other.'

Before each campaign a great deal of conventional boasting took place, the warriors asserting their own courage and warlike skill and promising for their leaders a quick victory and numerous prisoners. When a town or stronghold was besieged insults and taunts would be freely exchanged, but in the event there might be little fighting. It was considered bad form to attack enemies engaged in the war dance, or boasting, which were the recognized preludes to hostilities, and if one or two warriors were killed in the ensuing conflict honour was held to be satisfied and the combatants withdrew. There were, of course, exceptions when one side was able to overwhelm the other, killing a number of the warriors and slaughtering women and old people in cold blood, or carrying them off to be cooked and eaten in the victors' town. The villages of the conquered people would then be burnt and their crops destroyed, but many of the vanquished would escape and return after the departure of the victors to build their villages again. It might, however, be necessary for them to pay tribute to their conquerors, in foodstuffs or in women, to escape further molestation, and this would continue until some change in the balance of power made it safe for them to evade this obligation.

There was a great deal of treachery, and perhaps the worst example on record occurred as lately as 1841, a Wesleyan missionary being the helpless witness of the event. The chief of Viwa agreed with the chief of Mbau that he would entice some of the people of Verata to his island, by pretending that with their aid he would attack and defeat the Mbau warriors. Unsuspecting, the Verata men arrived at Viwa and there they were set upon not only by the men of Mbau but also by their false allies. More than a hundred bodies of their victims were cooked and eaten by the treacherous conspirators.

The Fijians were savage and cruel, and life was cheap. The punishments inflicted by the chiefs were sadistic and barbarous, the most merciful being death by clubbing. On the death of a chief a number of his widows were strangled, the closest relatives taking part in this tribute to convention. In 1852, when the chief of Mbau died, five of his widows were strangled, one being strangled by her own son, Cakobau, who later became a Christian and was the leading chief at the time of the cession of Fiji to the British Crown in 1874. The missionaries in Mbau at the time did their best to save the women, but in vain.

After the defeat of the Verata people at Viwa, at least eighty women, wives and other relatives of the dead, were strangled in mourning for the deaths of the warriors. There were other less unpleasant forms of mourning, such as the cutting off of the little finger or the shaving of the head, which to the Fijian, who is proud of his mop of hair, is a serious sacrifice. Indeed, Sir Basil Thomson has said that 'the self-assurance of a Fijian is as dependent on the length of his hair as was the strength of Samson'.

Infanticide was not unknown among Fijians and the treatment of the old and infirm was callous and horrible. Some were merely neglected and allowed to die, sometimes of starvation. Others were buried alive, the earth being thrown over them while they still spoke and moved. *Tui* Cakau, 'Lord of the Reef', the aged chief of Thakaumdrove (Cakaudrove), was buried in 1845 while he still breathed, his son and successor assuring the horrified missionary who was present that although his father's body moved the spirit had left the body. When a new house was being built for a chief, living men were sometimes buried in the holes in which the main uprights were to be planted, and it was over men's bodies, perhaps still living, that large canoes were launched.

In spite of all these horrors the people of Fiji were able to develop a respectable culture. With only primitive stone tools they felled great trees and shaped canoes that were better than any others built in the Pacific. The smaller Fijian canoes and some of the larger sailing canoes were made from a single log, but the great double canoes were built with planks. Large woven mats were used as sails, and huge oars, hewn from a single log and measuring more than thirty feet in length, were used in pairs for steering the larger craft; several steersmen must have been needed to handle one of these oars. Some of these oars and parts of large canoes can be seen in the Fiji Museum at Suva.

Besides those used for trade, large canoes with outriggers were used in war, the object being to sink enemy canoes by ramming and then to club their crews as they swam. The heavy double canoes were sometimes more than one hundred feet in length. William Lockerby describes one in which he was held as a prisoner in 1808. 'The canoe I was in', he says, 'was one of the largest size of double canoes; it consisted of two single ones joined together by a platform, in the middle of which the mast is fixed. Round the sides of the platform there

Double canoe

is a strong breastwork of bamboos, behind which they stand in engaging an enemy. There is also a house on the platform which is erected and taken down as circumstances require. The number of men on board amounted to two hundred. Captain Cook's account of the sailing of these vessels is quite correct, however incredible it may appear to those who have not seen them. With a moderate wind they will sail twenty miles an hour.'

Besides canoes, skilfully constructed bamboo rafts were used for transport on the rivers, and still are used on the Rewa by banana growers to bring their fruit to market.

The Fijians showed great skill in handling the large canoes they built and their bamboo rafts. They were quite at home in

31

the water and were, and still are, generally very good swimmers. Sir Basil Thomson considered that the Fijians' extraordinary powers of endurance in the water far surpassed anything recorded of Europeans. 'I have twice talked', he said, 'with people just rescued after being forty-eight hours in the water, swimming without support, in both cases from the capsizing of their canoes in mid-channel. They seemed little the worse, though they had been without food or drink for two days in a burning sun and in constant peril of sharks, which had eaten several of their companions, and their faces were raw, owing to their continually brushing the salt water out of their eyes.'

Sir Arthur Gordon relates a remarkable story of a Fijian and his wife who, after the canoe in which they were travelling was wrecked, swam for two days until they reached land. At first they swam with others who had been in the canoe but got separated from them during the first night. This is the man's account of their ordeal:

'My wife and I had with us one canoe scull and a medium-sized cedar box which contained our clothing and some government despatches. After swimming some time my wife got sleepy and I then took her by the hands and swam with her for some time, and when she awoke we continued our course again swimming side by side. I then got sleepy and my wife then took me me by the arm and kept me afloat until I got over my sleepiness, when we both swam on, changing and taking turn and turn with the box and the scull, for the box affording a better support than the scull, the one who had the latter became tired in course of time. This was our first night in the water away from the canoe.

'Next day we were still swimming and continued so up till mid-day. At this time my wife saw an old ripe coconut drifting, we picked it up, I husked it with my teeth, and we ate it. We kept on swimming until evening, at which time we sighted (land) but could distinguish no break in the reef and continued swimming till midnight. . . . A shark came up and passed close to my wife, touching her on the breast. She let go the box and clung to my neck. The shark swam away but soon returned and this time it caught hold of my foot. I then said to my wife "a shark has bitten me". I, however, managed to frighten it away with the scull but it soon returned again and caught hold of my wife's cloth and after a short struggle succeeded in tearing it away from her, and swam away with it; probably the cloth got over its head or else entangled in its teeth, for it never returned.

'I felt so weak from the effects of the bite of the shark that I grew faint and almost went down, when my wife let go the scull, to which she was clinging, and assisted me on to the box to rest myself, while she made an effort to get us both towards shore which we reached during the night, but did not land together in the same place. We were lifted by a wave, by which my wife succeeded in gaining a rocky ledge on the shore, to which she clung. I, however, was swept out again by the returning wave and was carried to some distance from where my wife landed.' He was able a little later to swim ashore and was found by his wife in the morning. The first thing they did was to open the box which had saved them, take out the despatches and clothing, and spread them out in the sun to dry. After this they lay down and slept until they were found by another Fijian who gave them food and carried them to safety in his canoe.

In spite of frequent casualties from sharks, the Fijians seem to be quite fearless in the water. A typical example of selfless Fijian courage was the effort of a young man, Waisea Valu, who recently risked his life to save a woman who had been attacked by a shark. When he heard the cries for help he ran from his village, some hundreds of yards away, and plunged into the sea, although, with the water stained with blood from the woman's wounds, he knew quite well that the shark had been made even more ferocious and that other sharks might have been attracted by the blood. The woman herself showed heroism when, seeing her rescuer swimming towards her, she called to him to go back and keep out of danger as the shark was still circling round her. In spite of her warning he swam on to the woman and helped her to the shore, where unfortunately she died from her injuries.

Perhaps the most extraordinary shark story from Fiji is that of the Tongan missionary, Joel Bulu, who was bitten on the thigh by a shark while wading into deep water with the intention of swimming across a river. There were a number of witnesses of the incident of which he himself gave an account. 'My flesh', he said, 'was torn and my blood was flowing.' He thought that he was going to die and said a prayer. The shark let go his thigh but turned back to attack him again. 'When he drew near', Bulu continued, 'and opened his mouth to bite, I thrust my hand down his throat—down, down as far as I could thrust it, for I thought that I could then tear out his heart and so kill him. His teeth closed on my arm and tore the flesh; but still I worked my hand downwards with all my might; and at length he could no longer bite me, but opened his mouth as if he were sick. Then I snatched forth my hand and, clasping him round the body with both arms, I lifted him as high as I could, holding my head down so that he could not bite me. Thus I staggered with him towards the shore, and I could hear his jaws clashing together over my head as he tried to bite, but I held him fast and I believe that I should have got him to land, only that, when I reached the shallow water, my right arm which he had bitten fell powerless to my side, whereupon he slipped out of my grasp, and began to swim away, though very slowly and feebly. So hot was my wrath against him that I turned and caught him again by the tail with my left hand; but now the shore and the trees and the people seemed as if they were going round and round. A deadly sickness crept upon my heart, a mist came over my eyes, there was a sound in my ears like the roaring of the surf; I fell down and knew no more. And this is how the Lord delivered me out of that fearful strife.' The European missionary who recorded this story said that the scar of the wound inflicted by the shark 'is frightful to look upon even now. It extends all round the arm and goes down to the very bone.'

The Fijians were also (and still are) expert house-builders, wooden posts and ridge poles being employed with walls of woven bamboo or thatching, and roofs thatched with reeds or the leaves of sugar-cane or palms. No nails were used, everything being fastened by cords made from coconut husk fibres. From the bark of the paper-mulberry tree a cloth known as *masi* was prepared and used for clothing or to decorate the interior of houses. *Masi* is still made and used. The bark is taken from the tree in long strips, and after being steeped in water is beaten with a hardwood club on a long low table for a couple of hours. I saw several houses in Fiji with the main beams and walls covered with stencil-patterned *masi*. The pattern is first roughly outlined and the stencil cut from banana leaves, the colours used being obtained from soot and a red clay. Pottery of various sizes and in many designs was made by hand, the use of the potter's wheel being unknown. Mats made of rushes or from the leaves of the coconut and *pandanus* trees were used as floor coverings, bedding and the sails of canoes, and there were many other crafts in which the Fijians excelled. The University Museum of Archaeology and Ethnology at Cambridge has an interesting collection of Fijian material, much of which was collected by Sir Arthur Gordon and Baron Anatole von Hugel who travelled in the interior of Viti Levu and other parts of the colony soon after the Cession, before the people had been greatly influenced by contact with other cultures.

While at Tonga in 1777 Captain Cook noted in his journal that:

> 'It appeared to me that the Feejee men whom we now saw were much respected here; not only, perhaps, from the power and cruel manner of their nation's going to war but also from their ingenuity. For they seem to excel the inhabitants of Tongataboo in that respect, if we might judge from several specimens of their skill in workmanship which we saw, such as clubs and spears, which were carved in a very masterly manner; cloth beautifully chequered; variegated mats; earthen pots; and some other articles; all which had a cast of superiority in the execution.'

Cook had already seen the crafts of other Pacific islands and was able to draw a comparison which was highly favourable to the Fijians. A later witness, Captain Wilson, of the London Missionary Society's ship *Duff*, who was at Tonga in 1797, said that 'the natives of the Friendly Islands, who are unwilling to give way to any, acknowledge that the Feejees excel them in many ingenious works; that they possess larger canoes, and are a brave, fighting people; but abhor them for their detestable practice of eating their unfortunate prisoners'. Later observers noted some of their feats of engineering, the terracing and irrigation of dry hillsides, the docks and reclamation work on Mbau island, a canal connecting two streams of the Rewa delta (still in use, and along which I passed in a launch), and a timber bridge of thirteen spans across the Rewa which was seen by a missionary in 1841.

Religious beliefs varied in different localities and were accepted without question by the common people. Mr. R. A. Derrick, the historian of Fiji, says that there is evidence that some of the high chiefs of historical times—men of high intelligence—had little faith in their gods and regarded ceremonies in their honour as a concession to public opinion. One of the first of the Wesleyan missionaries in Fiji, the Reverend Thomas Williams, wrote of the Fijians as they were before conversion to Christianity. 'The idea of Deity', he said, 'is familiar to the Fijian; and the existence of an invisible superhuman power, controlling or influencing all earthly things, is fully recognized by him. Idolatry—in the strict sense of the term—he seems to have never known; for he makes no attempt to fashion material representations of his gods, or to pay actual worship to the heavenly bodies, the elements, or any natural objects. It is extremely doubtful whether the reverence with which some things, such as certain clubs and stones, have been regarded, had in it anything of religious homage. The native word expressive of divinity is *kalou*.' Some of the gods worshipped were the deified spirits of famous ancestors, and there were numerous minor deities, as the Fijian peopled with invisible beings every remarkable spot, especially 'the lonely dell, the gloomy cave, the desolate rock, and the deep forest'. Each chiefdom had its own particular war god to whom offerings were made, especially before battle. The priests received the offerings made to the gods and spoke to the people in their name, promising success in war or warning them of possible disaster. They came from a priestly caste and to some extent their office was hereditary. Sickness or the failure of crops was attributed to sorcery, and competent sorcerers were in demand to deal with an enemy or to protect their clients.

The *meke* of the Fijians, which may be a song or a dance, or both, was and still is immensely popular among the people. For this the men and women performers dress elaborately in a kind of uniform, of which leaves and flowers form an important part. Frequent rehearsals ensure that the 'drill' is perfect, heads, arms and legs moving continuously in unison, with wooden gongs or the clapping of hands giving the time. The best of the men's *meke* are the wild war dances with clubs or spears, while the women's *meke* are quieter and more graceful.

The Fijians are a musical people and their singing is generally pleasant.

The Reverend David Hazlewood wrote, in 1850, that 'there is an abundance of poetry in the language on many subjects. The natives are passionately fond of it, and are incessantly at a humdrum kind of chant. They also frequently assemble and *meke* for whole nights together, and can, when they try, chant very agreeably. . . . Most of their poetry is in blank verse; but they have some—especially epigrammatic couplets—in rhyme.'

There are several dialects of the Fijian language, but owing to the adoption by the missionaries of the Mbau dialect for their translation of the Bible, this dialect is becoming the standard. There is, happily, no trace of that horrible language, 'pidgin' English.

Family feeling among the Fijians was very strong, and within the family groups, possessing land in common and working together in its cultivation, there was common ownership in most things and a common allegiance to the chiefs, the senior descendants of the common ancestor. There was little private property, and such as there was could with difficulty be retained owing to the custom of *kerekere*. This custom allowed a relation to ask the owner for anything he wanted, and there would be few brave enough to refuse such a request as public opinion would regard such a refusal as shameful. In the days when the Fijians enjoyed—if that is the right word—a subsistence economy, and everyone was more or less on the same level as regards the possession of property, there was little harm in *kerekere*, which meant no more than an exchange or loan of goods. But today the position is quite different and *kerekere* is a serious handicap to the progress of the Fijian people, as it is a powerful disincentive to individual effort and thrift. As Mr. Derrick says, 'a young man returning to his village after a year's work on a plantation may be the proud possessor of a wristlet watch, a new box, a gay shirt, or a well-tailored *sulu*; but it is probable that before a week is out the watch will be on another's wrist, the box in a friend's house, and the clothes either borrowed or appropriated by his relations.' When I was in Fiji I heard of a young man who worked for some time on an agricultural training farm, and, when he left, had earned about £80. Two months later he came back to borrow money with which to start a farm, explaining that all he had previously earned had been taken from him by his relatives and spent on a prolonged feast.

Even chiefs were liable to lose their property by *kerekere*, and Sir Arthur Gordon in his journal relates how Cakobau made safe his ownership of a large new canoe which he feared would otherwise have been taken from him by *kerekere*. He went through the form of presenting the canoe to Lady Gordon who then asked him to 'take care of the canoe for her, and use it'. This made it possible for him to say that it was not his to give away, but belonged to Lady Gordon who kindly allowed him to use it!

Another custom, *vasu*, is not unlike *kerekere* in its effects, although it is not reciprocal. In Fiji the Polynesian system of patrilineal inheritance had largely replaced the Melanesian matrilineal system, but traces of the latter survived in some areas and in the form of *vasu* was fairly general. *Vasu* gave to a nephew the right to demand from his maternal uncles anything they owned, and this right was freely exercised regardless of the loss or inconvenience to the unfortunate owners. Resistance to the most unreasonable demands was never made, and it is on record that a chief, during a quarrel with his uncle which had developed into civil war, used the right of *vasu* to supply himself with ammunition from his enemy's arsenal!

All transactions of importance among Fijians required the presentation of a *tabua* (pronounced *tambua*), a symbolic gift, which, formerly of wood and later of shell, is today invariably a whale's tooth, from the cachalot or sperm whale. The *tabua* is offered as a token of fealty on the visit of a chief or as an accompaniment to an apology or a request; when it is accepted failure to grant the request is held to be attended by misfortune. In olden days *tabua* was also offered as an act of propitiation before undertaking hostilities, the planting of crops, or house building. *Tabua* is also presented as a sign of respect to high officials and important visitors, and I value one presented to me, as chairman of the Commission of Enquiry, by the Fijian chiefs in 1959. On at least one occasion *tabua* was offered by missionaries in the hope of saving widows about to be strangled, and fifty whales' teeth were given by the captain of the *Nimrod* in 1838 to ransom some of his crew who had been kidnapped by a Fijian chief.

Whales' teeth for *tabua* were probably first obtained from the jaws of whales which had become stranded on the beaches and their early value was due to the rarity of such occasions. By the beginning of the nineteenth century they were being obtained from whaling ships in exchange for local produce, and later still they became ordinary articles of trade. William Lockerby, who was in Fiji in 1808 and 1809, tells of an occasion

Tabua

when the chief of Mbua was presented with a brass-laced hat and a brass crown, 'but he would much rather have had a whale's tooth, that being the most valuable article among them. They hang them about their necks on great festivals, and give them with their daughters in marriage—as their marriage portion—in short, he who is possessed of a quantity of them, thinks himself rich.' Captain Richard Siddons, who was trading in Fiji at about the same period, reported that 'one of the most extraordinary circumstances among them is, the excessive value they set upon large teeth, such as those of the whale or sea elephant. So that persons going to procure sandal wood from them generally take with them as many of these teeth as they can procure. The principal things they barter for are axes, knives or razors; but they will give as much wood for one large tooth as for five or six axes. The regard they put upon large teeth is the more extraordinary, as they do not seem to make any use of them except as ornaments. When a native, by purchase or any other means, becomes possessed of a large tooth, he hangs it up in his house, and for the first few days scarcely ceases looking upon it and admiring it. He frequently takes it down and rubs it with a particular kind of leaf, and polishes it; some of them almost for a month continue to labour upon it.'

In spite of the supicion and hostility between tribes there was inevitably a considerable amount of trade. The mountain tribes of Viti Levu exchanged *yaqona*, grown in the interior, for salt, mats and other articles produced on the coast. Certain areas produced the best mats, or *masi*, or canoes, and these were eagerly sought after by people from other areas who offered their own produce in exchange. There was also some trading between the eastern islands of the group and Tonga, where there was demand for Fijian pottery, sail-mats, and particularly for canoes.

There was no alcoholic liquor but throughout the islands quantities of *yaqona* were drunk on ceremonial occasions and at less formal parties. The making and drinking of *yaqona* is still such an important part of Fijian life that it merits more than a passing notice. It is described by Sir Harry Luke, who was Governor of Fiji from 1938 to 1942, as 'perhaps the most essential and most honoured feature' of their social life and, indeed, of that of Tongans and Samoans as well. Known as *kava* in other parts of the Pacific, *yaqona* is made from the powdered root of a shrub, *Piper methysticum*. Dried *yaqona* powder is often used and in this form can be bought in shops, but in all ceremonies the beverage is made from freshly grated green root, and this is said to produce the best flavoured drink. It is very popular with local Europeans and Indians as well as with Fijians and I have heard of an Australian, formerly resident in Fiji, who now lives in Sydney and has a regular supply of *yaqona* sent to him there. It is, no doubt, a taste that can be acquired, but although I attended many formal and informal *yaqona* parties while I was in the Pacific, and perforce drank many cups of it, I never learnt to like it. I agree with one writer who likened the taste of *yaqona* to that of 'magnesia, with a slight flavour of pepper'. Another considered that it had a 'taste resembling rhubarb and magnesia, flavoured with sal volatile', while Sir Harry Luke says that it looks and tastes like a mild Gregory powder.

The *yaqona* ritual, which is almost sacramental, is still faithfully observed. The root is cut into small pieces and pounded or grated into a powder. (In former days it was ceremonially chewed by young men or girls but this custom has fortunately been discontinued.) Those taking part in the ceremony wear the traditional skirts of grass or leaves, with the upper part of their bodies bare and their faces blackened. A large wooden bowl is placed in position opposite to where the guest of honour is seated. One end of a short rope of coconut fibre is attached to the bowl and the other end, which is decorated with cowrie shells, is taken forward so that the rope is pointing towards the principal guest. No one is allowed to cross this rope, and indeed in olden days such a breach would have been punishable with death. The powder is then steeped in water in the bowl and more water is added to get it thoroughly mixed. Then an attendant, squatting on the ground behind the bowl and facing the principal person present, with both hands and forearms in the water, strains the mixture through a bundle of hibiscus fibre. When this is done the serving begins and is carried on with slow and dignified grace. A cup-bearer approaches the bowl with a cup made of half a coconut shell, which is generally highly polished. The cup is filled by the attendant at the bowl, raised slowly by the cup-bearer so that all may see it, and carried by him, with knees bent and arms extended, to the guest of honour. He is expected to drain the cup at a single draught and then to spin the cup away from him along the ground. The others present are then served one by one in the same manner in strict order of precedence.

While the *yaqona* is being prepared traditional songs are chanted and hands are clapped as the cup is presented to each chief or guest; as each cup is emptied there is a cry of *maca* (it is dry).

The mixing of the *yaqona*, done with great care and deliberation, takes some time, as does the actual drinking. When the

cup-bearer hands the cup to each of those honoured he sinks
to the ground and remains sitting until the cup is emptied,
and then rises and returns to the bowl to fetch another cup.
When a large number are to be served the ceremony lasts for
a long while; as no discussion, formal or informal, can proceed
until the *yaqona* ritual is completed, the sacrifice of time can be
considerable. Even in public and business offices in the towns
there is often to be seen a bowl of *yaqona* from which the caller
can refresh himself. It was probably because I had no bowl of
yaqona in the office I used while I was in Suva that a kindly
Fijian magistrate in a neighbouring office sent me a cupful on
more than one occasion.

It is said that the drinking of a quantity of *yaqona*, which is
not fermented, does not affect the brain but paralyses the leg
muscles, so as to immobilize the drinker. As most of those who
drink *yaqona* do so in a squatting position and remain in that
position for long periods, it is possible that it is cramp, and not
paralysis, that affects them when they try to rise. However, as
I never drank much *yaqona*, and in any case was always provided
with a chair, I am not in a position to defend this theory against
others more experienced.

It is said by many people, and in general I agree with them,
that too much time is wasted in Fiji on ceremonies, and that the
yaqona ceremonies are the most wasteful of time, but the liking
for *yaqona* has saved a great many Fijians from addiction to more
harmful beverages and this should be remembered in its favour.

Wooden head rest, to keep hair off the ground while
owner is sleeping, and dish for cosmetic oil

2. THE FIRST EUROPEANS

IT was inevitable, sooner or later, in spite of navigational dangers and the reputation of its inhabitants, that Fiji should become known to the outside world. As long ago as 1643 some of the north-eastern islands and reefs of the group had been seen by the Dutch navigator, Abel Tasman, the first European, so far as is known, to have done so. More than a century later, in 1774, Captain James Cook sighted Vatoa, one of the most southerly of the Fiji Islands, during his second voyage to the Pacific. Faced by the menace of unknown reefs, neither of these explorers made any attempt to probe the secrets of the archipelago.

It would be proper here to anticipate a little and mention the discovery in 1820, by the Russian Admiral Fabian von Bellingshausen, of Oni-i-Lau and other small islands in the extreme south of the group. Approaching the islands in the evening, no reefs being visible, he says that suddenly 'we heard the tremendous roar of breaking surf and coral reef. I immediately gave orders to bring the wind aft; as we bore away we passed so close to the reef that notwithstanding the darkness we could clearly distinguish each wave breaking over it. A few moments' delay and we should inevitably have perished.'

In 1789, after the mutiny on the *Bounty*, Captain William Bligh, as stated on page 19, passed through Fijian waters in an open boat, sighting both Viti Levu and Vanua Levu and many of the smaller islands. Off the Yasawa islands, north-west of Viti Levu, the boat was chased by two Fijian canoes but escaped. In spite of bad weather and the handicap of an overcrowded boat, Bligh made careful observations of what he saw, and his chart of the channels through which he passed is remarkably accurate. For some years Fiji was referred to as 'Bligh's Islands'.

In 1791 a tender of H.M.S. *Pandora*, engaged in the search for the *Bounty* mutineers, was in Fijian waters for five weeks and her crew met with friendly and hospitable treatment from the inhabitants of one of the smaller islands, probably Matuku. This was the first known contact between Europeans and Fijians in the islands and a strange sickness broke out among the inhabitants after the visit, the first of the epidemics which seemed to be the consequence of such contacts. Bligh himself, now in command of H.M.S. *Providence,* visited the islands during the following year and 'formed no very favourable opinion of the country'. No landings were made but some barter trade was done with the people.

In 1794 Captain Barber anchored his small vessel, the *Arthur,* off the west coast of Viti Levu and tried unsuccessfully to obtain supplies from the local inhabitants. On the second day of his visit the ship was attacked by a number of canoes, two of the crew were wounded by arrows, and the canoes had to be driven off by gunfire and musketry. It should be remembered that at this period, and much later, even trading vessels, such as the *Arthur,* were armed with guns for self-protection, and muskets were invariably carried for use by the crews. As late as 1840 the American Commodore Wilkes commented strongly on the 'imprudence' of the captain of a whaling vessel which entered Fijian waters 'without any guns or arms on board', and added that very many ships had been lost and many lives sacrificed in the Pacific 'from over-confidence in these treacherous savages'. Ships that were well armed were fairly safe from capture by the Fijians provided that a careful watch was kept against treacherous surprise attacks which were sometimes successful. One such attack, which was very nearly successful, was that on the British brig, *Sir David Ogilby,* in the late 'thirties. According to the Reverend J. Hunt, Captain Hutchins, who was in command of the brig, had been kind to and was very popular with the Fijians and on particularly good terms with the chief who murdered him. This chief was standing on the deck of the vessel while the captain was giving orders to his crew and suddenly 'he laid him dead on the deck with one blow of his club'. The chief's followers immediately attacked the crew and drove them from the deck, the mate and several others being severely wounded. Fortunately, however, due to the foresight of Captain Hutchins, who knew the Fijians by experience, there was a case of muskets kept in the main-top and with these the seamen succeeded in clearing the deck, the chief being shot as he sat in the cabin. The only reason the Fijians had for murdering the captain was to secure his property. Fortunately for the trading vessels the Fijians were greatly afraid of the guns and for a long time dreaded even the muskets. They had no idea how the muskets were fired and what connection these weapons had with gunpowder. There is a tradition that the contents of a cask of gunpowder recovered from a wreck was used as hairdressing until one Fijian came too near a large fire and there was a sudden flash which burnt off the poor man's mop of hair.

In 1797 the London Missionary Society's ship *Duff*, under Captain James Wilson, sighted some of the small eastern islands of the archipelago and at two of them saw 'vast numbers of natives assembled upon the beach'. That night the ship struck a reef, but was backed off without having suffered serious injury. Those on board, however, went through some anxious hours after 'a misfortune which presented itself with a thousand frightful ideas. We knew that the Feejees were cannibals of a fierce disposition, and who had never had the least intercourse with any voyagers; consequently we could expect no favour from such. Imagination, quick and fertile on such occasions, figured them dancing round us, while we were roasted on large fires.' At sunrise they discovered that the ship was within a circle of reefs, 'probably the same as Tasman got entangled among', and, 'when the day showed us the dangers which lay hid on every side, it appeared wonderful how we had escaped so well, and made us very desirous to get clear of them as fast as possible'. They were lucky to get away safely.

Shipping was now increasing in the Pacific and more and more vessels passed close to the Fiji Islands on their voyages. Bad weather or head winds might compel some of these to enter Fijian waters, or the need for fresh water or food might tempt them to anchor close to the shore, but so far the contact between Europeans and Fijians had been slight and ephemeral, with little effect on the Fijian way of life and without adding much to European knowledge of the islands. In the first years of the nineteenth century the position was completely changed by the arrival of Europeans, shipwrecked sailors or men fleeing from civilization, who remained in Fiji and settled among the people.

The Reverend Thomas Williams, writing many years later, stated that 'about the year 1804 a number of convicts escaped from New South Wales and settled among the islands', and it has been suggested that these were the first Europeans to do so. In fact, there is no proof of any mass immigration of escaped convicts although some of those who came to Fiji in the early years had certainly been convicts, and others perhaps should have been. It is more likely that the first Europeans in Fiji were the survivors from vessels wrecked in Fijian waters.

The first wreck of which there is any record was that of the American schooner *Argo*, which ran on a reef east of Lakemba, probably in 1800 although the exact date is uncertain. Some of the crew were taken to Tonga in Tongan canoes, others joined in local fights and were killed, but the remainder settled down in Lakemba or moved to other islands. Another epidemic, worse than that which followed the visit of the *Pandora's* tender, was introduced by the *Argo's* crew and spread through the islands, killing thousands. The Fijians spoke of it as 'the wasting sickness' but it is not possible to say what it really was; cholera and dysentery have been suggested.

One of the survivors of the *Argo's* crew, an American called Oscar Slater, travelled as far as the western end of Vanua Levu and there saw growing a number of sandalwood trees. He was picked up by another ship at Mbua (Bua) Bay in 1802 and after various adventures reached New South Wales where he reported what he had seen. At this time sandalwood, which was used by the Fijians for perfuming the coconut oil with which they anointed their bodies, was also in great demand in India and China for ceremonial and religious purposes (for example, the making of incense) and high prices were offered for it. When Slater's report became public property, small vessels from Port Jackson in Australia, American ships from New England ports, and East Indiamen from Calcutta, flocked to Mbua Bay to purchase this valuable commodity. The heyday of the sandalwood trade was between 1804 and 1812. At the end of this period the slow-growing trees were almost completely cut out and it was difficult to obtain supplies, but while it lasted the trade brought rich returns to successful traders. So important did the trade become that Vanua Levu was known for a while as Sandalwood Island, and the chief of Mbua, made wealthy by the trade, was perhaps at this time the most powerful of the Fijian chiefs.

In 1808 one ship, the *Jenny*, of which we shall hear again, obtained 250 tons of sandalwood, in exchange for trade goods valued at not more than £50, which was worth £20,000 in China. Captain Bligh, whose name keeps cropping up in early Fijian history, was governor of New South Wales for a short time, and in 1808, justifying a tax he had imposed on the traffic, described in a report how it was carried on by Australian-based vessels. 'The Sandalwood', he wrote, 'has been procured with old iron, made into a kind of Chisels, and Nails, Beads, and Trinkets of any kind, and on very fair principles which the Estimates shows. I put a duty of £2. 10s. per ton on exportation, which was paid by the Purchaser and not at all felt by the Merchant. I valued the sandalwood at only £50 per ton while it sold here for about £70, on an average, to Vessels going to China.'

In addition to the trade articles mentioned by Bligh, axes were in great demand by the Fijians, but the most highly prized were whales' teeth. There were numbers of whaling vessels working in the Pacific and the sandalwood traders would have had little difficulty in obtaining supplies. The ivory of elephants' tusks from India, cut into the shape of whales' teeth but larger than normal size, proved particularly successful for trading purposes as they were much admired by the Fijians, although doubtless the size of these false teeth would have astonished even a large whale.

The captains of some of the vessels that came to Mbua Bay for sandalwood were honest men who treated the Fijians fairly, but others were unscrupulous in their dealings and ruthless in the use of force to promote business. At first the Fijians were friendly and traded willingly with the ships, but the treatment they received from some of the Europeans made them increasingly suspicious and hostile. Much of the treachery of which the Fijians were accused at that period and later was the direct result of the dishonesty and violence of previous visitors. Samuel Patterson, one of the crew of the American brig *Providence*, which was wrecked on a Fijian reef in 1808, said that 'some of our men were so unwise as to go with the natives into their battles with muskets and kill many of the opposite party, who had never injured them, and pleased their employers much'. Some of the ships' captains were willing to join the local chiefs in attacks on their neighbours in return for supplies of sandalwood, and two captains are known to have received each a gift of ten tons of sandalwood as a reward for assisting in the defence of a town against hostile attack. The power of the ships' guns and the muskets of the crew made them powerful allies in local warfare.

The best contemporary account of the sandalwood trade in Fiji, and of the savage fighting that often accompanied it, is given in the Journal of William Lockerby (published by the Hakluyt Society in 1925) who was at Vanua Levu for about fifteen months in 1808 and 1809.

Lockerby, who was born in Scotland, was a sailor. As first mate of the American ship *Jenny*, he sailed to Mbua Bay to buy sandalwood in 1808, but was unable to do much trade for a while because of the presence of rival Australian purchasers. This led to friction and quarrels, blows sometimes being exchanged, but Lockerby put the time to good use by becoming friendly with the chief of Mbua and learning to speak Fijian 'in a tolerable manner'. He was generally employed ashore in the purchase of sandalwood and in charge of the boats which brought it to the ship.

Boats from the American and Australian vessels were now moving along the coast as far as Wailea Bay, some fifty miles from Mbua, in search of sandalwood which was already becoming scarce at the latter place. One of the boats from the Australian vessels fired upon a canoe and in the fighting that ensued three Europeans were killed and two Tahitian members of the boat's crew were taken prisoner. On his own initiative Lockerby took three armed boats to rescue the prisoners and recover the bodies of the dead. By detaining as a hostage the local chief who came to discuss terms, Lockerby was able to recover the Tahitians who were, however, badly mutilated; the bodies of the Europeans had already been cooked and eaten. In revenge for this, and as the Fijians refused to give up the boat they had captured, they were fired on by Lockerby's boats as they pulled away.

Lockerby had not been getting on well with his captain, and one day in July, to his astonishment, he found that the *Jenny* had sailed, leaving him and five others of the crew on shore. Captain Dorr stated afterwards that he was driven to sea by bad weather and could not regain his anchorage, but Lockerby believed, with some reason, that he was deliberately deserted. In this predicament, as he was unwilling to go on board the Australian vessel, he sought the protection of the chief which was not refused. As Lockerby wrote later, 'from the good old King I had received kindnesses which I should remember while I live with gratitude. Left as I was on his island without the least means of subsistence, to the mercy of the lower class of natives, who might have plundered me of the few articles I had left, and even deprived me of life, he not only supplied me with food when there was a great scarcity all over the island, and granted me his protection from the insults of his people, but he taught me by his advice how to acquire their goodwill'. One way in which he acquired this goodwill was by dressing as they did, or rather, as he put it, by going 'naked with only a belt made from the bark of a tree round my waist, that hung down before and behind like a sash', and with his hair 'at times painted black, at other times red'.

Lockerby and the white men with him had built a boat in which they hoped to leave the island, but had to conceal their intention from the chief who counted on their aid in the face of a threatened attack by some of his rebellious subjects assisted by the people of Mbau (Bau). Fortunately, before this happened, in October, the American brig *Favorite* arrived at Mbua Bay and took the castaways on board, but Lockerby's troubles were by no means over. He was away in a boat collecting sandalwood for the captain of the *Favorite* when the anticipated attack materialized and he was taken prisoner. A second ship, the *General Wellesley*, had now arrived and the guns of the two ships covered the approaches to Mbua, so the attack was diverted to a small island which was loyal to the Mbua chief. Lockerby, as a prisoner, was a witness of the fighting which followed, the capture of the island and massacre of non-combatants, and the cooking and eating of the prisoners taken.

Meanwhile the captain of the *Favorite*, believing that Lockerby had been killed, fired on his supposed murderers and killed many of them, to the dismay of Lockerby who hoped that he would be given up on payment of a ransom. However, two chiefs were detained on board the *Favorite*, where they had gone to discuss terms, and it was agreed that they should be exchanged for Lockerby. Unfortunately, the chiefs were killed when they tried to escape from the ship but this was success-fully concealed from their people until the ship's boat and the canoe with Lockerby on board approached one another. Then, contrary to orders, the seamen in the boat opened fire on the Fijians and Lockerby only escaped by diving overboard and swimming to the boat. The ship then fired on the canoes, killing many of the Fijians.

The Mbau warriors now left for home and the chief of Mbua organized a punitive expedition against those of his subjects who had rebelled against him. Lockerby, who had recovered from the injuries received while a prisoner, and other Euro-peans from the ships, joined the expedition, small guns being mounted in their boats. The main stronghold of the rebels was attacked, the guns and muskets of the Europeans doing con-siderable damage, and it was captured after severe fighting with heavy casualties on both sides, Lockerby himself being wounded. Before the attack the chief had promised Lockerby that the women and children taken prisoner should not be killed, but his followers could not be restrained and the taking of the fort was followed by a massacre and a cannibal feast.

In return for their services the chief supplied a large quantity of sandalwood to both ships, and the *Favorite* left with a full cargo. The *General Wellesley* was not yet fully loaded and Lockerby transferred to her and was employed once more in the search for sandalwood. While doing this, one boat in which he was travelling was wrecked on a reef. On another occasion he was present at the strangling of a widow whom he tried to save by offering a number of whales' teeth, but was told by the local chief that 'she was an old woman, and would be of no use to me. I made him understand that my motives were quite different from those he entertained.' No arguments were of any avail and the woman was strangled. On yet another occasion Lockerby nearly lost his life when his boat was attacked by hostile Fijians. At last the *General Wellesley* was loaded and, after an affectionate farewell to the Mbua chief, Lockerby sailed away. He lived to be a successful merchant and ship-owner in Liverpool and died there in 1853.

In addition to the story of his own adventures, which gives such a vivid picture of conditions at Vanua Levu and the hazards of the sandalwood trade, Lockerby in his Journal mentions the wreck of the American brig *Eliza*, in May 1808, an incident which revealed the Fijian idea of values at that time and gave to Mbau, through Charles Savage and his musket, the means to attain power. When the crew of the *Eliza* got ashore in their boats on the small island of Nairai, 'they were soon stripped naked by the natives, and plundered of everything they had saved from the wreck of their vessel', which included more than thirty thousand dollars in coin. The captain and a few men were allowed to leave in one of the boats and reached Mbua Bay where they found the *Jenny* at anchor. Lockerby went with an armed party to the rescue of the other shipwrecked men, and a large proportion of the dollars was recovered as the Fijians put no value on them and were glad to give them up in exchange for some iron and trinkets.

The captain and most of the *Eliza's* crew got away, with some of the dollars, in ships from Mbua Bay, but a few went to Verata and one, a Swede named Charles Savage, was taken to Mbau. Here he quickly made himself useful to Naulivou, the chief of that small island, just then beginning to become important. At some time early in the eighteenth century the Mbau tribe had moved from its original home in the mountains of Viti Levu to the coast, and later, about 1760, to the island now named Mbau. Comparatively few in numbers, they had had to fight hard to maintain their independence against their stronger neighbours, Rewa and Verata, but the strange white man was going to change the balance of power. So important, in fact, did Mbau become that early writers gave the name of this tiny islet to the whole of the large island off which it lies; to English ears the emphasis on the initial letter made the word sound as *Ambau* and it is under this name that Viti Levu was sometimes referred to.

Savage had a musket and was a good shot, and he accompanied the Mbau warriors on their expeditions against enemy tribes. None of these had muskets or indeed had ever seen such weapons, and, keeping out of range of arrows, Savage was able to shoot down the opposing warriors with ease and immunity, though he was once wounded when he ventured too close to enemy bowmen. As a result of the casualties caused by Savage's musketry, and the terror caused by this novel weapon, Mbau won quick victories over Rewa and Verata and became the most powerful of the chiefdoms. Savage was soon joined by the Europeans at Verata and elsewhere, who were also armed with muskets, and in return for their services to Mbau these mercenaries were given women and almost unrestrained licence. Some of them, however, went too far in their depravity and were killed, but Savage continued to live in comfort at Mbau with a large harem, his principal wife being the daughter of the chief. He had several children and one daughter was still living in 1840, but it is said that his sons were all eliminated soon after birth to prevent them becoming candidates for chieftainship.

Another dissolute beachcomber was Paddy Connel (or Connor), an ex-convict, who was for some time a kind of court jester to the chief of Rewa; he claimed to have had a hundred wives and forty-eight children.

When not engaged as mercenaries some of the Europeans made themselves useful to the captains of vessels as intermediaries in the purchase of sandalwood and by working the boats which brought it off to the ships. Their knowledge of the language and understanding of the people were valuable, and they were able to obtain from the ships, in payment for their services, the arms and ammunition which made them useful to the chiefs, as well as liquor and tobacco for their own consumption.

In 1813 Savage and some other white men went to Mbua for this purpose and joined with the crew of the *Hunter*, one of the sandalwood ships, in an expedition against the people of Wailea, who were threatening to attack the ship. This was in retaliation for what seems to have been unprovoked firing on them by the *Hunter's* crew. Peter Dillon, mate of the *Hunter*, who later wrote an account of what followed, says that 'Captain Robson had been at these islands twice before, and had obtained considerable influence over the natives of a part of the Sandalwood coast, by joining them in their wars, and assisting them to destroy their enemies, who were cut up, baked and eaten in his presence'. The party sent by Captain Robson against Wailea was ambushed and suffered heavy casualties. Savage, Dillon and three others managed to escape from the ambush and took refuge at the top of a small but steep rock, from which they could see the *Hunter* lying at anchor in the distance. With four muskets they could defend themselves for a while in this temporary refuge, but between them and the shore were thousands of Wailean warriors who were even then preparing the ovens in which the bodies of those killed in the ambush were to be cooked. A similar fate was obviously in store for them if they were captured. Savage saw among the Waileans some men whom he knew and, confident that their old friendship would protect him, left the rock and joined them. For a short time he was not molested, but when a Chinese seaman followed him from the rock both were killed, the Chinese being clubbed and Savage held head downward in a pool of water until suffocated. The survivors remaining on the rock saw the bodies of their late companions cut up and placed in the ovens to be cooked.

The captain of the *Hunter* now sent ashore eight hostages he had kept on board, together with presents to the chiefs, in the hope that the few remaining survivors might be spared and allowed to return on board, and one of the Wailean priests came to the rock to parley with the Europeans. Dillon, who did not trust the offer of a safe-conduct, seized the priest and threatened to shoot him if he attempted to escape or if any of his party were molested. With the muzzles of three muskets at his head and back the priest was anxious to co-operate and persuade his people not to interfere. Keeping the priest between them covered with their muskets, the survivors then left the rock and proceeded to the shore between rows of hostile warriors, got into a boat that awaited them there and were taken to safety on board the *Hunter*.

In addition to six members of the *Hunter's* crew, eight white men from Mbau had been killed, besides a number of Mbau warriors. These deaths were quickly avenged, a strong force from Mbau destroying Wailea and killing a large number of its inhabitants. The prisoners taken were carried to Mbau to be slaughtered and eaten.

The influence of Charles Savage on the future of Fiji was considerable. He was the first to use a firearm in tribal warfare and was the leader of the small band of whites who increased the military power of Mbau and made its chief the most powerful ruler in Fiji. It was to this chief and his successor that European missionaries, traders and settlers were later to look for protection and grants of land. The ruler of Mbau came in time to be regarded by Europeans as the King of Fiji, *Tui Viti*, although other chiefs would not have been prepared to acknowledge him as such.

Savage and his associates were guilty of many crimes and their participation in tribal warfare added greatly to its intensity and the amount of bloodshed. Many of those killed by them were cooked and eaten by their Fijian companions, and they well knew beforehand that this would be the fate of the men they shot and of the prisoners taken. It is true that they did not themselves join in the cannibal feasts that followed the victories secured by their weapons, but they were at least accessories. Their influence on the uncivilized Fijians of their time was wholly evil.

Toad

3. THE MISSIONARIES

SOON after the death of Savage in 1813 the sandalwood trade came to an end, as most of the trees had been cut out, but there was a demand for *béche-de-mer*, the sea-slug beloved of Chinese epicures, which was found in Fijian waters. The *béche-de-mer* was taken by Fijian divers and after being washed was parboiled and smoked, often under the supervision of white beachcombers who acted as agents for the captains of trading vessels. A fair quantity of *béche-de-mer* was bought by these vessels and taken to Chinese ports. Whaling ships also called at the islands, particularly at Kandavu, for fresh water and provisions, and they also made use of the beachcombers. In addition, a number of white men were kept as retainers by the chiefs, as mercenaries or gunsmiths, or merely because it added to the chief's prestige to have a tame white man in his retinue. Even more prized, because of their comparative rarity, were Negroes, who sometimes were landed from American ships. Sir Basil Thomson wrote that 'the natives as a body appear to have treated the white men with tolerant contempt, as being destitute of good manners and the deportment proper to those who consort with chiefs'. William Diapea (Cannibal Jack) says that he spent his time collecting tortoiseshell and *béche-de-mer*, 'mending muskets and amassing property, and living quite content with my three wives'. Gunsmiths were very necessary to mend the old Tower muskets sold to the chiefs by trading vessels, as these weapons were sometimes as dangerous to the man firing them as to anyone else. At first the use of muskets was confined to the whites, as the Fijians were greatly afraid of these weapons, but gradually they came into common use by the warriors and added greatly to the carnage of tribal wars.

The wars themselves were made more frequent by the ambition of the chiefs of Mbau, whose military prestige had been so greatly increased by the musketry of Charles Savage. By these wars, and sometimes only by the threat of war, as well as by dynastic marriages, the power and territories of Mbau were added to. Even as far away as the Lau islands the influence of Mbau was felt in spite of the presence there of a number of Tongan immigrants. Several large war canoes were maintained and the naval power of Mbau enabled it to levy tribute on distant tribes.

Mbau was at the zenith of its power in 1829 when the chief Naulivou died and was succeeded by his brother Tanoa, a man of unprepossessing appearance, despised by the Europeans (who called him 'Old Snuff') and unpopular with his own subjects. He was described by the captain of a trading vessel as 'a little man of most savage appearance'. His tyrannical conduct resulted, in 1832, in a rebellion led by his younger brother and certain minor chiefs, and Tanoa fled into exile. By promising to provide a cargo of *bêche-de-mer* in return for help, Tanoa persuaded the captain of an American trading ship to bombard his rebellious subjects in Mbau, but a gun manned by the Europeans resident there inflicted some damage on the ship which withdrew without doing Mbau much harm.

In consequence of the disturbed conditions in Mbau, the more respectable of the Europeans there decided to move to the island of Ovalau. Here they established themselves under the protection of the chief of Levuka who was allied, if not tributary, to Mbau, and engaged in boat-building and trade with passing vessels. Apart from supplying locally grown foodstuffs to the ships, they also dealt in *bêche-de-mer*, coconut oil and tortoiseshell, while some of them made 'genuine' antiques and curios for sale to the gullible. Most of these Europeans were married to Fijian wives, and were the ancestors of many of the present Part-Europeans.

For the sailing ships of the period Levuka was a comparatively safe and convenient port, with deep water within the reef close to the shore, and fresh water available in abundance. It became, and remained for many years, the trading centre of Fiji, and after the Cession it was the capital of the Colony for eight years. Today its glory has departed, but it is still a picturesque and pleasant little town.

Meanwhile, the chiefs who controlled Mbau after the rebellion sought to capture and kill Tanoa, and they persuaded Captain des Bureaux, of the French trading brig *L'Aimable Josephine*, to transport their warriors in an expedition against

Somosomo, where Tanoa had taken refuge. The attack on Somosomo was repulsed and a little later the Mbau rebels captured the vessel at Viwa, the captain and most of the crew being massacred. Worked by the few surviving French sailors, the vessel was then taken to the Rewa river to bombard a town which had long resisted all attacks from Mbau; the town was destroyed but *L'Aimable Josephine* was soon afterwards wrecked on a reef.

Meanwhile, Tanoa's young son Cakobau, at that time known as Seru, who had been allowed to remain in Mbau after his father's flight, was steadily building up a following, although he concealed his activities behind a façade of frivolity which caused him to be regarded as no more than a 'play-boy'. By 1837 (the year Queen Victoria came to the throne), when Cakobau was about twenty years of age, the time was ripe for a counter-revolution, and one night his adherents rose against the rebels and completely defeated them. Tanoa was restored as chief, but Cakobau was the power behind the throne and virtually regent. Within a few months of this event the first missionaries visited Mbau.

Missionaries had been in other Fijian islands before this. Driven out of Tahiti in 1808, some missionaries of the London Missionary Society were on board the brig *Hibernia* when she struck a reef off the coast of Vanua Levu, and for three weeks they lived on a small island while the brig was being repaired. They had little contact with the Fijians, of whom they were greatly afraid, and made no attempt to proselytize.

In 1830 two Tahitian teachers of the London Missionary Society were sent to Lakemba by the Wesleyan missionaries at Tonga, and moved later to the small island of Oneata. In 1835 two European missionaries, of the Wesleyan Methodist Missionary Society, the Reverend William Cross and the Reverend David Cargill, who had been in Tonga for some years, arrived at Lakemba. King George of Tonga had sent a message to the chief of Lakemba, asking him to receive the missionaries, and on account of this they found little opposition to their work. Some of the first to accept Christianity (*lotu*) were Tongans resident in Lakemba.

In January 1838 William Cross went from Lakemba to Mbau, hoping to establish a mission at this important centre.

Tanoa had been re-instated as chief a few months earlier, and his son Cakobau was in power and perhaps not unwilling to receive the missionaries. 'But', in the words of the Reverend James Calvert, 'the storm of the great rebellion was scarcely calmed, and the work of vengeance was at its height. Cakobau told the missionary plainly that he could not guarantee his safety in the present state of affairs, neither would the active pursuit of war permit his own attention to religion for some time to come. Mr. Cross, finding that the island was densely crowded with savage people, infuriated with war, and that two rebel chiefs had just been eaten, and two more were in the ovens when he arrived, determined to wait for a better time.' He therefore went on to Rewa where he was welcomed by the chief and allowed to open a mission.

It is probable that Cross misunderstood what Cakobau meant for no more than a warning as a definite refusal, and when a year later he wished to establish a mission at Mbau he was refused permission 'because he would not trust himself at Bau on his first visit, but turned aside and opened a mission at Rewa'. As Rewa was the chief rival of Mbau at this period Cakobau resented the priority given it as a mission centre. For years, as a result of this misunderstanding, there were no missionaries at Mbau, but Cakobau allowed them to start work on the small island of Viwa, two miles away, and he himself frequently received visits from the missionaries who sought to convert him. To all their preaching he turned a deaf ear for many years, replying with flippancy to their admonitions. He asked, for example, whether, being a chief, he would get special precedence in heaven, and when Cross told him that those who did not repent of their sins would be cast into hell fire, he replied: 'Ah, well! It is a fine thing to have a fire in cold weather.'

Other missions were opened by white Wesleyan missionaries at Somosomo in 1839 (abandoned in 1847), on Vanua Levu in 1847, at Levuka in 1851, and finally at Mbau in 1854. In these places and elsewhere Tongan and Fijian converts had prepared the way for Christianity and no appraisal of the work of the missions in Fiji should overlook the heroism of these devoted men. It has been pointed out by Professor G. C. Henderson that there was not a single mission station in any part of Fiji where the way had not been prepared for the white missionary by a native teacher or local preacher. Unprotected by the prestige which surrounded the European missionaries, they ventured into districts where Christianity was unknown or resented, and many lived in constant jeopardy. The most famous of these men was Joel Bulu, the Tongan who was converted while quite young and sent to Fiji to work for the Wesleyan mission. His autobiography, translated into English, was published in 1871, and gives a vivid account of the difficulties and dangers to which he was exposed. At a much later date, about 1875, some Fijian Christians went as missionaries to New Guinea where some of them were killed and eaten by the savage inhabitants.

The European missionaries, in spite of their prestige, were often in danger also, and they, with their heroic wives, suffered much from illness. In view of their uncompromising attitude to the evils they saw around them, and to the tactlessness they sometimes displayed, it is perhaps surprising that only one of them, the Reverend Thomas Baker, was killed (as late as 1867), although several were threatened with death and narrowly escaped being clubbed. They fearlessly protested against cannibalism and the strangling of widows, though seldom with success. They were unyielding in their opposition to polygamy and, according to the Reverend James Calvert, 'any man having more than one wife who offered himself as a candidate for membership (of the Wesleyan community) was required to select one to whom he should be duly and religiously married and reject all the rest'.

The missionary attitude in all these matters ran counter to the established customs of the people and involved those who tried to interfere with these customs in considerable peril. One dangerous but partially successful intervention, by wives of missionaries, deserves special notice. These two ladies were at Viwa, their husbands being away on mission work, when they heard that fourteen women were to be killed and eaten at Mbau. They immediately went there by canoe, insisted on seeing the chief, Tanoa, and implored him to spare the women. Nine of the women had already been killed but Tanoa was so impressed by the courage and sincerity of these ladies from the mission that he reprieved the other five. On their errand of

59

mercy these missionary wives had run much risk from the excited crowd through which they passed on their way to see the chief.

In the matter of tribal warfare the missionaries took a strong line. They did what they could to prevent fighting and when war broke out they forbade their converts to take any part in it. The chiefs, not unnaturally, resented the refusal of these conscientious objectors to follow them to battle but were remarkably patient under this provocation. One outburst by Cakobau probably reflected the feeling of all the chiefs. When asked by the Reverend James Calvert to assist a Christian tribe in hostilities which had been forced upon it by heathen enemies during the 1849–52 war at Mbua, he refused, saying, 'I shall not protect them; and I rejoice that you have now a fight of your own. When I ask you *lotu* people to help me in war you say "No, it is not lawful for Christians to fight!" and here are we breaking our backs by steering our canoes, catching dysentery by sleeping abroad in the dews and rains, and being shot in great numbers, whilst the Christians sit quietly at home all the time. Now you have a fight of your own and I am glad of it!'

In the end, although they continued to do all they could to discourage tribal warfare and to mitigate its savagery, the missionaries were gradually compelled to relax their pacificism and to allow their followers to fight in self-defence. It was, indeed, the victory of the converted Fijians and Tongans at Kamba (Kaba), in 1855, that finally decided the Christian future of the Fijian people.

The influence of naval commanders, American, French and British, to which the missionaries frequently paid tribute in their letters, also helped considerably. Fear of the ships' guns and the verbal remonstrances of naval officers had a restraining effect on warlike chiefs and ensured that the missionaries and their followers should be treated in a fairly reasonable manner. In 1852 Sir Everard Home, in H.M.S. *Calliope*, stopped the war at Mbua in which, as related above, Cakobau had refused to intervene. The heathen forces then outnumbered the Christians and Mr. Calvert recorded the debt owed to 'Sir Everard in going to Bua Bay with H.M.S. *Calliope* and for his earnest endeavours to bring about and establish peace with the long hostile parties. . . . Other commanders of ships of war have done excellently in trying to prevent evil and promote good in Fiji; but Sir Everard has excelled them all.'

Naval commanders had, in fact, done a great deal to discourage warfare, cannibalism and the strangling of widows, and to protect the missionaries. Captain Erskine, of H.M.S. *Havannah*, in 1849, spoke to Cakobau of cannibalism 'in terms of horror and disgust', and later the same year Captain Fanshawe of H.M.S. *Daphne* wrote urging him not to allow the strangling of his father's widows. Captain Magruder of the U.S.S. *St. Mary* spoke to Cakobau in similar terms and there are other instances of the support given by naval officers to the missionaries in their reforming work and of the protection they afforded them. Especially noteworthy were the efforts made by Commodore Wilkes, commanding the United States Exploring Expedition which visited Fiji in 1840, who warned the chief at Somosomo that he would be held responsible if any harm befell the missionaries there. The naval officers respected and admired the early missionaries in Fiji and gave them at all times their sympathy and support.

Notwithstanding this support, which in any case was not always available, the missionaries had a difficult time, especially during their first years in Fiji. They were often witnesses of savage fighting, cannibalism and stranglings which they were powerless to stop. 'Well do I remember', wrote Joel Bulu, the Tongan missionary referred to above, 'the day that Bau and Viwa had smitten Teilau, the little island opposite Viwa which stands empty at this day—how a large war-canoe came in laden with the dead, who were taken ashore and piled up in a great heap on the low flat opposite to our houses; and when the Bau messenger had finished his report the king said "Do what you like with them", whereupon there rose a sudden yell. A great rush was made down to the waterside and the bodies were dragged hither and thither as the people struggled with one another over them, many clutching the same body, cutting them up limb from limb, tearing them asunder, and snatching the pieces out of one another's hands. And the yells rose louder and louder as the people grew ever fiercer in their eagerness; women and children also mingled with them in the struggle, their shrill voices rising high amid the uproar.'

It was against a background such as this that the first

missionaries worked to bring the Fijian people to the Christianity they now profess. The greatest credit is due to them and to their helpers, to Europeans, Tongans and Fijians alike, for what they accomplished, and credit must also be given to the Fijian people as a whole, who turned within a few short years from utter savagery to a peaceful and civilized life. Men who had been practising cannibals for years changed completely when at last they decided to embrace Christianity, in many cases braving public opinion and defying the bestial conventions which previously governed their behaviour. The courage necessary for this should not be under-rated.

Professor Henderson has suggested that most of the Fijians who became Christians were converts, not to the Christian religion, but to the belief that the white man's God conferred greater material benefits and was more powerful than their own deities. He quotes a story told by the Reverend Thomas Williams of a better catch of turtles by Christian canoemen than by unconverted Fijians, who attributed the difference in result to divine intervention, adding that 'the arguments of all the divines in the world would not convince or silence the heathen so effectually as the above little fact' Henderson admits however, that after the Fijians had become associated with the church the missionaries were then able to lead them on to a higher and nobler conception of religion. Apart from the material benefits which the Fijians expected from Christianity, many undoubtedly became Christians because their chief had been converted and desired them to follow his example. Some of the simultaneous conversions of entire tribes were too good to be true, but similar wholesale conversions occurred in Britain when Saxon kings became Christian. The recently converted Fijians at any rate took their religion seriously. An English beachcomber, named Danford, who had played a dishonest trick on his best friend, was nicknamed by the other Europeans, on account of this, 'Harry the Jew'. The Christian Fijians thought he really was a Jew and refused to have anything to do with a man who 'belonged to a people who had killed Christ'. He therefore took refuge among the heathen hill people of Viti Levu and married many wives.

The Wesleyan missionaries have been accused of tactlessness in their dealings with the Fijians and some of them were undoubtedly narrow in their views and regardless of Fijian susceptibilities, destroying sacred groves and insulting the emblems of local religious belief. They introduced regulations to control the morals and behaviour of their recently converted followers, such as singing and dancing on a Sunday, any breach of which was punishable by fine or corporal punishment. They required the cutting off of the mops of hair, the crowning glory of men and women alike, for sanitary reasons but perhaps also as a sign of conversion.

Perhaps the worst example of missionary narrow-mindedness (by no means confined to the Wesleyans) was the hostility between the Wesleyan and Roman Catholic clergy. French Catholic missionaries of the Marist Order first went to Lakemba in 1844, some nine years after the Wesleyans, but abandoned their mission there in 1855. They failed also in attempts to establish missions at several other centres and were only successful at Levuka, where Father Bréherét, who lived there for many years, had considerable influence. Levuka was for some time the headquarters of the Catholics in Fiji. The mutual bitterness and back-biting of Wesleyans and Catholics was a credit to neither side and must have been perplexing to the Fijians. The Catholic priests, generally French, were often brought to the islands by French warships and it was later suggested that Wesleyan support for the annexation of Fiji by Great Britain was largely due to fear that French annexation would be the alternative and would lead to the victory of Catholicism. Fortunately, open warfare between French Catholics and British Protestants, such as afflicted Uganda in the 'eighties, did not occur in Fiji, although several persons were killed at Rotuma in 1871 in a battle between Wesleyans and Catholics.

With all the human faults of the missionaries, even their critics admit that they did far more good than harm. Not the least of the benefits they conferred on the Fijians was the example of God-fearing, sober-living men and women, whose behaviour was in marked contrast to that of the majority of white men who first came to the islands, dissolute ruffians who gave to the Fijians their earliest impression of 'Christian' Europeans.

On a more material plane, although this contributed greatly to the spread of Christianity, they gave the people a written language which they did not possess before, taught the Fijians to read and write and started them on the road to a fuller education.

The first book published in Fiji was a translation into the vernacular of the first part of the Catechism which was printed by the Wesleyan Mission Press at Lakemba in 1839. The Press was later moved to Viwa and the translation of the New Testament into Fijian (the Mbauan dialect), by the Reverend John Hunt, was printed, bound and published there in 1847. The Reverend David Hazlewood's *Dictionary and Grammar of the Feejeean Language* followed in 1850, and *A Short English and Feejeean Dictionary* in 1852. A second edition of this latter work, edited by J. Calvert, appeared in 1874, and in 1941 *A New Fijian Dictionary*, by Dr. A. C. Capell, based on Hazlewood's work, was published in London. (The first book printed in the Fijian language was a small 'spelling' book compiled and printed in Tahiti in 1825 by missionaries of the London Missionary Society.)

At the time of the Cession in 1874 it seemed as though Christianity would quickly become universal throughout Fiji, and today almost all Fijians are professing Christians. The over-all position, however, was changed by the arrival of indentured labourers from India who were Hindu or Moslem by religion. There are today comparatively few Indian Christians in Fiji. At the time of the 1956 Census the proportion of the total population belonging to each of the principal religious groups was approximately as follows:

	per cent
Methodist (Wesleyan)	40·0
Hindu	39·7
Roman Catholic	8·0
Moslem	7·3
Church of England	1·5
Seventh Day Adventist	1·2

Of the Fijians, 85·7 per cent were Methodists and 11·7 per cent Roman Catholics. Of the Indians 81·0 per cent professed the Hindu religion and 15·0 per cent followed Islam. Of the Part-Europeans about half were Methodists and half Roman Catholics.

4. TONGAN INTERVENTION

SOON after the missionaries had established themselves in Fiji, warships of various nations began to visit the archipelago at irregular intervals, British ships being the most frequent. One of the first was H.M.S. *Victor*, which came to Lakemba in 1836 to punish the murderers of four British seamen from the wrecked schooner *Active* who had been killed a short time before. As it was found impossible to capture the guilty parties without fighting, which would have endangered a number of innocent persons, the captain of the *Victor* was persuaded by the missionaries to take no action other than giving a stern warning to the people.

In 1838 two French corvettes, *Astrolabe* and *Zélée*, under the command of captain Dumont D'Urville, the explorer, visited Viwa to avenge the massacre of the crew of *L'Aimable Josephine* four years earlier. The inhabitants were given time to escape and the town was then destroyed.

In 1840 an American squadron, the United States Exploring Expedition, commanded by Commodore Charles Wilkes, carried out extensive surveys in Fijian waters. The opportunity was taken to arrest a brother of the chief of Rewa who had been responsible for the murder of ten of the crew of an American vessel six years before; he was taken away as a prisoner and it is not certain what became of him. Wilkes also made treaties with the chiefs of Mbau, Mbua, Thakaundrove, Mathuata and Rewa, for the protection of foreign consuls and other Europeans and for regulating the terms on which water and provisions were to be supplied to vessels visiting Fiji.

In most places the American squadron had peaceful contacts with the inhabitants, but at Mbua two villages were burnt in retaliation for the seizure of one of the ships' boats, and a more serious incident followed. At Malolo island, west of Nandi, two American officers were murdered (one of them the nephew of Commodore Wilkes) while attempting to purchase provisions; a strong force was landed from the ships, two villages were burnt, the crops on the island destroyed, and fifty-seven Fijians were killed, the Americans suffering no casualties. Some of Wilkes's officers, who had been sent home in disgrace, subsequently reported unfavourably on his conduct in these matters, and he was accused of murder.

He defended himself, however, by pleading the need to show the Fijians that 'they could no longer hope to commit acts of this description without receiving punishment', and that 'it was not weakness or fear that had thus far stayed our hands'.

One must be chary of judging by modern standards the conduct of those who were in Fiji more than a century ago, but it is a fact that none of the warships of other nations found it necessary to take such drastic action as was taken by Commodore Wilkes at Malolo. Indeed, Wilkes says he was aware that the Fijians 'had ridiculed and misunderstood the lenity with which they had been treated by the French and English men-of-war'.

In the meanwhile the power of Cakobau in Mbau was increasing. His father, Tanoa, who had been reinstated as chief in 1837, was very infirm and most of the real power lay with Cakobau, who was an ambitious and warlike man. Mbau had risen to its pre-eminence partly because it was the first (thanks to Charles Savage) to use firearms in tribal warfare, and partly because of the naval power it possessed through the number of its war canoes. An indication of the extent of Cakobau's power in the more accessible parts of Fiji is given by William Diapea's statement, in his book, *Cannibal Jack*, that he was compelled, after he had offended this chief, to fly to Tonga, 'the only outlet for me out of Thakobau's clutches, unless I buried myself in the heart of the bush of Viti Levu among those very petty cannibals'. The Mbau chiefs (except Tanoa, who was noted mainly for his tyranny and cruelty) had been men of ability, and Cakobau was the ablest of them all. He is undoubtedly the most outstanding figure in Fijian history.

Cakobau's appearance was described by Captain Erskine, R.N., who met him in 1849 when he was thirty-two years of age. 'It was impossible', he wrote, 'but to admire the appearance of the Chief; of large, almost gigantic, size, his limbs were beautifully formed and proportioned; his countenance, with far less of the Negro cast than among the lower orders, agreeable and intelligent; while his immense head of hair, covered and concealed with gauze, smoke-dried and slightly tinged with brown, gave him altogether the appearance of an eastern Sultan. No garments confined his magnificent chest and neck, or concealed the natural colour of the skin, a clear but decided black; and in spite of this paucity of attire—the evident wealth which surrounded him showing that this was a matter of choice and not of necessity—he looked every inch a King.' Years later, in 1874, Sir Arthur Gordon wrote that 'he is a far more striking man than the photographs would lead you to suppose, very kingly in bearing and with a most intelligent head'.

The years which followed Cakobau's accession to power were years of savage warfare on a scale, as Mr. Derrick says, and of a barbarity hitherto unknown to Fiji, and this was largely due to Mbau aggression, mainly directed against Rewa and Verata, the principal rivals to Mbau. This aggression, and jealousy of Mbau power, led to a combination of other chiefdoms against it, and there was, moreover, active opposition to Cakobau by a section of the Mbau people, rebels against the authority of their chief.

War began against Verata in 1839 and against Mathuata the following year, and in neither case was Mbau altogether successful. An appeal by Cakobau to the white traders at Levuka for help against his enemies was refused and this was the first cause of his subsequent hostility to the Europeans there. In 1841 Mbau was raided by Verata warriors and in retaliation a number of Verata men were slaughtered at Viwa as the result of the treacherous conspiracy between Cakobau and the Viwa chief, referred to on page 29.

Then in 1843 began the war between Mbau and Rewa. The immediate cause was the destruction by Rewa of the village of Suva, which was on the site now occupied by the Botanical Gardens. Suva was tributary to Mbau but was dangerously close to Rewa, and in 1843 it was suddenly attacked and its inhabitants massacred. Mbau was bound to react to this deliberate provocation and the war that followed lasted for eleven years, the town of Rewa being twice destroyed, in 1845 and 1847.

This war had a direct effect on the fortunes of the Europeans at Levuka, which by now had become a fairly prosperous settlement, protected to a certain extent by the local chief who was an adherent of Cakobau. The Europeans there were of a better type than the earliest settlers and for the most part endeavoured to earn an honest living by boat-building and trade. A. B. Brewster, who went to Fiji first as a settler in 1870, when he was only sixteen, and lived there until his retirement from the Colonial Service in 1910, knew many of these men, the 'old hands' as they were called. Accustomed to the semi-starvation and hard drudgery of the sea life of those days, he says that they found life in Fiji easy and pleasant, with plenty of *yaqona* and tobacco and affectionate Fijian wives. According to Brewster 'the trades of carpenter and canoe builder were hereditary in Fiji, and the half-caste progeny of the old hands mainly carried on the tribal traditions of their mothers and so followed the occupations of their sires, and they gradually collected together in villages of their own. In my days they were very useful people, as not only did they carry on the trades just mentioned, but in addition they were good seamen and pilots.'

In 1844, angered by the support that one white man had given to Rewa, Cakobau ordered all the Europeans to leave Levuka, and it was not until 1849 that they were allowed to return. In the interval most of them lived, with their families, in Vanua Levu.

Cakobau by now had few friends, and his enemies, including the Mbau rebels, were gradually closing in for what they hoped would be the kill. In the eastern islands there were a number of resident Tongans prepared to resist Mbau aggression and the situation was made more critical by the arrival at Lakemba, in 1848, of the Tongan chief Ma'afu. King George of Tonga, to whom he was closely related, considered Ma'afu a possible pretender to the throne and banished him to Fiji where he soon became the recognized leader of all the Tongans resident there and a rival in power to Cakobau.

In 1846 John Williams, the first United States representative, as Commercial Agent, established his office in Fiji, and in addition to holding agencies for several American firms began to acquire land for himself, considerable areas being purchased from Cakobau and other chiefs, payment being made in muskets and other trade goods of trifling value. During a salute by cannon on his property at Nukulau island in celebration of

Independence Day, on the 4th July 1849, one of the guns burst, setting fire to his house, and the Fijians took advantage of the confusion caused to loot a quantity of his property which he valued, in the first instance, at 5,001 dollars and 38 cents. This incident was later to have important results for Fiji.

Ships of war were now paying more frequent visits to Fiji. In 1848 H.M.S. *Calypso* destroyed a town near Viwa which had been responsible for the murder of two Europeans the year before. In 1849 Cakobau and his chiefs were entertained on board H.M.S. *Havannah* at Ovalau and witnessed a demonstration of naval power, a target being set up on a rock about eight hundred yards from the ship and quickly knocked to pieces by the guns. Cakobau was greatly impressed by this and told a missionary who was with him: 'This makes me tremble. I feel that we are no longer secure. If we offend these people they will bring their ship to Bau, where, having found us out with their spy-glasses, they would destroy us and our town at once.' There is no doubt that this demonstration, and other examples of naval power, had a great effect in Fiji and made it possible for Europeans to live in fair security.

It did nothing, however, to curb Cakobau's arrogance

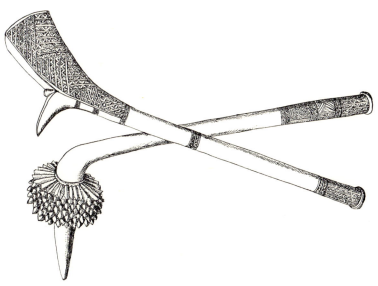

Types of war club

towards other Fijians and his ambition to be recognized as *Tui
Viti*, King of Fiji, a title to which he had no claim either in
theory or in fact. While being careful that his warriors did no
harm to the white missionaries, who, he realized, were held in
particular regard by naval commanders, Cakobau in 1850
levied war on all Christian Fijians, sending a strong force to
attack Viwa where the missionaries and many of their followers
lived. An appeal by the missionaries to Ma'afu and his Tongans
led to their intervention and Cakobau thought it wiser to withdraw his warriors.

In order to enhance his dignity he decided to order a ship from
America, which he thought would be more suitable to his rank
than the largest canoe, agreeing to pay for it with a thousand
piculs of *bêche-de-mer*. (The *picul* is a Chinese weight, equivalent
to $133\frac{1}{3}$ pounds.) The ship did not arrive as quickly as he had
expected and in his impatience he accepted the offer of a ketch
from Australia for which he promised to pay five hundred
piculs of *bêche-de-mer*. The ketch arrived and a start was made
on the collection of *bêche-de-mer* to pay for it, but before this was
completed the American ship arrived and Cakobau preferred
the larger vessel. The purchase of the ketch was therefore repudiated, only a portion of the agreed payment having been
made, and Cakobau sailed happily around the islands in his
American ship to impress friend and foe alike. To pay for it,
however, was not so easy as he could not get together sufficient
bêche-de-mer by ordinary means, the Fijians preferring to sell
what they collected to the European traders at Levuka who
paid a better price than Cakobau offered. He therefore imposed a levy on each district under his control but was met by
a campaign of passive resistance against the payment of a
tribute which was not justified by Fijian custom or tradition.
(Shades of ship-money!) Even a show of force led to small
results; in some cases only a trifling amount of *bêche-de-mer* was
produced, in other cases the chiefs flatly refused to co-operate.
Cakobau realized that he was powerless against public opinion
and the opposition of those he regarded as his subjects or clients.
The full amount due on the ship was never paid.

From this set-back Cakobau suffered a loss of prestige which
was, however, temporarily restored when he succeeded his
father, Tanoa, who died in December 1852. For years he had

been *de facto* chief but now he held the title *de jure* and was installed with due ceremony as *Vunivalu* (or Commander-in-Chief, literally The Root of War) and Chief of Mbau. In spite of the pleading of the missionaries and the exhortations of naval officers, five of Tanoa's widows were strangled, as related on page 30, Cakobau himself assisting in the strangling of his own mother.

In 1853 when the Lovoni tribe from the interior of the island of Ovalau raided and set fire to the town of Levuka, the European traders there suffered heavy loss. They believed, but could not prove, that the attack had been instigated by Cakobau, and this incident worsened the already bad relations between him and the white inhabitants. A league against Cakobau was soon formed in which the Europeans joined with the chief of Rewa and other enemies of Cakobau, and Mbau was practically blockaded, no trading vessels being allowed to go there. On account of this Cakobau's supplies of arms and ammunition began to run short. The position was made more serious for him when the garrison of Mbau warriors on the strategically important peninsula of Kamba, on Viti Levu, some five miles from Mbau, rebelled and joined the Rewa forces; Cakobau led a strong expedition against Kamba and suffered a severe defeat, which led to further defections among his own people and a strengthening of the morale of his enemies.

At this time Cakobau was in very poor health and everyone and everything appeared to be against him. The American Commercial Agent, Williams, wrote a letter which was published in a Sydney newspaper giving a lurid description of conditions in Mbau and appealing to the civilized nations to destroy this 'sink of iniquity'. The Wesleyan missionaries who visited him from Viwa warned him that his troubles were due to his opposition to Christianity, and King George of Tonga wrote urging him to mend his ways and become a Christian. For a few days after the receipt of King George's letter Cakobau hesitated, but on the 30th April 1854 he publicly renounced his heathen beliefs and accepted Christianity. He was baptized a few months later under the name of Ebenezer. A Wesleyan mission was opened at Mbau, the old temples were destroyed, and most of the inhabitants followed the example of their chief and became Christians.

The immediate result of Cakobau's conversion was a further weakening of his position, as his heathen enemies were more than ever determined to destroy him and hated Christianity the more because it was now the religion of Cakobau. Some of his own people also, disliking the idea of Christianity, deserted him and joined the enemy. The Europeans as a whole were against him and only the missionaries now appeared to be his friends. So serious were the prospects that one of the missionaries urged him to grant a liberal constitution to his people, which at such a period would have been entirely impractical. Even at this critical time, when his fortunes were at their lowest ebb, Cakobau was not prepared to surrender the power he had partly won for himself and partly inherited, and he replied to the missionary's suggestion with spirit: 'No. I was born a chief and I will die a chief.' This was in keeping with the pride and strength of character which never deserted him. A little later he was challenged by the chief of Rewa to settle their differences by a duel. 'It is shameful,' said the Rewa chief, 'that so many warriors should perish; let you or me die.' To this Cakobau replied: 'Are we dogs that we should bite one another? Are we not chiefs? Let us fight with our warriors like chiefs.'

It was, however, very likely that Cakobau was near his end. His enemies talked hopefully of the day when he would be killed and eaten. He was now the leader of only a small section of the Mbau people and the few Fijian Christians in other parts, while against him were ranged the Mbau rebels, the Europeans of Levuka, and all the heathen chiefs whom he had alienated by his former arrogance and aggression and had now infuriated by his conversion. At this critical time he was saved by the intervention of his friend, King George of Tonga.

King George came from Tonga in March 1855, with a fleet of thirty canoes and two thousand warriors, and was joined at Lakemba by Ma'afu and a number of other Tongans. It is probable that he came only to mediate between Cakobau and his enemies, with a show of force to strengthen his hand in negotiation. An unlooked for incident led to his taking an active and decisive part in the struggle between Cakobau, the converted Christian, and his heathen rivals. One of the Tongan canoes called at Levuka to deliver some letters and was fired on by some of Cakobau's opponents, in spite of a safe conduct promised by the chief of Levuka and the Europeans. During the firing a Tongan chief was killed and in spite of missionary efforts to avoid hostilities King George decided to join with his friend and fellow-Christian, Cakobau, to defeat the heathen enemy.

On the 7th April 1855 a combined attack was made on the fortified position at Kamba, and an impetuous charge by the Tongans, who did not observe the Fijian battle-conventions, resulted in an overwhelming victory. Cakobau's own warriors, who had not taken so prominent a part in the fighting, butchered many of the enemy, including women and children, but the carnage was stopped and Cakobau refused to allow the prisoners taken to be killed and eaten, their certain fate in the bad old days. He even spared the lives of some of his greatest enemies among the chiefs who had rebelled against him. This second battle of Kamba was, in fact, a victory of Christianity and Christian ideals over heathendom and the customs of the past.

The Tongan King then used his influence to stop further fighting and terms were agreed between Cakobau and his enemies. Rewa remained a separate chiefdom but recognized the suzerainty of Mbau, the Mbau rebels returned to their allegiance, and the whites at Levuka were reconciled to Cakobau. He himself turned over a new leaf, changing from a bellicose cannibal savage into a comparatively peaceful and civilized Christian ruler, from being the leader of the anti-Christian element in Fiji to being the strongest supporter of Christianity. He was married by the missionaries to his principal wife, while suitable provision was made for the other ladies of his harem who were dismissed to their former homes. He did not, however, abandon his desire to be *Tui Viti*, and he was now in a better position to achieve his ambition, but he could not ignore the fact that he owed almost everything, including his life, to Tongan assistance.

King George took as his reward Cakobau's largest canoe as well as the American ship which had cost Cakobau so much trouble and expense. He joined in the suppression of a rebellion against the chief of Thakaundrove and took the island of Rambi as payment for his services. He left Ma'afu in a strong position at Lomaloma, from where he was able to exert Tongan influence in Fiji.

Ma'afu was a skilful military leader and an even more skilful diplomat. He took advantage of the interminable disputes between the Fijian chiefs to improve his own position as holder of the balance of power. He became the ruler of the northern group of Lau islands and virtual overlord of the chiefdoms of Vanua Levu. As a professing Christian he did not permit cannibalism but he was ruthless in his wars against the people of Vanua Levu and allowed his followers to pursue a policy of 'frightfulness' which terrorized his opponents and facilitated the collection of tribute. Ma'afu was as ambitious as Cakobau and in many ways more efficient, and had he come to Fiji a little earlier might well have become the ruler of all Fiji. But times were changing. European immigration and the visits of naval ships were having their effect and it was now too late for an adventurer to succeed. Nevertheless, for many years Ma'afu and his Tongans had considerable influence on Fijian affairs and Ma'afu himself became the principal rival of Cakobau.

Moated Fijian village, pre-Cession

5. THE FIRST OFFER OF CESSION

THE two decades which followed the second battle of Kamba saw a steady increase of European influence in Fiji. In February 1855, shortly before the battle of Kamba, a new house at Lauthala (Laucala) Point belonging to Williams, the American Commercial Agent, was deliberately burnt by the people of Rewa. He had received no compensation for the loss of his property at Nukalau and he now used his official position to press his claims. There were other Americans who had suffered in one way or another as a result of the general lawlessness in Fiji, especially those in Levuka whose property had been destroyed when the Lovoni tribesmen set fire to Levuka in 1853. In September 1855 Commander Boutwell, in the U.S.S. *John Adams*, arrived to enquire into these outrages. Ignoring the reasonable recommendations made by arbitrators appointed by a previous American naval commander (one of whom was the highly respected American, David Whippy, who was referred to a few years earlier by the American Commodore Charles Wilkes as 'a prudent, trustworthy person') to enquire into Williams's earlier claim, Boutwell assessed the total damages at 43,531 dollars and decided that Cakobau was responsible and should pay this sum as compensation.

It was a most unjust decision. Some of the outrages had been committed at places where, at the time, Cakobau had no power or control; the damages, especially those claimed by Williams, had been grossly exaggerated; and Boutwell's bluster and bullying gave Cakobau no chance to defend himself. He was summoned on board the *John Adams* and threatened with deportation if he did not sign a document acknowledging his liability and promising to pay the full amount within two years, on pain of punishment by the next American ship to visit the islands. He signed under duress and at once protested in a letter to the American Government against Boutwell's 'unrighteous, tyrannical and unwarrantable' action. Another American captain later reduced the amount of the indemnity but in the end, as

75

we shall see, the American Government received the money. Williams was utterly unscrupulous in his claims, as in many of his land transactions, Commander Boutwell was unfair in forcing Cakobau to sign a document acknowledging the justice of an unjustified claim, and the whole business was discreditable to the American citizens concerned. Boutwell's conduct was severely criticized by an American merchant captain who had been in Fiji in a letter to the *New York Herald* published on the 9th November 1856.

An interesting comparison was drawn by William Diapea, who did not then know that the Americans would ultimately get the money, between the protection given to their citizens by the various nations. 'Uncle Sam', he said, 'is generally very prodigal of his awards . . . but then, by some means or other, it is hardly ever forthcoming. . . . But then, John Bull is much worse. He seldom awards at all, and hardly ever enquires, and if he does it is generally settled against the poor unfortunate white. . . . The Germans and French located in these seas are the best Governments for their subjects to seek redress from, for injuries received at the hands of these savages, either by fine, when practicable, or by pitching straight into them by fire and sword.'

International interest in Fiji was now increasing. French warships called at Levuka in 1856 and 1858 and a treaty for the protection of missionaries and other Europeans was concluded between the French Government and Cakobau. In 1857 United States ships called and negotiated a similar treaty. A British ship, H.M.S. *Herald*, carried out survey work in Fijian waters during 1855 and 1856 and the river Rewa was explored by a party from the ship. In 1857 W. T. Pritchard was appointed British Consul in Fiji. The nations were, in fact, watching one another with suspicion, none anxious to assume responsibility for Fiji but each unwilling to see the islands come under some other country's flag. The Wesleyan missionaries feared French annexation which they thought would give their Catholic rivals an advantage over them, and tried, without success, to persuade the British Government to take the islands.

In 1858 the U.S.S. *Vandalia* came to Fiji to avenge an American citizen who, with other members of the crew of a trading vessel, had been killed and eaten by the people of Waya, one of the Yasawa islands. With the loss of five men wounded, the stronghold of the Waya murderers was stormed and destroyed and twenty Fijians were killed. The warship then went to Levuka and Cakobau was sent for. He was told that he must pay within one year the amount of the indemnity which had been imposed on him by Commander Boutwell three years before, and he signed another document promising to do so although he knew that he had little chance of finding the necessary money. Four days later he signed another document, prepared at his request by Consul Pritchard and witnessed by two missionaries, offering to cede Fiji to Great Britain under certain conditions. In this document he was described as:

'Ebenezer Thakombau, by the grace of God, Sovereign Chief of Bau and its Dependencies, *Vunivalu* of the Armies of Fiji and *Tui Viti*',

and the document continued:

'Whereas We, being duly, fully and formally recognized in our aforesaid state, rank and sovereignty by Great Britain, France, and the United States of America respectively, and having full and exclusive sovereignty and domain in and over the islands and territories constituting, forming, and being included in the group known as Fiji, or Viti; and being desirous to procure for our people and subjects a good and permanent form of government . . . and being ourselves unable to afford to our aforesaid people and subjects protection and shelter from the violence, the oppression, and the tyranny of Foreign Powers. . . . And being heavily indebted to the President and Government of the United States of America, the liquidation of which indebtedness is pressingly urged, with menaces of severe measures against our person and our sovereignty. . . . We do hereby . . . transfer and convey unto Victoria, by the grace of God, Queen of Great Britain and Ireland, Her heirs and successors for ever, the full sovereignty and domain in and over our aforesaid islands and territories.'

There were two important conditions provided for, first, that the Queen 'shall permit us to retain the title and rank of *Tui Viti*, in so far as the aboriginal population is concerned and shall permit us to be at the head of the department for governing the aforesaid aboriginal population, acting always under the guidance and by the counsels of the representative of Great Britain'; and secondly, that the British Government should pay the debt due to America, receiving in return two hundred thousand acres of land in fee simple. Pritchard left at once for England to urge acceptance of the offer, and in doing so he stressed the possibility of developing the growing of cotton on the two hundred thousand acres of land mentioned in the document and in other parts of Fiji.

Cakobau was moved to this first offer of cession not only by the need for money to satisfy American demands but also by fear of Tongan aggression. He feared that King George was scheming to conquer Fiji and he knew that Ma'afu was taking steps that might be a prelude to such conquest. While professing friendship with Cakobau, Ma'afu was engaged in hostilities against the allies of Mbau in Vanua Levu and had seized the island of Mbengga (Beqa) and the district of Rakiraki on Viti Levu, both of which were under Mbau suzerainty. The next step would probably have been an attack on Mbau itself but, fortunately for Cakobau, Pritchard returned from England in time to save him.

Cakobau and Ma'afu both appealed to Pritchard for support. Ma'afu pointed out that if Pritchard did not help Cakobau, and merely remained neutral, 'that old savage' would quickly be eliminated and he, Ma'afu, a friend of the Europeans, would become chief of all Fiji and would cede the islands to Britain, giving his full support to the government. Pritchard hesitated for a while but decided to support Cakobau, who, although his claim to be *Tui Viti* was as doubtful as his authority to dispose of 200,000 acres of land, had at any rate a better claim than Ma'afu, who was not even a Fijian.

With a warship, H.M.S. *Elk*, in the harbour to support him, Pritchard convened a meeting in the consulate at Levuka, in December 1859, of all the leading chiefs. At this meeting Ma'afu was persuaded to sign a document renouncing all Tongan claims in Fiji and agreeing to restore all the territories he had conquered. He and the other chiefs present ratified Cakobau's offer of cession and an agreement was signed which provided, *inter alia*, for the protection of Christians of all races, for the prohibition of cannibalism and infanticide, and for recognition of the right of Europeans to hold land and to trade. The chiefs went further, and gave to the Consul 'full, unreserved, entire and supreme authority to govern Fiji and to make what laws he pleased'.

In virtue of this authority Pritchard established a consular court where disputes between Europeans were settled, with the co-operation of the American Consul in cases where United

States citizens were concerned. Pritchard also attempted to regulate the growing number of land transactions between Europeans and Fijians. The Fijians, with their communal conception of land ownership, did not usually understand that they were parting with their land when they sold it to Europeans, and sometimes the amounts paid for this land, chiefly in arms and ammunition, were ludicrously small. At the same time, the purchasers, with European ideas of freehold rights, in many cases paid what was thought at the time, by both parties to the bargain, to be a reasonable price, and believed that they had fairly and fully acquired the land they paid for. In such cases Pritchard registered the purchase, but where he considered the transaction to be irregular and unfair he ordered that the land should be restored to the Fijian owners. This naturally made him extremely unpopular with the worst type of Europeans who were unscrupulous in their complaints against him. Another cause of his unpopularity with these people was resentment at what they considered to be his interference in their private arrangements for the purchase of young Fijian women, 'ostensibly', as he described it, 'as servants or housekeepers, but in reality as so many wives'.

Pritchard was, in fact, making an honest effort to give Fiji an effective and responsible administration in the place of chaos, and although he lacked Foreign Office authority for his extra-consular activities his actions were approved by the Fijian chiefs and by the better type of European residents. Until he decided a case between Catholic and Wesleyan clergy in favour of the former he was supported by the Wesleyan missionaries, who were tending to become, as Mr. Derrick suggests, 'spiritual dictators, jealous of their power'. In the circumstances then prevailing in Fiji, such initiative as Pritchard showed was in the best interests of the country and of British prestige, and it is unfortunate that the Foreign Office took a narrow view of his activities and, instead of applying the brake gently, administered to him a sharp rebuke. Pritchard at once gave up his judicial and administrative work and confined himself strictly to purely consular duties.

The British Government had, in the meantime, sent Colonel W. T. Smythe to Fiji to examine the matter and report whether it would be expedient to accept the offer of cession. With him was associated a botanist of standing, Dr. Berthold Seeman, who was to report on agricultural possibilities in Fiji and particularly on the prospects of cotton growing which Pritchard had recommended. Seeman considered that high grade cotton could certainly be grown in the islands and that there were other possibilities. Smythe, however, submitted a most unfavourable report, advising against acceptance of the offer of cession.

In his report, dated the 1st May 1861, he wrote that Cakobau had 'no claim to the title of King of Fiji. There is, in fact, no such title. He is only one, although probably the most influential, of the numerous independent chiefs of Fiji, and has consequently no power to cede the sovereignty of the entire group to Her Majesty. He is of an ambitious disposition and his object seems to be, through the assistance of England, to become the ruler of Fiji, and to be protected from France and the United States of America, of both of which Powers he has great apprehensions. He is most desirous to get quit of the claims of the latter country, for which the United States officers, for their own convenience, have made him responsible although the amount of the claims has been apportioned by them among several tribes.'

Smythe also pointed out that Cakobau did not possess the 200,000 acres of land which he had offered. He did not believe, in spite of Seeman's better qualified opinion, that there were good prospects for a cotton industry, and he disagreed with naval experts on the advantage of finding in Fiji a port of call for vessels on the Pacific routes. He considered that the cost of administration would greatly exceed the revenue which could be expected. He was completely out of sympathy with Pritchard and appears to have been quite unable to take a broad view of the problem he was sent to study.

Of the permanent white residents in Fiji, amounting at that time to less than two hundred, he had little opinion. They were, he wrote, 'composed chiefly of men who have left or run away from vessels visiting the islands. They are principally British subjects, citizens of the United States, Frenchmen and Germans. The two former are the most numerous. They traffic with the natives for produce which they dispose of to vessels. They do nothing to civilize or impr   s; on the con-

Above: Sugar train. 'After the cane is cut it is loaded on trucks which are hauled into the fields on portable lines.' *Below:* Coconut plantation, Taveuni. Coconut products are the second most important export

Right: A Fijian holding a *dalo* plant

Below: 'The bananas grown in Fiji are of excellent quality'

Facing page, above: Cane cutters at work

Facing page, below: Inside the Emperor Gold-Mine, Vatukoula

Overleaf: A Fijian fish drive

Above: Fijian copra cutters. After the copra has been cut from the shell it goes to the drying sheds. *Below:* More than half of the total land area of the colony is under forest, which includes both hard and soft woods

Above: A student small holding at Navuso Agricultural School. Each student farmer has approximately eight acres
Below: Packing butter at a modern factory, Rewa

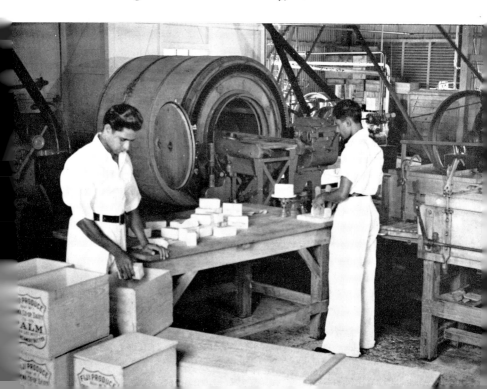

Right: Fishermen landing a turtle. These are usually presented to chiefs or caught on special occasions for feasts

Below: Tourists on the beach near the Beachcomber Hotel. The number of visitors to Fiji has been rising and additional hotels are being built

trary, they have in many instances fallen to a lower level. Whenever they can obtain spirits most of them drink to excess.'

Of the Fijian population, 'less than one third profess the Christian religion; among the remainder, cannibalism, strangulation of widows, infanticide, and other enormities, prevail to a frightful extent'.

So, finally, he said, 'on a review of the foregoing considerations, and the conclusions derived from a personal examination of the Islands and the people, I am of opinion that it would not be expedient that Her Majesty's Government should accept the offer which has been made to cede to Her Majesty the sovereignty over the Fiji Islands'.

In view of later decisions regarding land policy, and the claims of Europeans who had purchased land from the chiefs, it is interesting to quote a further extract from Smythe's report. 'On the subject of the purchase of land by whites, I made particular enquiry of the chiefs at each of the public meetings; the general reply was that an agreement made with the owners, if approved by the chiefs, would hold good.'

The British Government unfortunately accepted Smythe's report and rejected the offer of cession, the decision being made known to Cakobau in July 1862. Pritchard, against whose conduct Smythe and others had laid complaints, was removed from office in January 1863. He was replaced by Captain H. M. Jones, V.C. The acceptance of Smythe's report and the dismissal of Pritchard were disasters which led to another twelve years of confusion and strife in Fiji. Pritchard, the son of a missionary in Tahiti who afterwards became British Consul in Samoa, spent many years in the Pacific and had a considerable knowledge and understanding of local customs. He was liked and respected by the Fijians and could have done much good if he had been allowed to complete the work he had begun and had received adequate support. The official reason for his dismissal was that he had drawn bills for expenditure beyond the amounts authorized by the Foreign Office, but there is little doubt that behind this was the dislike of Whitehall officials for a man who displayed excessive initiative, and their acceptance of the mischievous tales told by dissolute Europeans.

There were many people, besides Pritchard, who were disappointed by the refusal of the British Government to accept the offer of cession. In 1859, while the matter was still being considered, the legislature of New South Wales forwarded an address to the Queen urging annexation, and one public-spirited Australian offered to provide the $45,000 necessary to satisfy American claims. Apart from those who hoped to obtain lands and settle in Fiji if it became a British colony, there was the fear that if the islands were not annexed by Britain they would be annexed by France or the United States. There was, in fact, a strong belief that the offer of cession could not possibly be refused, and Pritchard's enthusiastic propaganda, published in the Australian press, led many to regard Fiji as the land of promise.

As a result, during the year 1860 numbers of people came to the islands from Australia and New Zealand seeking land on which to cultivate cotton or raise sheep. Some were disappointed in the conditions they found prevailing and quickly left, but the majority remained, buying land from the chiefs and settling along the coasts of Viti Levu and in other islands. They needed labour to work on their plantations and, as the Fijians disliked steady and regular work, although they were (and still are) capable of very hard work for short periods, it was not long before recruiting agents were bringing labourers from the New Hebrides, the Solomons, and other island groups in the Pacific. This led to a scandalous trade in human beings, little different from slavery, which will be referred to later.

The more immediate result of the refusal of the offer of cession was a revival of strife and near anarchy in Fiji. In spite of the undertaking he gave when he signed the document in the Consul's office in 1859, Ma'afu had already, by 1861, resumed his former swashbuckling activities in Vanua Levu. Once again, this time on board a warship, Pritchard required him to sign a document promising better behaviour, and once again Ma'afu went back on his promises and sent his war canoes to support the Rewa chiefs against Cakobau and the European settlers in the Rewa territories. Later that year H.M.S. *Harrier* arrived to punish raids and attempts to burn the settlers' houses, and two villages were burnt after the inhabitants had been warned to leave. At about the same time the French corvette *Cornélie* arrived at Levuka and carried off as a prisoner to New Caledonia a Tongan chief, one of Ma'afu's lieutenants, who had flogged Catholic Fijians in the Yasawa islands. This strong action did not deter Ma'afu from further violence and intrigues, and in April 1862, Pritchard visited Tonga and persuaded King George to sign an agreement that there should be no more Tongan aggression against Fiji pending a decision by the British Government on the offer of cession.

Notwithstanding that the offer was declined there was no further overt aggression by Tonga after that date but Ma'afu continued to interfere in religious disputes between Wesleyan and Catholic Fijians, in every case to his own advantage.

Shortly after this, the refusal of the offer of cession and the dismissal of Pritchard, as related above, threw Fiji once again into a state of political turmoil, although the economic position was improving as a result of the increasing number of European settlers. A sugar factory was set up on Wakaya island and several cotton plantations were established. When the American Civil War cut off from the world's markets the supply of cotton formerly provided from the Southern States, the demand stimulated production from Fiji and good prices were obtained. Exports of coconut oil, *bêche-de-mer* and tortoise-shell, were also increasing and generally, in comparison with a few years earlier, trade was booming. The European settlers, however, had little security and a Foreign Residents' Self-Protection Society was formed which, after a short and ineffective life, passed out of existence. Cakobau did what he could to safeguard the lives and property of the settlers but lacked the power to give them effective protection. Areas controlled by Ma'afu, in Vanua Levu and Lau, had a little more security.

6. CAKOBAU REX

COLONEL SMYTHE'S report on the problems of Fiji was not entirely negative. As an alternative to British rule he suggested 'a native government aided by the counsels of respectable Europeans' and this appeared, to Fijians and Europeans alike, to be the only solution. On the 8th May 1865 the seven leading chiefs of Fiji, those of Lakemba, Mathuata, Mbau, Mbua, Nanduri, Rewa and Thakaundrove, signed an agreement at Levuka, constituting themselves a General Assembly with legislative powers, competent to make laws for the whole of Fiji, and with an annually elected President. Each state was to be self-governing in internal affairs and to levy its own taxes, but tribal wars were prohibited except with the approval of the General Assembly. For a short time this constitution appeared to be working, and Cakobau was elected President for two consecutive years, but in 1867 Ma'afu contested the election. He was not elected, but the contest led to disagreements among the chiefs and the Fijian Confederacy split into two.

Mbua, Lau and Thakaundrove, where Ma'afu's influence was strongest, agreed to form a Confederation of North and East Fiji, with Ma'afu as the real authority although at first the chief of Thakaundrove was allowed to be the nominal Chieftain Supreme. The ability of Ma'afu and of his British adviser, R. S. Swanston (later acting British Consul and a Magistrate under the Colonial Government), led to a reasonably efficient administration, especially in Lau which was under Ma'afu's direct rule. The German firm of Hennings Brothers, which had its headquarters at Lomaloma, carried on an extensive business under Ma'afu's protection, rivalling that of the merchants at Levuka.

In the rest of Fiji the situation was not so satisfactory, as Cakobau and his white advisers were less efficient and less capable of enforcing order. There were, however, more European residents and they were anxious to have a stable government under which they could work and trade in security. In April 1867 a meeting was held at Mbau, attended by more than sixty Europeans, and a constitution was drawn up, to be, in the first instance, for a trial period of three years. By this constitution Cakobau was recognized as king of all that part of Fiji which was not included in the Confederation of the North and East, and given full authority to govern and make laws. On the 2nd May the flag of the new kingdom was hoisted, and at a coronation ceremony which had its comic side, a tawdry crown, made by a local carpenter and studded with imitation jewels, was placed on Cakobau's hirsute head. A. B. Brewster, who was in Fiji before the Cession, says that Cakobau, 'with the innate good taste of a native gentleman, despised the tawdriness of the ceremony thrust upon him by his rugged white advisers, flung the bauble away and never used it again'. Later in the month nearly three hundred Fijian chiefs accepted the new constitution and swore allegiance to King Cakobau. All documents were signed by him as 'Cakobau R.'. A Chief Justice and several European Ministers were appointed, the principal being S. A. St. John, an American, and W. H. Drew, a British subject.

The new government did not last long as the European community refused to pay taxes and the treasury was soon bare. More serious was the arrival of the U.S.S. *Tuscarora* in July 1867, to demand payment of the debt due by Cakobau, the little matter of nearly $45,000 which seven years earlier he had promised, under duress, to pay. The American Civil War had postponed the day of reckoning but it seemed now to be at hand. Threatened with a bombardment of Levuka by the *Tuscarora*, Cakobau reluctantly signed another agreement to pay the amount due in four annual instalments, giving three of his islands as security.

Troubles did not come singly to Cakobau for during the same month a Wesleyan missionary, the Reverend Thomas Baker, with a number of Fijian Christians who accompanied him, were murdered near the headwaters of the Singatoka river, their bodies being afterwards cooked and eaten. Although it was considered that this part of Viti Levu lay within Cakobau's dominions, he was not in fact able to exercise much control over the wild mountaineers of the interior, but he nevertheless admitted his responsibility and promised J. B. (afterwards Sir John) Thurston, a former cotton planter, who was now acting as British Consul (Jones having been transferred to another post), to punish the murderers. Nothing was done for a while and in October H.M.S. *Brisk* arrived to investigate. On Thurston's advice it was decided to leave it to Cakobau to deal with the matter and at last, in April 1868, an expedition was launched. After a small initial success, one detachment led by Cakobau himself was ambushed and suffered heavy casualties. Another detachment, which Thurston accompanied, was also defeated and Cakobau was compelled to withdraw his forces having failed completely to enforce his authority.

The true reason for the murder of Mr. Baker has never been satisfactorily established. It has been said that he was imprudent in visiting an area where the people were notoriously savage, that he had insulted a chief, and that as a Wesleyan missionary he was associated with the hated Cakobau and killed for that reason. He was the first and last missionary to be killed in Fiji.

In the meantime, through the United States Vice-Consul in Levuka, some Australian interests were induced to negotiate with Cakobau for the settlement of the American debt in return for the grant of two hundred thousand acres of land and other privileges. In May 1868 Cakobau signed a charter granting to these Australians, incorporated as the Polynesia Company, a large area of land and extensive privileges in consideration of the company paying off the $45,000 claim by the United States Government and giving Cakobau himself an annuity of £200. The company was to receive a large area of land and the right to acquire any other land they might later need; to possess all minerals found on such land; to have a banking monopoly; to have the right to impose customs and other duties; to make laws binding on all Fijians and Europeans in their territory; and to administer such laws. A mutual obligation bound Cakobau and the company to support one another, if necessary by force.

Thurston, who was away at the time the charter was signed, protested against it as soon as he returned, on the grounds that it gave the company power over British subjects and that Cakobau had given away more than was his to give. He had, in fact, been persuaded to sell for about £9,000 a very large area of his peoples' land and had given governmental powers to a trading company. When H.M.S. *Challenger* arrived soon afterwards, Cakobau was persuaded to revoke the charter, the terms of which, he said, he had not fully understood. It was alleged that one of the Wesleyan missionaries had advised him to sign this deplorable charter, hoping to benefit himself by speculation in land at the expense of the Fijian people. One of the promoters of the Polynesia Company, and for a time one of its directors, was General Latham, the United States Consul-General at Melbourne.

In July, at the American Consulate, Cakobau signed a second charter which, although less favourable to the company than the first, still gave it considerable benefits, including the grant of much land round Suva harbour and in other parts of Viti Levu and Vanua Levu. Thurston again protested but was unable to veto this charter. And so, after a further futile and partial inquiry by the captain of yet another American warship, the United States Government received its pound of flesh in the shape of the dollars paid by the Polynesia Company, and Cakobau was relieved of one of his anxieties.

The company was not very successful in its enterprise and its reputation never stood high. Some of the land it sold to settlers was quite unsuitable and in some cases did not even exist. In other cases the settlers had considerable difficulty in establishing themselves, as the Fijian occupiers of the land refused to recognize Cakobau's right to dispose of their property, and Cakobau was not strong enough to compel them. In the opinion of the British Consul, 'Cakobau deceived the company and the company cheated its clients, who in their turn settled themselves on the debatable land and thus commenced an epoch of quarrels and outrages between the whites and the Fijians'. Most of the company's settlers were confined to the Suva area and the banks of the Rewa river, and even there trouble arose. In 1868 H.M.S. *Challenger* despatched a boat expedition up the river to protect settlers who were prevented from occupying land they had bought. A hostile village was burnt, but as the naval party had strict orders not to fire on the Fijians, it was forced to retire in the face of a determined attack and suffered casualties, the settlers being obliged to abandon their property.

The company later disposed of most of its rights to a group of people popularly known in Fiji as the 'Forty Thieves' who had advanced the money needed to pay the American claims. After Fiji became a British colony (in 1874) a claim was made to the land originally granted by Cakobau to the Polynesia Company and this was referred to by Sir Arthur Gordon in a despatch to the Secretary of State for the Colonies which explained the position. 'In 1870', he wrote, 'the Polynesia Company sold or professed to sell 100,000 acres of the land alleged to be granted to it under Cakobau's charter to the "Forty Thieves". Into the motives of this sale it is unnecessary to go. Ostensibly at all events, the "Forties" paid to the Polynesia Company a sum of £10,000 and received from it a transfer of 100,000 acres of land. So far the case is simple. The "Forties" could not receive from the Polynesia Company a better title to the land than that which it possessed itself, *i.e.* one absolutely worthless. . . . The Government will I think be slow to admit that such a grant has alienated, without the consent of the occupants, large tracts of inhabited country, full of populous towns, thickly studded with gardens and cultivation, and of which neither the Polynesia Company nor the "Forties" have at any time yet attempted to take possession.'

In his interesting book, *King of the Cannibal Isles*, published in 1937, A. B. Brewster gives his personal reminiscences of the settlers who came to live on the company's land at Suva and the kind of life they led there just before Fiji became a colony. 'Taking us all round,' he says, 'we were an inefficient happy-go-lucky crowd, with inadequate capital, who had not sat down and counted properly the cost of the venture, but had been caught by the glamour of the islands, and always trusted that something would turn up which would lead us to fortune. The inadequacy of capital did not matter so much, as in those days Fiji was a soft and easy country where, if a man had a little land, nearly everything he required could be produced on it. Not much clothing was required; as a rule we went barefooted, and a shirt, a pair of duck trousers and a Tokelau hat made up the rest of our kit.'

Notwithstanding the company's difficulties and the risks run by Europeans on isolated plantations, there was a steady increase of immigrants from Australia, and the European population rose from little more than eight hundred in 1867 to over two thousand by 1870.

Considerable areas of land were acquired directly from the chiefs of various districts and cotton exports in 1869 were valued at £57,000. The first sugar mill was erected at Suva in 1872 by two shareholders in the Polynesia Company. Reading matter was provided for the residents of Levuka by the *Fiji Weekly News and Planters' Journal*, first published in 1868, and replaced by the *Fiji Times* the following year.

In the Confederation of North and East Fiji, under Ma'afu's strong rule, there continued to be peace and comparative good order, but in the area controlled, or partially controlled, by Cakobau there was still disorder and no security of tenure for European settlers. In March 1869, a number of Europeans met at Mbau to draw up another constitution to replace that agreed to in 1867. Cakobau was again recognized as King, and it was decided that there should be two Houses of Parliament, one of Fijian chiefs and the other of whites elected from the various districts. The approval of both Houses and of the King was necessary for the enactment of a law. The executive consisted of a number of Europeans, W. H. Drew becoming Chief Secretary. In spite of the hopes raised by the acceptance of this constitution it was no more successful than the previous one, as once again the Europeans refused to pay the taxes imposed.

The British Consul at Levuka, H. M. March, who had taken over from Thurston in December 1868, refused to recognize the authority of the new government over areas which were not under its control and warned British subjects that they could not be nationals both of Fiji and of the United Kingdom. The traders at Levuka, with a long tradition of hostility to Cakobau, also ignored the Mbau constitution and supported the chief of Levuka who was now no friend to Cakobau.

From Levuka in 1869 no less than three memorials were forwarded asking for annexation, to Prussia from some German settlers, to the United States from a minority of the Europeans, and to the United Kingdom from the majority of the settlers, most of whom were British, as well as from Cakobau, Ma'afu and other chiefs.

During the same year H.M.S. *Rosario* seized a ship in Levuka harbour which had brought men, kidnapped from the New Hebrides, for disposal in Fiji, and there was other evidence of an unholy traffic in human beings to supply the planters with labour. Many of the better type of Europeans deplored the way in which this labour was recruited and the British and American

Consuls did what they could to stop it, but it was obvious that only a strong local administration could put an end to the irregularities which were giving Fiji a worse name than it had already. The settlers did not themselves kidnap men, but they were at the receiving end and paid the 'blackbirders' who did so for their human cargoes.

More and more Europeans were coming to Fiji, several hundred living in Levuka and others scattered around the coasts of the larger islands. Most of the planters were educated men with a certain amount of capital, but many even of these were blind to the scandals of the labour traffic. Of the remainder, some were honest men anxious to make an honest living; some were criminals, safe in Fiji because of the absence of extradition treaties; some were men who had fled from importunate creditors; and others were just thriftless and irresponsible persons who hoped to make money without working too hard for it. There was a great deal of drinking and gambling in Levuka in which whites and Fijian chiefs joined. (A case of German or Dutch gin, containing four gallons, cost then only seventeen to twenty shillings.) It would in any case have been difficult for the Cakobau administration to maintain order in Fiji at this time, although the behaviour of most of the Fijians compared favourably with that of the more dissolute Europeans, but the rush of immigrants who did not take kindly to any form of control made it quite impossible.

In these circumstances attempts were made in 1870 by the more responsible Europeans to establish a practical form of government for the whole group but it proved hopeless to reconcile the conflicting interests of the planters and the inhabitants of Levuka and the matter was dropped. Later that year, however, Cakobau authorized the whites at Levuka to elect a corporation for local government and some improvements were effected, but nothing much could be done in face of a legal ruling that British subjects could not be coerced by the corporation.

The United Kingdom Government was being particularly unhelpful. It had refused to accept the offer of cession made in 1858, it would take no action in 1870 in spite of appeals from Fiji and urgent requests from the Australian colonies, and it would not even grant magisterial powers to the British Consul at Levuka or recognize local governments set up in the islands. It is no wonder that the New South Wales Cabinet felt that this attitude was 'very much to be regretted'.

It was therefore with a sense of frustration and exasperation that one group of Europeans in Fiji encouraged Cakobau to make yet another attempt to establish a government. The need for stability was more than ever necessary owing to the collapse of the cotton market, which ruined most of the planters, and the falling off of trade which brought disaster to the merchants.

On the 5th June 1871, at Levuka, Cakobau was again proclaimed as King of Fiji and several European and Fijian Ministers were appointed. (Postage stamps were issued bearing the initials C. R. (Cakobau Rex) surmounted by a crown.) There were immediate protests from a minority of Europeans, and the British Consul refused to recognize the authority of Cakobau's government and warned British subjects against it. On the other hand, there was surprising co-operation from Ma'afu who took the oath of allegiance to Cakobau and accepted for himself the office and title of Viceroy of Lau. Ma'afu's example was followed by other chiefs. A House of Delegates was opened on the 1st August, about half of the members being Fijian chiefs and the remainder Europeans elected for various constituencies, with J. S. Butters, the representative in Fiji of the Polynesia Company and a former Speaker of the Legislative Assembly of Victoria, in the chair. As the Fijian members took little interest in the proceedings of the House, and seldom attended (except when brought in to support the Government against the Opposition), it was decided to confine membership to the elected Europeans, the Fijians becoming members of the Privy Council. A constitution was agreed to and writs were issued for elections to a Legislative Assembly which was opened on the 3rd November, Butters being elected Speaker. The Cabinet Ministers were mainly Europeans, the most important being S. C. Burt, formerly an auctioneer in Sydney, and G. A. Woods, a retired naval officer, both of whom were extremely unpopular with other Europeans. In March 1872, Burt resigned his office and after some delay Thurston was persuaded to take his place. He had acted as British Consul on the departure of Jones in 1867 until

March assumed office and since then had been planting cotton in Taveuni. It was fortunate for Cakobau that so able and so honest a man was available to help him at a critical time.

Cakobau's previous administrations had failed because of the lack of funds but on this occasion, although financial difficulties were later encountered, an immediate way of raising money was found. The Lovoni tribe in the mountainous interior of Ovalau, which had long been a menace to the whites in Levuka, refused, at the beginning of 1871, to pay the taxes imposed on them by Cakobau, and raided villages inhabited by his followers, killing and eating one of the chiefs. They were then attacked by Cakobau's warriors and after a long struggle were persuaded by the missionaries to surrender at the end of June. They were taken, men, women and children, to Levuka and sentenced to transportation, being handed over to European settlers to work on their plantations on payment to Cakobau of a premium of £3 a head and a yearly sum for their hire. This outrageous arrangement, in no way different from slavery, lasted until 1874, when Fiji became a British colony, and provided Cakobau with a large revenue.

In August 1871 two Europeans who had settled on the banks of the Mba (Ba) River were murdered by Fijians, and other plantations were threatened by the mountain tribes of the interior of Viti Levu. A punitive expedition was promised, but before it could take action a force of European settlers, with some warriors of the Mba tribe, advanced into the hills and, after failing to make contact with the tribes responsible for the murders, withdrew without effecting anything.

The European settlers in the more remote and uncontrolled areas took considerable risks with equanimity. Brewster tells of a war between a hill tribe from the interior and a small Fijian Christian settlement which was established on the coast of Viti Levu Bay. 'Between the belligerents', he says, 'was a plantation belonging to a man named Hannah. His house was in the direct line of fire; the walls inside were lined with bags of cotton and there was a shelter pit sunk in the centre of the floor into which the placid-minded owner retired when shooting commenced. . . . He was regarded as strictly neutral, living on no man's land, where both sides could meet and arrange the fight according to the customs of Fijian warfare, and, by means of trade, impartially get their ammunition replenished.'

In addition to his troubles with the Fijian population Cakobau's government had to deal with some serio-comic disturbances in Levuka. Some of the more lawless Europeans defied the government and forcibly released a British subject who had been committed to prison by the magistrate. They formed a secret society which they called the British Subjects' Society and Volunteer Corps, but which was generally known as the Ku Klux Klan (scarcely more respectable than its American namesake) and bound themselves to resist the government by force, parading under arms to prevent the arrest of another European accused of murder. They were, however, disarmed by Cakobau's constabulary, Fijians under British officers, and by pro-government Europeans who styled themselves the Mutual Defence Corps.

A German corvette was at Levuka at this time and her captain warned German citizens not to join in any demonstrations against the government. March, the British Consul, on the other hand, would take no action and it is believed that he secretly supported the opposition and encouraged British subjects not to pay taxes. March was suspiciously popular with the worst type of Europeans in Fiji and his bias against Cakobau's government did considerable harm until he was finally recalled by the Foreign Office in January 1873.

It is fortunate that British naval officers were more helpful than the Consul. In May 1872 the Ku Klux Klan again attempted to defy the government by releasing prisoners from the Levuka gaol. Thurston, who was now acting Premier, was determined to enforce the authority of the government and ordered the constabulary to fire on the Europeans if they used force. At this moment Captain Douglas in H.M.S. *Cossack* arrived at Levuka and intervened to prevent bloodshed. He warned the members of the Ku Klux Klan that whatever their nationality they were subject to the laws of the country in which they were resident, and he assured Cakobau of British sympathy for his government.

In February 1873 a settler on the Mba River named Burns with his wife and children and a number of unarmed foreign labourers were brutally massacred by Fijians of a mountain tribe. This outrage was apparently unprovoked, but was no doubt the result of the 1871 murders in the same district having gone unpunished.

The settlers blamed the government for the disaster as it had forbidden the arming of labourers who were thus unable to defend themselves, and resolved to deal with the murderers on their own responsibility and prevent the government forces, which had quickly been despatched to Mba, from taking action. When the constabulary and European pro-government volunteers from Levuka arrived they were met by a larger body of armed settlers who ordered them to withdraw. For some days the two parties faced one another and there would probably have been fighting had it not been for the fortunate arrival of H.M.S. *Dido* which anchored off the Mba River on the 18th March. Captain Chapman insisted that the settlers should lay down their arms and removed two of their leaders, a lawyer named DeCourcy Ireland and Colonel T. W. White, both notorious opponents of the government, who were deported to Australia. The government forces, joined now by many of the settlers, then advanced against the mountain strongholds of the murderers, with a number of Fijian auxiliaries who were, however, not very reliable. After some severe fighting, in which the government forces and the settlers suffered heavy casualties, these strongholds were destroyed and many of the murderers were captured. Some of these were sentenced to death but their sentences were commuted. A number of other prisoners taken, including women and children, were sentenced to penal servitude, and offered to the planters on the same terms as in the case of the Lovoni tribe. Very few planters accepted the offer owing to protests by Commodore Goodenough who arrived in Fiji before the transactions were effected; the prisoners were, however, detained until the colonial government set them free.

Shortly after these events, in May 1873, the government was defeated on a vote in the Legislative Assembly and the Ministers submitted their resignations to Cakobau, but he, preferring his Ministers to the obstreperous members of the opposition, dissolved the House on the 11th June and retained the Ministers in office. Although perhaps unconstitutional, this action was justified by the factious behaviour of the white members of the

94

legislature who wished to use their position for their own advantage without any consideration for the welfare of the Fijian population. The poll tax which had been imposed by the government had proved oppressive, those Fijians who could not pay being sentenced to work for the planters for a wage of about one shilling a week, while the Europeans resisted the payment of taxes by themselves.

Thurston did what he could to protect the people from the oppression of their chiefs and the tyranny of the planters, and in so doing earned the hatred of most of the Europeans but remained popular with the Fijians. In July writs were issued for a new election and the Ministers arranged that the Fijians should be allowed and encouraged to vote, a step which the Europeans denounced as a breach of the constitution, which provided for white voters only. Meanwhile, when the Ministers attempted to raise revenue without legislative authority, the Europeans at Levuka again defied the government and only the presence of H.M.S. *Blanche* prevented actual hostilities. The government troops were in position and ready to fire on the rebels but the ringleaders were taken into preventive detention in the warship and Captain Simpson issued a proclamation forbidding the use of force by either the rebels or the government. Thurston at once protested against this interference which had prevented the government from asserting its authority, as he was confident it could do, and Simpson withdrew his proclamation. The trouble died down for a while and when it began again a few weeks later the agitators were dispersed by the government constabulary without bloodshed.

The position, however, was becoming impossible. Faced with the selfish opposition of a majority of the Europeans, most of them unprincipled men who cared nothing for the Fijian inhabitants, the Cakobau Ministers, led by Thurston, were carrying on a dictatorial administration which was nevertheless better than the chaos which appeared to be its only possible alternative. The Fijians themselves were governed to a great extent in accordance with custom through their own chiefs and no constitution was necessary for this. The Legislative Assembly, the courts of law, and the expensive administration were foreign institutions made necessary by the presence of white immigrants who refused to pay the taxes needed to maintain the government. Power had indeed passed from the hands of the Fijian chiefs into the hands of members of an alien minority, and the government of King Cakobau was conducted in his name entirely by Europeans who continued to rule after being rejected by those who had originally elected them. It was due almost entirely to Thurston's personal influence and strength of character that the position did not further deteriorate.

It was obvious, however, that the existing arrangements could not continue indefinitely. The government was in debt and Australian debenture holders were anxious about their investments. Cakobau and Thurston were in favour of ceding the islands to the British Crown and made tentative enquiries as to whether cession would be acceptable. Public opinion in Britain and elsewhere was concerned by the scandals connected with the labour traffic and the Aborigines Protection Society asserted that Fiji was 'the real focus of the slave trade' in the Pacific. Two years later the Secretary of this Society declared, in an address to the Royal Colonial Institute, that 'civilization can only make real progress in the Pacific under the guidance of a powerful and united Empire—an Empire which is determined that human rights shall be respected wherever its authority extends, and that just laws shall be established in the remotest island which yields obedience to the sceptre of the Queen'.

In the House of Commons, on the 13th June 1873, a resolution was moved that the United Kingdom should either annex Fiji or declare a protectorate over the islands, which would provide a proper government and stop the bringing of kidnapped labourers to the territory. In response to this pressure the British Government at last, and with reluctance, sent commissioners to Fiji to examine the situation and report.

7. THE CESSION

IN 1873 Commodore J. G. Goodenough, in command of the Australia station (killed two years later by the savages of Santa Cruz, one of the Solomon Islands), and E. L. Layard, who had been selected to succeed March as Consul in Fiji, were appointed as Commissioners to examine the Fiji question. The Gladstone government in England was still reluctant to accept responsibility and made it clear that it was 'far from desiring any increase in British territory', being unwilling to annex Fiji unless this were proved to be 'the only means of escape from evils for which this country might be justly held to be bound to provide an adequate remedy'.

The Commissioners arrived in Fiji early in 1874 and found that practically all the Europeans, Ma'afu and his Tongans, and most of the Fijian chiefs were in favour of annexation. On the other hand Cakobau and his principal adviser, Thurston, who had previously been in favour of cession, now wavered for a while. They thought it possible that Cakobau's government, under Thurston's management, could be continued, and withdrew the offer of cession. This led to strong protests from the Europeans and from Ma'afu, and the Commissioners made it plain that they had no confidence in Cakobau's government. In these circumstances Cakobau again changed his mind and on the 20th March announced formally that he was prepared to cede the islands to Great Britain. On the following day, accompanied by Thurston, he met the Commodore on board H.M.S. *Pearl* and presented a letter stating that 'it is our mind to give the government of our kingdom to the Lady Queen of Great Britain'. Later, referring to Queen Victoria, he said: 'We trust in her goodness: we give ourselves this day to her.'

The Commissioners were now in a position to report and they strongly recommended that Fiji should be annexed as a British colony as they could 'see no prospect for these islands should Her Majesty's Government decline to accept the offer of cession but ruin to the English planters and confusion to the

Native Government'. Before leaving Fiji the Commissioners were able to persuade Cakobau to form an interim government, with Thurston as Chief Secretary and a provisional legislature which included the foreign Consuls. Government expenditure was drastically reduced and, apart from a few irresponsible Europeans who disliked the prospect of orderly administration, there was general satisfaction in Fiji.

Meanwhile in England the Gladstone government had fallen and Disraeli had taken office as Prime Minister. The Australian colonies and New Zealand urged the acceptance of the offer of cession and the United Kingdom Government was at last prepared to agree. Sir Hercules Robinson (afterwards Lord Rosmead), Governor of New South Wales, was instructed to proceed to Fiji, with discretion, and after discussing the matter fully with the chiefs and the European inhabitants, to accept or refuse the offer. Robinson was welcomed at Levuka by the European community and two days later he met Cakobau on board H.M.S. *Dido* and explained to him that, while Her Majesty's Government was willing to accept the offer of cession, the offer must be unqualified as the Government could not accept the conditions attached to the formal offer. Cakobau made a characteristic reply: 'The Queen is right, conditions are not chieflike.'

Cakobau continued with a speech in which he gave his opinion of the Europeans who had tormented him for so many years. 'If matters remain as they are,' he said, 'Fiji will become like a piece of drift-wood on the sea, and be picked up by the first passer-by. The whites who have come to Fiji are a bad lot. They are mere stalkers on the beach. The wars here have been far more the result of interference of intruders than the fault of the inhabitants. Of one thing I am assured, that if we do not cede Fiji the white stalkers on the beach, the cormorants, will open their maws and swallow us. The white residents are going about influencing the minds of others so as to prevent annexation, fearing that in case order is established a period may be put to their lawless proceedings.' So far as many of the Europeans in Fiji were concerned, Cakobau was justified in this outburst. Some of the worst characters left when Fiji came under British rule and settled in Samoa, to the detriment of that territory.

The Commissioners then asked Cakobau to consult the Council of Chiefs, which decided to 'give Fiji unreservedly to the Queen of Britain, that she may rule us justly and affectionately, and that we may live in peace and prosperity'. On the 30th September King Cakobau and four of his principal chiefs signed the Deed of Cession, which was also signed later by Ma'afu and the other High Chiefs of Fiji. A copy of this document, which was referred to in evidence before the Commission of Enquiry of 1959 as 'our Fiji Magna Carta', is at Appendix A.

On the 10th October 1874 at Levuka, the Deed of Cession was signed and sealed by Sir Hercules Robinson on behalf of Her Majesty's Government, and Fiji was declared to be a British colony. The flag of Cakobau's government was lowered and the British flag hoisted, a salute being fired by the warships in the harbour. During the proceedings Cakobau gave his war-club to Robinson, with a message to Queen Victoria which was interpreted by Thurston. 'Before finally ceding his country,' the message ran, 'the King desires to give Her Majesty the only thing he possesses that may interest her. The King gives Her Majesty his old and favourite war-club, the former, and until lately the only, known law of Fiji. . . . With this emblem of the past he sends his love to Her Majesty, saying that he fully confides in her and in her children, who, succeeding her, shall become kings of Fiji, to exercise a watchful control over the welfare of his children and people; and who, having survived the barbaric law and age, are now submitting themselves, under Her Majesty's rule, to civilization.' The club was kept in England until 1932 when King George the Fifth sent it back to Fiji to be used as the mace of the Legislative Council. With it he sent a message which was read to the Council by the Governor: 'Since its presentation by King Thakombau to Her Majesty Queen Victoria,' ran the message, 'this mace has had an honoured place among the royal treasures in Windsor Castle. His Majesty now returns the mace for ceremonial use in the Legislative Council as a visible token of his abiding concern for the welfare of his Fijian people, of whose unswerving loyalty he is deeply sensible.'

When Robinson returned to New South Wales the former Consul, Layard, remained in Fiji and administered the government under the interim arrangements, with Thurston as

Colonial Secretary. Cakobau and two of his sons also went to New South Wales on a visit and there contracted measles. By the time they got back to Fiji in H.M.S. *Dido*, on the 12th January 1875, they were convalescent but still infectious, and in the absence of any quarantine precautions the crowds who assembled to welcome them home quickly caught and spread the disease. It ran rapidly through all the islands of the group and is remembered as the worst disaster that ever affected the colony. In a few cases, as for example among the Fijian constabulary under military discipline and proper care, the deaths were not excessive, but for the most part a very high proportion of those infected died for lack of proper treatment. Many went into water to cool themselves when tormented by fever, with fatal results, and the death roll was so heavy that there were scarcely sufficient left to bury the dead. Provisions ran short owing to the number incapacitated by illness. One of the Wesleyan missionaries reported from Mbau that 'daily the canoes were to be seen carrying the dead to their resting places on the opposite shore, and day and night was the death-drum beating, and the wails of the mourners rose on the air. Strong winds and heavy rains added to the horrors of the situation; and the Bauans almost starved for food, the people being unable to get to the mainland where their gardens were.' A planter at Savusavu wrote that 'the greatest trouble is to get the dead buried. The whites have done all they can in their several neighbourhoods (but the Fijians) seem quite indifferent about one another and, unless some white person is near, neglect the sick, and sit and look at them dying for want of a drink or a bit of food.' The people were, in fact, stunned by a disaster without parallel in their history. It is not known how many actually perished but it is believed that the number was about 40,000, perhaps a quarter of the total population, and most of the deaths occurred between February and May 1875. It was a particular mischance, as will be seen later, that towards the end of January representatives of the wild mountain tribes from the interior of Viti Levu came to Navuso, on the Rewa river, to meet Layard and Thurston. They agreed to renounce heathen practices, especially cannibalism, to live at peace among themselves, and to acknowledge the supremacy of the government, but unfortunately they carried back the infection to their villages. As the epidemic spread among these unsophisticated people, causing considerable loss of life, the belief grew that it had been deliberately spread by the government or was a punishment for the desertion of the old gods and acceptance of the white man's religion.

The epidemic was almost at an end when the first Governor, Sir Arthur Gordon (afterwards Lord Stanmore), arrived at Levuka on the 24th June. A younger son of the fourth Earl of Aberdeen, Gordon was recognized as an aristocrat by the chiefs of Fiji who placed (and still place) a high premium on dignity and good manners. He had been Lieutenant-Governor of New Brunswick and Governor of Trinidad and Mauritius and thus had much experience of colonial administration. He was determined to govern Fiji in the best interests of the indigenous population and to protect them from that section of the white traders and settlers who thought only of their own profits.

These were the people he referred to in a paper read to the Royal Colonial Society in 1879. 'The white settlers', he said, 'had apparently imagined that by some magical process the assumption of sovereignty by Great Britain was to be followed by an immediate change from poverty to wealth, from struggling indigence to prosperity, that their claims to land would be at once allowed, that an abundant supply of labour would be at once found for them, and that their claims to supremacy over the natives, which the Government of Cakobau—whatever its faults—had steadily refused to recognize, would be at once acknowledged. They were, therefore, bitterly disappointed to find their hopes not realized.

'The natives', he continued, 'were cowed and disheartened by the pestilence (of measles), which they believed to have been introduced purposely to destroy them—a belief encouraged, I am ashamed to say, by some of our countrymen, and which was probably the main cause of the disturbances in the highlands of Viti Levu in the following year.'

It is not surprising, in view of his policy, that Gordon made himself unpopular with a number of Europeans but he was greatly admired and loved by the Fijians, who still revere his name. It was largely due to Gordon's efforts on their behalf both as Governor and later as a member of the House of Lords, that the right of the Fijians to their communally owned land was recognized and respected. With his background it was natural for him to see, in the chiefly hierarchy of the Fijians, a valuable stabilizer that was worth preserving. Professor Spate, in his report on the Fijian people, says that Gordon's ultimate ideal 'was probably a society in which hereditary rank should retain all the traditional respect still accorded to the chief of a Scottish clan, in which social ceremonial should still be actively observed, but in which a chief could not demand political leadership, still less economic privilege, simply on grounds of birth'. To a great extent, like Lord Lugard in Nigeria a quarter of a century later, he was compelled, on account of the shortage of staff and money, to use the chiefs in the administration of the infant colony. Miss Perham, biographer of Lord Lugard, quotes Gordon's opinion of Lugard as a man possessing that quality 'essential to the successful government of native races, the power to make them act in their own way, under their own leaders, and of their own free will, in the direction in which he wishes them to go'. Gordon might have been speaking of himself.

This was the man who was faced with all the problems of a new, practically bankrupt, colony, to which law and order were as yet unknown. These were the days when Britain's dependencies were expected to be self-supporting, which meant, in effect, that their development was gravely retarded and the local officials were given an almost impossible task. It is typical of the niggardly attitude of successive British governments in the nineteenth century, that the money provided by the United Kingdom to start the administration of Fiji, £100,000, was not made as a grant but as a repayable loan. Having suffered under Treasury control as Governor of a grant-aided colony I can appreciate the difficulties and frustrations which Gordon must have endured in the task of making bricks without straw.

For some weeks after his arrival Gordon studied the situation and, although he quietly took command, he left the administration formally in the hands of Layard. It was not until the 1st September that the Royal Charter constituting the Colony of Fiji was publicly read and Gordon sworn in as Governor. Before this, however, Cakobau had made what Gordon described as his 'personal feudal submission in proper style', laying an immense root of *yaqona* at his feet, breaking off 'one of the smaller portions of it and placing it on my hand. This was the decisive act of vassalage . . . probably the first time in his life that he ever performed a personal act of homage to another, and that too in presence of his people.'

Gordon also described the Fijian constabulary which provided his guard of honour. They 'were armed with short rifles and dressed in a very full garment of thick fringes like a kilt reaching to the knee, under the knee a sort of garter of black water-weed. They all had great heads of hair, for the most part dyed yellow', and were commanded by Lieutenant Olive of the Royal Marines.

The first serious problem with which Gordon had to deal was a rising of several of the mountain tribes of Viti Levu in the upper Singatoka valley. These people, as related above, held the government, or the Christianity which the government supported, responsible for their sufferings during the measles epidemic. Known as the 'devil tribes', they attacked and burnt villages belonging to Christian Fijians, killing and eating several of the inhabitants, and threatening government posts. Any delay in dealing with the situation would certainly have resulted in further raids on Christian villages and would probably have led to other tribes, which were wavering, joining the anti-government party. In these circumstances Gordon acted at once, and on his own responsibility. Without calling for assistance from the small detachment of Royal Engineers engaged in Fiji on construction works, or asking for other military assistance or advice, he decided to treat the suppression of the outbreak as a police matter and to use for the purpose only such local forces as were available to him. A few hundred men of the Fiji Constabulary were the only 'regulars' at his disposal, but an appeal to the chiefs of the coastal tribes of Viti Levu met with an enthusiastic response and thousands of warriors, led by their chiefs, joined the government force. Several columns, commanded mainly by members of the Governor's personal staff, moved against the hostile villages and after some difficult operations in mountainous and rugged country the 'devil tribes' were defeated and their strongholds destroyed. A number of prisoners were taken and, after trial, several were convicted of murder and executed.

The loyal chiefs gave their aid as feudal service without pay, and the total cost of this police action was less than £3,000. Nevertheless, Gordon was attacked in the House of Commons regarding the expenditure incurred, which, owing to a misunderstanding, was thought to have exceeded £13,000, and he was called upon by the Secretary of State for the Colonies to explain why he had ventured on these completely successful operations without asking for military advice or assistance.

The second problem, and one of more lasting importance, was that of land. There was, according to Fijian ideas, no such thing as individual property except as regards 'the dwelling house and what in England is called the curtilage'. The fields, which were the property of the village, were portioned out from time to time to cultivators and the waste belonging to it was available to the whole commune. Before the Cession, however, a considerable amount of land had been sold by the chiefs to Europeans and this was clearly admitted in the fourth clause of the Deed of Cession, which read as follows:

> 'That the absolute proprietorship of all lands not shown to be now alienated so as to have become *bona fide* the property of Europeans or other foreigners or not now in the actual use or occupation of some Chief or tribe or not actually required for the probable future support and maintenance of some Chief or tribe shall be and is hereby declared to be vested in Her said Majesty her heirs and successors.'

There was considerable doubt whether all the land claimed by Europeans had, in fact, been acquired *bona fide*, and, on the recommendation of Sir Hercules Robinson, the Secretary of State for the Colonies had directed 'that with the view of disturbing as little as possible existing tenures and occupations, and of maintaining (as far as practicable, and with such conditions only as justice and good policy may in any case appear to demand) all contracts honestly entered into before the Cession, the Colonial Government, to which the rights of the Crown are delegated in that behalf, should forthwith require all Europeans claiming to have acquired land by purchase to give satisfactory evidence of the transactions with the natives on which they rely as establishing their title, and if the land appears to have been acquired fairly, and at a fair price, should issue to the persons accepted after due enquiry as owners a Crown grant in fee simple of the land to which they may appear entitled'.

A Land Claims Commission was accordingly set up in 1875,

under the chairmanship of the Chief Justice, which examined several hundred claims and submitted its findings for the decision of the Governor in Council, the final report of the Commission being dated the 2nd February 1882. According to this report no less than 1,683 applications were received, but, as several of these related to the same land or to more than one piece of land, this total is misleading. The Commission actually dealt with 1,335 claims which they classified as follows:

Granted as claimed	517
Disallowed as of right, but granted *ex gratia* wholly or in part or with modifications	390
Disallowed	361
Withdrawn and otherwise disposed of	56
Not finally decided	11
	1,335

Some of the Commissioners' comments on special cases illustrate the conditions existing in Fiji before the Cession and incidentally explain the time taken by the Commission in arriving at its conclusions. Nine of the claims disallowed were 'merely the inevitable results of the preposterous proceedings of white men. . . . Two gentlemen having purchased, as they believed, some 9,000 acres, proceeded to sell lands to the extent of 16,000 acres, a transaction which might appear strange had it not been given in evidence . . . "that they had about that time 'got on the spree' or, in plain English, were in a chronic state of intoxication".'

The Commissioners drew attention to the fact that many of the documents relating to alleged sales of land were irregular and could not have been fully understood by the Fijians. 'In many cases the so-called deed has been merely a sale note of the most irregular and informal character, written on any scrap of paper procurable, and by any person who could be found to write it, but the largest allowance has always been made for informalities where no defect graver than informality has attached to them, and, considering the class of persons who constituted the majority of the early land purchasers in Fiji, and the rough half savage manner in which they lived, it is perhaps surprising that the informalities and irregularities have not been even greater than they are.' They also cited the case where the mark of a young chief was obtained to a document at a time when he was a child of about five years of age.

A large proportion of the land sales were effected by Fijians in order to obtain arms and ammunition for offensive and defensive purposes. 'By Fijian custom, that is by Fijian law, the absolute alienation of land as understood by us was unknown, and therefore, strictly speaking, illegal: yet can it be doubted they had a perfect right in common prudence to procure by any means in their power the safety of their lives and the lives of their wives and families? Where would be the utility of preserving land when by so doing they subjected themselves to extinction altogether, and consequently left no posterity to enjoy the lands thus spared by a too rigid adherence to their old customs?'

The Governor in Council approved generally of the Commission's recommendations and an attempt by certain Europeans whose claims had been disallowed to appeal from these decisions to a court of law was frustrated. For those lands in respect of which claims had been allowed, amounting to more than 400,000 acres, Crown grants were issued, and it is on the titles so established that the ownership of most of the freehold land in Fiji now depends. The 75,000 acres now belonging to the South Pacific Sugar Mills, Ltd., a subsidiary of the Colonial Sugar Refining Company, the largest freehold property owners in Fiji, were bought from some of the original grantees.

The German Government protested against the disallowance of claims made in respect of alleged grants to Hennings Brothers and after long negotiations compensation was paid to the German claimants by the United Kingdom Treasury.

The success of the German claim prompted the renewal of claims by United States citizens, the most celebrated (or notorious) of these being G. R. Burt. The claim of this man, who had a reputation for making false claims to the ownership of lands and had withdrawn some of them when threatened by Cakobau with being charged with nine murders, was finally acknowledged by the United Kingdom Government and a sum of £10,000 was paid in 1923.

Having settled the claims of those Europeans who had a reasonable title to their lands, the government took pains to ensure that the Fijians should be left in undisturbed possession of the rest of the country (with the exception of Crown Land). In spite of much opposition and criticism by would-be purchasers, Fijian land was declared by law to be inalienable to non-Fijians, and except for a short period between the years 1905 and 1908 this has been the consistent policy of the colonial government, with the result that the Fijians still own, under 'native customary tenure', more than 83 per cent of the total land acreage of the colony.

For this fortunate position the Fijians are indebted, as stated above, to Gordon's persistent efforts to prevent them, even when they wished to do so, from selling their birthright. In the House of Lords, on the 16th July 1907, Gordon, then Lord Stanmore, opposed any alteration of the law which he had enacted some twenty-seven years before to safeguard the Fijians' ownership of their land. 'All who are acquainted,' he said, 'with the Fijian race know perfectly well that if you separate them from their land the race will die out, and that would be a violation of the express conditions on which alone we took possession of the Fijian islands. We told the natives that we had come to protect them against the lawlessness of the white settlers; we told them that their lands should be kept to them inviolate; we told them that their customs and laws, so far as they were not absolutely objectionable and immoral, should be maintained; and to that we are pledged by despatches without number from successive Secretaries of State, and in speeches equally without number of successive Governors; and what is more important than all, by the solemn word of Her late Majesty the Queen. On two separate occasions Her late Majesty did me the honour to convey to me her commands from her own lips that I was to tell the Fijian people that their lands were theirs and should never be taken from them. I told them so on the authority of our Sovereign, and I do trust that that pledge then given will be maintained.'

It was these repeated pledges, and the terms of the Deed of Cession, which led the 1959 Commission of Enquiry to declare that it was 'quite impossible to ignore the Fijians' right to the ownership of all land in the colony other than Crown Land and land under freehold'.

Gordon thought, however, that the Fijians could be secured 'in the full possession of their rights without entirely blocking the progress of settlement by white settlers', by permitting the leasing of their land, so that 'there should always be some money coming in to the commune as long as the lease lasted, and that it should not be whittled and made away with by being given a lump sum once for all to those who really have no right to dispose of the property and who possessed only a life interest in it'. This is the policy that obtains today and should be perpetuated, but, as will be shown later, it has been interpreted in so narrow a spirit in some cases as to retard the progress of the colony.

The third serious problem with which Gordon had to deal was that of labour, which will be considered next.

8. THE INDIANS

PRIOR to the Cession, as we have seen, the demand of European settlers for labour had been met by the introduction of men from the Solomon Islands, the New Hebrides, the Gilberts, and other island groups. Most of these were of the Melanesian race but in Fiji they were always spoken of as 'Polynesians'. In some cases, especially at first, the recruitment of these labourers was carried out in a humane and honest manner, but the traffic soon passed into the hands of unscrupulous schooner captains who, if unable to obtain their labourers by fair means, did not hesitate to kidnap them and treat them, while aboard their vessels, with great brutality.

These 'blackbirders' were, in fact, slave traders of the worst type, whose conduct led to a general distrust of all Europeans by the islanders of the Pacific. It was because of their enormities that other white men, desirous only of helping the people of these islands, were murdered by unsophisticated and suspicious savages who had come to believe that all Europeans were their enemies. There is no doubt that the murders in the Santa Cruz islands of Bishop Patteson in 1871, and of Commodore Goodenough in 1875, were in retaliation for outrages committed by white men.

So long as Fiji provided a market at which labourers could be disposed of they were brought there in their hundreds in spite of the attempts of British warships to intercept the slavers. The foreign consuls accredited to Cakobau's government did their best to regulate the traffic but it was seldom possible to protect the men from ill-treatment by their employers or to ensure that they were repatriated at the end of their term of engagement, in some cases because the employers had not the means to pay for repatriation. After Cession one of the first duties of the colonial government was to start sending back to their homes numbers of labourers who had been detained in Fiji far beyond the time when they should have been repatriated. Owing to lack of transport and other difficulties there was much delay and in 1876 there were still nearly 3,000 whose period of service had expired.

Although most of the settlers treated their labourers humanely there were some who did not. In a despatch of the 22nd July 1875, Sir Arthur Gordon refers to the 'trial of two Europeans whose brutal inhumanity and neglect led to the death, in a few weeks, of twenty-four out of thirty-one labourers'. A jury of their fellow-countrymen found them 'not guilty' of man-slaughter, but the judge considered that one at least of them, though acquitted, had been guilty of gross inhumanity. At a later date, in October 1879, Gordon referred to 'cases of labourers being habitually supplied with insufficient food, of their being lodged in improper dwellings, and of an entire want of medicine in cases of sickness, followed by a heavy mortality'. Sir Arthur was of the opinion, however, that the imported labourers were, in general, well off and well treated in Fiji and that, as the abuses connected in the past with the recruitment of labour were almost wholly abolished, no reasonable fault could be found with the system or the condition of the labourers during their term of service.

Nevertheless, as early as September 1875, Gordon had pointed out to the settlers that the supply of 'Polynesian' labour was decreasing and the cost of it increasing, and suggested that it would be wise to supplement this labour by that of Indian coolies. In view of the present attitude of the Fijians to their Indian fellow-citizens, it is important to recall that it was Sir Arthur Gordon, one of the greatest champions of the Fijian people, who first proposed the immigration of Indians. He had previously been Governor of Mauritius, where Indian inden-tured labour had been introduced as early as 1834. Nothing was done for a while but as 'Polynesian' labour became scarcer (partly because of competition from Queensland) and the Fijians, depleted in numbers by the measles epidemic, were unable or unwilling to perform regular work, Gordon revived the proposal in 1877. After long negotiations with the Govern-ment of India a scheme for indentured labour was agreed upon.

The principal features of the scheme were that volunteers were recruited by agents in India and after signing contracts were transported to Fiji at the expense of the employers to whom they were later assigned. The contract in each case was with the Fiji Government and the labourer bound himself to work where he was directed for a term of five years in return for agreed wages and accommodation. He could then work for another five years for whom he pleased and was after this entitled to free passages back to India for himself and his family. It was stipulated that forty women should be brought to Fiji for every one hundred men.

The first immigrant ship arrived from India in May 1879, with 481 labourers on board. Between that date and 1916, when the indenture system was abolished, some 62,000 Indians were brought to Fiji under indenture and of these only about one-third exercised their right to repatriation; some even of these subsequently decided to come back to Fiji. There were also a few immigrants who came from India at their own expense, but the greater part of the present Indian population in Fiji (205,068 at the end of 1961) are the descendants of indentured labourers. It is estimated that over 92 per cent of the Indians now in Fiji were born in the colony.

The majority of the immigrants were agriculturists from different parts of India. In the report on the 1956 census of Fiji the number of Indian households were classified according to the languages spoken within them as follows:

Hindustani	17,164
Hindi	3,644
Tamil	1,498
Urdu	1,223
Gujarati	830
Telegu	797
Gurmukhi	468
Malayalam	134
Other languages or not stated	273
	26,031

A form of Hindustani which pays scant attention to grammar is most generally used in Fiji. Less than one-sixth of those now in the colony are Moslems, the remainder Hindus, and among the latter there is little evidence of caste distinctions. In the first place, caste was lost by leaving India and crossing the sea, and secondly, the unavoidable mingling of passengers in the

immigrant ships and in the 'coolie lines' where the labourers
lived in Fiji had a levelling effect.

There were inevitable abuses in the indenture system and a
report by C. F. Andrews and W. W. Pearson in 1916, after their
visit to Fiji, mentions some of them. The greatest evil of the
system appears to have been the sex disproportion which led to
a corruption of morals, murders caused by jealousy, and a surprising number of suicides. The accommodation in the 'coolie
lines' was also condemned, as were the frauds perpetrated by
recruiting agents in India who gave misleading accounts of the
conditions and in some cases practically kidnapped women.

In spite of these handicaps the immigrants were probably
much better off in many respects than they had been in India,
and some of them, and their descendants, became prosperous.
Their numbers have greatly increased and in recent years, as
the sex disproportion has disappeared, they are increasing very
rapidly indeed. They now comprise nearly 50 per cent of the
population while the indigenous Fijians are only about 43 per
cent, and it is estimated that in another twenty years the pro-
portions will be 53 per cent and 40 per cent respectively.

The reasons for the more rapid growth of the Indian population are firstly that their women marry at a much younger age
and secondly that infant mortality among the Indians is considerably lower than among the Fijians. In the report on the
Census of 1956 it is shown that 702 out of every thousand Indian
women aged twenty or over had borne their first child before
they were twenty. The comparative figure for Fijian women
was only 298. Whatever the causes, there can be no doubt that
the Indian population is increasing at a rate which fills the
Fijians with alarm, and this has led to some friction.

The year after the first Indians arrived in Fiji, the Colonial
Sugar Refining Company, of Australia (generally referred to as
the C.S.R.), purchased its first land in the colony, on the Rewa
river, and began to plant sugar-cane. Later it bought other
lands and now owns 75,000 acres, most of which is leased to
Indian cane farmers. The company also built, or acquired from
previous owners, all the sugar mills now operating in Fiji and
for many years has completely controlled the sugar industry of
the colony.

At first the company used 'Polynesian' labour but later

nearly all of their labour was Indian and they were the principal employers of the indentured labourers who came to Fiji. When the indenture system came to an end in 1916 it became difficult for the company to obtain labour to work its fields, especially as many of the Indians whose indentures had expired were growing cane and other crops as independent farmers on lands leased from Fijians. The company therefore decided to give up the direct cultivation of their lands and to subdivide these lands into farms of about ten acres each for leasing to tenant farmers. It was considered that a farm of this size would allow the tenant to make a living for himself and his family by growing cane and vegetables and keeping a cow or two.

Most of these tenants were Indians and today most of the cane crop is produced by Indians. In 1958 they were cultivating cane on 118,184 acres as against 8,448 acres of cane cultivated by Fijians. The latter were not in the past attracted by the demanding work of cane farming which requires constant attention, while today most of their land best suited to growing cane and near to the sugar mills has been leased to Indians.

To the Indians, on the other hand, sugar-cane appears to be the only popular crop. As will be shown on page 189, so much has been done for them by the Colonial Sugar Refining Company that they have few responsibilities, and in recent years they have received good payment for their cane. This has had the effect of making the Indian farmer believe that no other crop is worth while, and he wishes to be allowed to grow and sell more cane than the company is in a position to buy, owing to the limitations imposed by International and Commonwealth Sugar Agreements on the amount of sugar that may be exported from each territory.

It is clear that on account of these Agreements the sugar-cane crop cannot be increased and indeed, owing to the use of better-producing varieties of cane and improvements in agricultural practice, the permitted quota of sugar can be produced from a smaller acreage of cane than was previously planted. In these circumstances it is imperative that the Indians should turn their attention to alternative crops and, indeed, in view of their increasing numbers, they should look for land other than the very best cane-growing land which they now consider essential for farming. At present a map showing the distribution of the

Indian population would be almost identical with one showing the cane-growing areas of Fiji, but other areas, and other crops, are worth consideration.

While most of the Indians are engaged in agriculture, a number have entered the professions or business and many of these are wealthy. Some are in the Civil Service. A Fijian-born Indian is now Commissioner of Labour. Another is a Crown Counsel. Of the 56 lawyers in Fiji 38 are Indians, and out of 10,245 persons or businesses assessed for income tax in 1957 no less than 9,076 were Indian.

As long ago as 1919 there was published in a pamphlet a list of names of several Indians who had prospered since their arrival in Fiji. One who started on a small area of land at Lautoka on which he cultivated sugar-cane and other crops was then the owner of 2,482 acres of freehold which he leased to tenants; he and his family owned several motor-cars. Another came to the colony some sixteen years earlier without any capital; he borrowed £200 to procure the leasehold of 120 acres of land and paid off all his debts in a few years by growing cane. Yet another had given up work altogether, having amassed considerable wealth.

At the same time, while some Indians have acquired wealth and many of the farmers are comfortably off, a number live in a permanent state of indebtedness to shopkeepers and money-lenders. It is said that 'men in comparatively poor circumstances spend extravagant amounts at the marriage of their daughters and incur debts in this connection which cripple them financially for the rest of their lives'.

There is little doubt also that some shopkeepers who give credit to their compatriots take advantage of their less literate clients and fleece them unmercifully. It is significant that many Indians in their evidence to the 1959 Commission of Enquiry complained of their treatment by shopkeepers and money-lenders of their own race and suggested the deportation of all Punjabis and Gujaratis who are held particularly responsible.

Many Indians have given up agriculture in favour of shop-keeping, or to work as tailors or barbers. Some run bus or taxi services and several are in domestic service in hotels or private houses. In the early days of the colony they were particularly valued by the Europeans as domestics, and Brewster writes feelingly on the subject. 'The Indians', he says, 'have added considerably to the comforts of the British colonists, who are now able to enjoy the services of first-class cooks and domestic servants.'

When it is remembered that the Indians in Fiji are largely of peasant stock, and came to the colony as indentured labourers without capital, one is bound to admire the industry and initiative which have led to such a change in their fortunes as is described above.

The implications of the rapid increase in the Indian population, with its effect on the Fijians, will be referred to in a later chapter. We must first consider some of the other events which followed the Cession of 1874.

9. COLONIAL GOVERNMENT

IN the two preceding chapters an account has been given of three serious problems with which Sir Arthur Gordon had to deal soon after he assumed the government of Fiji—the rising in Viti Levu, land, and labour. There was also the important matter of administration. Sir Hercules Robinson, in establishing the interim government after the Cession, had recognized twelve of the leading chiefs as *Rokos*, each in charge of a provincial area, and Gordon confirmed this arrangement and developed the system of administering the Fijian population through their own chiefs. The traditional district and provincial councils were retained and a council of chiefs was inaugurated which brought together, for friendly consultation, the leaders of the various tribes who had, in the past, known little contact other than war. This council, which included some Fijian officials not of chiefly rank, drew up regulations dealing with a number of matters particularly affecting the Fijians, and in cases where Fijians were concerned (apart from serious crimes) Fijian magistrates presided in courts which administered Fijian law.

A new system of taxation was also devised. The former poll-tax imposed by Cakobau's government had proved a heavy burden on the Fijians, who were forced in most cases to become labourers on European estates in order to earn the money by which the tax could be paid. On Thurston's advice, Gordon levied a tax in kind on the various provinces, which the *Rokos* collected from the districts or villages within their jurisdiction in the form of locally grown produce. The produce was then sold by tender and the proceeds credited to government revenue up to the amount of the tax due, any balance being paid to the Fijians. This system was acceptable to the Fijians but was criticized by the white population—by the settlers because it was no longer necessary for the Fijians to work for wages and by the traders because it gave to the growers a better idea of the value of their produce.

It was denounced even in England as slavery or forced labour. In reply to criticisms Gordon pointed out that the scheme had both a financial and a social object. As to the former there could be no doubt of its success as the revenue had rapidly increased. As to the latter, he wrote, 'the cultivation of articles of export by the natives has been largely promoted. Fijians are by no means habitually indolent, as by many careless observers they are supposed to be, and they are passionately fond of agriculture; but their cultivation, though very neat and careful, is chiefly that of food plantations and articles for domestic use . . . although coconuts and yams in large quantities have long been sold, or rather bartered, to the white traders. Under the new system the area of native cultivation is rapidly increasing, and the lesson which it was desired to inculcate has been already partially learnt. Another consequence of the adoption of this law has been that of giving to the people a juster idea of the value of the produce which they raise.'

In the past, Gordon continued, the Fijian 'only received for his produce about half the price which the very same traders are now ready to give to the government for a similar amount of produce. . . . This has opened the eyes of the natives, and in their private trading transactions they now, in many cases, ask and obtain prices more nearly resembling the true market value of the article.' The system also had the effect of checking what Gordon called 'the entanglement of the natives in debt to the traders'. Whatever objections there may be in principle to such a form of taxation, there can be no doubt that it was suitable to the conditions prevailing in the infant colony of Fiji, and that it was in the best interests of the local inhabitants. As late as 1890, according to the annual report for that year, the taxes due from the Fijians were collected principally in copra and sugarcane, but maize, tobacco, yams, *yaqona* and *bêche-de-mer* were also received. Not until 1902 were cash payments substituted.

There were other problems of minor importance, and not the least of these were the people with whom Gordon had to deal. His opinions of some of them are on record, and are often pungent. Of one of his senior officials whom he thought self-seeking he writes that 'the man is repulsive to me'. One settler he describes as 'feeble, foolish and knavish', and another as 'presumably a rascal'. But for the most part his comments are generous, although he cannot resist telling of a Chief Justice (whom he liked personally) whose 'ever present sense of his own dignity and importance used sometimes to place him in comical situations'. This pompous individual took his exercise and recreation by rowing a small boat about Levuka harbour, wearing a 'black swallow-tailed coat and tall black hat, which he deemed essential to the maintenance of his official dignity. The figure he cut, with his swallow-tails hanging down to the water in the bottom of the boat as it washed about from side to side, and with his tall hat bending to each stroke of the oar, was ridiculous.'

Of Thurston he had a high opinion and considered that he stood far above the other white men in Fiji in ability and resource, and perhaps for that reason as much as any other was hated and feared by those who did not understand him. Owing to his unpopularity with the white residents, Gordon thought it politic not to continue him in the post of Colonial Secretary, the second post in the administrative hierarchy, to which Sir Hercules Robinson had appointed him. For a while, therefore, he served as Auditor General but gradually overcame the prejudices against him and rose through various offices until, as Sir John Thurston, he became Governor of Fiji in 1887. He was always greatly respected and beloved by the Fijians.

For Cakobau also Gordon had nothing but praise. In a speech he made in 1878 he pointed out that 'if, on ceasing to reign, Cakobau had cherished any ill-will towards the new order of things, or had even given way to a feeling of sullenness, it would have been in his power to cause the government very considerable trouble and annoyance; had he merely passively held aloof from affairs, embarrassment would probably have followed. But from the first day of British rule up to this moment the cordial co-operation of the *Vunivalu* has never been wanting, and his efforts to render the new order of things intelligible and palatable to his people has been unceasing.' Two years later Gordon spoke in the same sense. 'Had he listened,' Gordon said, 'to the whispers of those—whites, alas, not natives—who have vainly endeavoured to make him discontented the work of the government might have been most seriously embarrassed. But this has never in the slightest degree been the case. ... The whole of his vast influence has been invariably exercised in furtherance of the objects of the government.'

A later Governor, Sir William Des Voeux, also found Cakobau 'wise in council, just in decision and loyal in speech and action. He had, moreover, an indescribable dignity and a manner indicative of mingled pride and courtesy.' There can be no doubt that Cakobau was, in his own way, a great man. Without education and barely able even to sign his own name, he had been for the first thirty-seven years of his life a savage and a cannibal, delighting in bloodshed and the foremost champion of Fijian heathendom against Christianity and civilization. When, however, he accepted Christianity in 1854 he did so whole-heartedly and changed his ways completely. Until the Cession, so far as he was allowed to by unscrupulous Europeans, he tried to govern his people efficiently and honestly. Ambitious as he was to be King of all Fiji, he became convinced that the best thing for the country was to cede it to the British Crown, and after Cession he never faltered in the loyalty to which he had sworn. He died in 1883 and at his funeral a British warship fired a salute and the Last Post was sounded over the grave of a great Fijian chieftain who, in his youth, had been a brave and dangerous warrior.

Ma'afu, Cakobau's old rival, died three years before him in 1880. He too proved loyal to the colonial government, and did good work as *Roko Tui* of Lau. He is buried at his old base, Lakemba.

One of Gordon's difficulties was the attitude of the Wesleyan missionaries who resented their replacement as advisers to the Fijians by officials of the government. A particular cause of friction lay in what Gordon described as 'an impudent attempt to extort money for missionary collections' from their congregations, with the assistance of Fijian magistrates and threats of imprisonment in case of non-payment. As the people were led to believe that this mission tax was legally collectable, a number of them paid before the government became aware of the situation and took steps to have the money refunded. From this time, says Gordon, the chief effort of the head of the Mission 'was to regain his lost ascendancy, or, failing that, to destroy what had superseded it, namely, the colonial government'. According to Gordon, the head of the Mission had occupied in the past 'very much the position of one of the political bishops of the Middle Ages . . . accustomed to rule very autocratically in much outside the spiritual sphere'. In the opinion of the Chief Justice it was the general decay of their authority which was vexing the missionaries.

There was, however, more in it than that. The missionaries objected to government recognition of the validity of marriages contracted in accordance with Fijian custom, and to the refusal of the government to support their own puritanical objections to dancing and other innocent pastimes. A letter from the Governor to the head of the Wesleyan Mission in 1880 explains the official attitude. 'You may rely', he wrote, on 'officials seconding to the utmost the prohibition of nocturnal, immoral or indecent dances but then I hope it will be clearly understood that such prohibition does not extend to harmless dancing in the daytime, wrestling, running, or playing at ball (all of which seem to have been proscribed), for these I should certainly not only not discountenance but distinctly encourage, believing that where harmless and open recreation is forbidden, resort will be had to such as can be indulged in secret, and which will probably be of a less innocent nature. . . . As an example of the needless rigidity of puritanism which had been enforced, I may mention that when I was in Rotuma in December last I found it was considered sinful to wear flowers, or to make artificial flowers of feathers, at which the girls are very expert.'

The cold war between the Governor and the Wesleyan missionaries was the more remarkable because Gordon admired their work and liked personally several of them, giving support to the Mission whenever he could lawfully do so.

The over-riding problem in the early days of British rule in Fiji was how to carry on the administration and development of the colony with an inadequate revenue, for no help was given by the United Kingdom Government which at that period and for many years later required every colony, no matter how poor, to balance its budget without external aid. The solution was generally found in rigid economy, by the reduction of official staff, and the postponement of work which was essential to development. For example, when Thurston became Governor in 1887 he dispensed with a Colonial Secretary and a Secretary for Native Affairs and performed the duties of both offices in addition to his own.

So impoverished was the colony that economy had to be

exercised in the issue of postage stamps, the surcharged stamps of King Cakobau being used for some years and the design being followed for an even longer period. The philatelic history of Fiji is, in fact, very interesting. The first stamps were those issued in 1870 by the *Fiji Times* newspaper which arranged for the transport of mails, and although this private issue was not recognized abroad the stamps were used to pay postage among the Fiji islands. They were printed in Levuka and bore the plain inscription, *Fiji Times Express*, and the value. The *Fiji Times* was required to discontinue the issue of these stamps when the first stamps of the Cakobau government were issued at the end of 1871. These stamps, which were printed in Sydney, were more ambitious in design, with *FIJI* at the top and *Postage* and the value at the bottom. Within a circle in the middle of the stamp were the initials *C.R.* (Cakobau Rex) surmounted by a crown.

After the Cession in 1874 the Cakobau stamps were overprinted at Levuka with the initials *V.R.* (Victoria Regina) and these overprinted stamps remained in use until 1876. In that year a new issue was made, using the original frame of the Cakobau stamps, with the initials *V.R.* instead of *C.R.* It was not until 1881 that Queen Victoria's head appeared on any of the stamps of Fiji. Although the values of the *Fiji Times* stamps and of those issued by the Cakobau government were shown in shillings and pence, the latter were later surcharged to show the values in cents, as at that time dollar currency was more common in Fiji than sterling. Incidentally, in the 1938 pictorial issue there was a curious mistake, the 1½d. stamp showing a canoe in full sail without a crew; this was corrected later. The four shilling 'parrot' stamp issued in 1959 won the Grand Prix Gold Medal for the best stamp from Oceania at the Monaco International Stamp Exhibition of 1960.

When in 1880 Gordon was offered the governorship of New Zealand he hesitated for some time before accepting it as he was reluctant to leave Fiji, fearing that his successor might depart from the policy of governing the Fijians through their chiefs and of protecting them in the possession of their land. He suggested that he might be allowed to continue as Governor of Fiji in addition to his Governorship of New Zealand but this was considered impracticable. It was, however, agreed that he should continue to supervise 'native' affairs in Fiji as long as he remained Governor of New Zealand. His fears, as a matter of fact, were groundless, as his two immediate successors, Sir William Des Voeux and Sir John Thurston, both of whom had served under him in Fiji, were in full agreement with his policy and continued faithfully to implement it. It was not until Sir Everard Im Thurn was Governor in 1905 that a law was passed which permitted the sale of Fijian land, subject in each case to the approval of the Governor-in-Council, and another the following year giving the government authority to acquire Fijian land for any purpose which it might consider 'desirable as directly benefiting the colony'. This meant, in effect, that the government might acquire land for disposal to private persons for agricultural or other use which, in the government's opinion, might be of advantage to Fiji.[1]

There was considerable argument over these departures from the spirit of Gordon's policy and, as we have seen, Gordon himself intervened successfully in a debate in the House of Lords. The offending laws were repealed but not before some 20,000 acres of Fijian communal land had been sold.

When the time came for Gordon to leave Fiji, in November 1880, there were touching scenes as chiefs and people bade him farewell. Cakobau was too infirm to attend the last meeting of the Council of Chiefs at which Gordon was present, but Ma'afu was there to speak feelingly of the work the Governor had done. 'In former times,' he said, 'there were no such gatherings as these. In those days there was no unity and one-mindedness. We were divided, each in his heart pulling his own way. From the time that the *Vunivalu* decided to give Fiji to Great Britain we have been united. Union has followed, and we are today found one in consequence, enjoying peace and prosperity. But now, Sir, you are about to go and leave us behind. One thing let me say, let me urge. Do not forget us—do not forget us. Still think of us and act for us.'

A few months later the chiefs sent a letter 'To our Lady the Queen of Fiji and Great Britain' asking that they might be permitted to present Gordon with two small islands 'in order that he shall continue to be one of us and named among us in all time to come, that it may be known that it was he who estab-

[1] See page 138.

lished the working of good and suitable government in our land, which has brought us prosperity, rest and peace'.

After Gordon left Fiji he was Governor in succession of New Zealand and Ceylon, and in 1893 he was raised to the peerage as Lord Stanmore. He never lost his interest in Fiji or his affection for its people. He died in 1912.

The Devil's Thumb, Ovalau

10. THE LATER YEARS

THE later history of Fiji is one of careful building on the foundations laid down by Sir Arthur Gordon, with, perhaps, too little recognition of the fact that conditions were changing. The revenue and the value of the trade increased steadily, but very slowly, and, as has been pointed out, the revenue was at first insufficient for the proper development of Fiji's resources. The niggardly policy of the United Kingdom Government in the nineteenth century precluded any substantial financial assistance to the young and struggling colony. A grant-in-aid of £100,000 was swallowed up by expenses incurred in the establishment of the administration immediately after the Cession, and in paying off and repatriating the large number of Polynesians who had been brought to Fiji as labourers prior to annexation. It has been pointed out that in the nineteenth century individual failure in the economic struggle was regarded as a sign of lack of effort and therefore blameworthy. Charity was no remedy for poverty as it merely encouraged such moral shortcoming, and by analogy charity must also be bad for dependencies, which should be required to 'live of their own'.

Fiji was indeed treated no worse than any other colony at this period. It was the policy of the United Kingdom Government that each colony should be self-supporting and that the British taxpayer should not be called upon for direct financial assistance to overseas territories. It is true that when a colony suffered from some natural disaster, such as a hurricane or an earthquake, the United Kingdom Government provided such funds as were urgently required, and that when an impoverished colony was unable to raise sufficient revenue to balance its budget a grant-in-aid might be made to fill the gap. But such funds were grudgingly given and on condition that the United Kingdom Treasury should exercise control over the colony's expenditure, a deadening control which insisted on the most rigid economy in expenditure to the detriment of the territory's development.

It was not until after the first world war that a more generous and sensible policy was adopted, and that the colonial territories received through Colonial Development and Welfare funds, and by direct grants, the money that so many of them needed so badly. In recent years the United Kingdom Government has provided considerable sums for the economic and social development of the colonies and Fiji is getting its share of this largesse. Under the Colonial Development and Welfare Act of 1945, £1,000,000 was allocated to Fiji, and under the Act of 1955 a sum of £800,000. Under the 1959 Act, there have been further considerable allocations.

The pity of it is that help was not given to the young colony in its early days when so much was needed. In the first year after the Cession, 1875, the revenue was only £16,433 and the expenditure was £41,522. By the following year these figures had risen to £40,524 and £68,636, and until 1888 there were only two years in which the revenue exceeded the expenditure. The revenue, however, steadily increased and by 1904, thirty years after the Cession, it had reached £139,404. By 1924 the annual revenue had risen to £484,834 and in 1960 it was £7,411,116.

As the revenue increased so did the annual expenditure, which in 1960 amounted to £7,052,874. It is thought that in the past there has been too great expenditure on social services to the neglect of economic development, and in this connection the following comparative figures of expenditure for 1960 may be of interest:

Education £1,179,411   Agriculture £238,124
Medical   £844,881   Forestry   £85,794

The public debt of the colony at the end of 1960 amounted to £5,477,193.

As in most colonial territories a very large proportion of the annual revenue of Fiji is derived from customs duties. In 1960 import and export duties and excise (with port charges, light and tonnage dues) amounted to £3,756,863 and income tax to £1,832,984. In 1960 the income of 42 persons was assessed at over £5,000 per annum; of these 21 were Europeans, 16 Indians, and 5 Chinese.

There was no material change in the constitution of Fiji during the first thirty years of colonial administration. The colony was established by a Royal Charter of the 2nd January 1875, which, after referring to the Cession, created the post of Governor and a Legislative Council consisting of the Governor 'and of such other public officers and persons not being less than two in number' as might be appointed by the Queen or by her instructions, all holding their places in the Council 'during Our pleasure'. There was also an advisory Executive Council composed of official members. It was a typical 'Crown Colony' constitution of that period, with a law-making body which, under the supervision of the Secretary of State for the Colonies, was completely controlled by the Governor. At least half of the members of the Legislative Council were, at all times, government officials who voted in accordance with the directions of the Governor.

The first change was made by Letters Patent of the 21st March 1904, which revoked the Charter of 1875 and other constitutional documents, set up the post of Governor and Commander-in-Chief, and established as before an advisory Executive Council. The composition of the Legislative Council was changed, and then consisted of the Governor as President, ten Official Members, six Elected Members, and two Native Members. The Native Members were selected by the Governor from a list of six Fijians submitted by the Fijian Council of Chiefs. The Elected Members, who had to be qualified as electors, included two representatives for Suva, one representative for Levuka, and three others 'who are engaged, either on their own behalf or in the employ of other persons, in the cultivation of land or the management of farms within the colony of not less than 100 acres in extent, or in the production and manufacture of sugar, provided that the annual salary or wages derived from such employment be not less than £120'. This bias in favour of agriculturists disappeared later.

Under the 1904 constitution, an elector had to be a British subject, the son of parents of European descent, and possessed of freehold or leasehold property of a yearly value of £20 or an annual income of £120. The Indian population, which at this period numbered about 22,000, had no representation. The Elected Members, all Europeans, and the Fijian Members, could attack or oppose the government in the Council but could not seriously embarrass the Administration.

The next change of any consequence was made by Letters Patent of the 31st October 1910, which established three Electoral Divisions, with one (European) representative for each, in addition to the two members for Suva and the one for Levuka. In 1914 the number of Official Members of the Legislative Council was raised to eleven and the number of Elected Members to seven, Levuka losing its direct representation and being included in one of the five Electoral Divisions set up, in addition to the constituency of Suva. In 1916 the composition of the Council was again changed to include twelve Nominated Members, of whom eleven were officials and one an Indian; the other membership remained as before.

An important change was made by Letters Patent dated the 9th February 1929, which for the first time provided for elected Indian representation in the Legislative Council. The Council was now to consist of the Governor, as President, not more than thirteen Nominated (official) Members, six European Elected Members, three Native Members, and three Indian Elected Members. As before, the Governor selected the Native (Fijian) Members from a panel submitted by the Council of Chiefs. Two European Members were elected for the Southern Electoral Division which included Suva, and one European Member for each of four other Divisions. The Indian Members were each to represent one Indian Electoral Division, these not being identical with the European Electoral Divisions.

An Indian elector was required to be the son of parents of Indian descent, a British subject, able to read and write in English or one of the Indian languages spoken locally, and in possession of freehold or leasehold property of a yearly value of £5 or an income of £75 per annum.

The first entry of elected Indian members into the Legislative Council led immediately to friction. An Indian member moved that Indian electors should be placed on a common roll with other British subjects and when this proposal was negatived (only the three Indians voting for it) the Indian members resigned their seats. New writs were issued but no nominations were forthcoming for a time. In 1932 Indian members were again elected and took their seats.

A further change was made by Letters Patent of the 2nd April 1937, which with amendments are still in force although it is expected that changes in the constitution will shortly be made.[1] The composition of the Legislative Council is now the Governor as President; sixteen Official Members (including three *ex-officio*); five European Members, of whom three are elected and two nominated; five Native Members chosen as before; and five Indian Members, of whom three are elected and two nominated.

Letters Patent of the 24th November 1954 provided for the appointment by the Governor of a Speaker of the Legislative Council, who presides at meetings in the absence of the Governor; neither the Governor nor the Speaker has an original vote in the Council but may give a casting vote if on any question the votes of the members are equally divided. The first Speaker was *Ratu* Sir Lala Sukuna, K.C.M.G., K.B.E., who was appointed in 1956; on his death in 1958, Mr. Maurice Scott, C.B.E., D.F.C., was appointed Speaker.

The Executive Council as constituted in 1962 consists of three *ex-officio* and five appointed members, these latter including three unofficial members of the Legislative Council, one European, one Fijian, and one Indian, chosen in each case by the representatives of his own race in the Legislative Council. The Governor is required to consult with the Executive Council in all matters of importance but may act in opposition to the advice he receives from members of the Council, in which case he must report the circumstances to the Secretary of State for the Colonies.

European electors to seats in the Legislative Council are required to be sons of parents of European descent, British subjects, and in receipt of an income of £75 per annum or the owner of property of an annual value of not less than £20. Similar qualifications are required of Indian electors except that they must be of Indian descent, in receipt of an annual income of £75 or owning property of an annual value of not less than

---

[1] The proposed changes in the Legislative Council will probably provide for the election by adult suffrage of four representatives of each race—European, Fijian and Indian—and the election by the Council of Chiefs of two further Fijian members. The Governor will also nominate two European and two Indian members. The number of official members will be increased so that there should still be a majority of official members.

£5, and must be able to read and write English or one of six specified Indian languages.

One of the peculiarities of the Fijian constitution is that the five Fijian members, who are regarded as 'unofficial' members, are in fact, without exception, all salaried officials of the Government. The five Fijian members are, at present, three Administrative Officers, one Education Officer, and one Economic Development Officer.

The Civil Service of the colony consists of an Administrative Service and the usual departments of a colonial administration. The Judiciary consists of a Chief Justice and one Puisne Judge. Most of the senior posts are filled by Europeans, generally from the United Kingdom, though many of the Education Department officials and teachers in the schools are seconded on temporary agreements from the New Zealand Educational Service. The Police Force is officered mainly by Europeans, the rank and file being Fijians and Indians.

Side by side with the central government of Fiji is the Fijian Administration which has jurisdiction over all Fijians in the colony and the power to make regulations having the force of law. The Fijian Affairs Regulations, to quote the official annual report for 1959, 'serve three purposes. First, they ensure the continuance of the Fijian communal system and the customs and observances traditionally associated with the system, subject to such modifications as may appear desirable from time to time in the light of changing conditions. In the complex structure of Fiji's society, resulting from the influx of non-indigenous races, it has long been accepted that legislation must intervene to reinforce the moral and customary sanctions which in earlier times bound Fijians together in the communal fold.' This, then, is the first and apparently the most important purpose of the Regulations, to preserve intact the customs of the Fijian people. The policy implicit in this will be discussed later.

'Secondly,' the report continues, 'the regulations provide a simple code of civil and criminal law, comprehensible both to Fijian Magistrates and the people. They are adaptable to situations arising in the communal way of life, and enforce, in some instances, traditional Fijian moral standards. Thirdly, they enable cases to be heard locally and justice to be carried out speedily.'

As already mentioned, for much the same reason that led Lord Lugard to introduce the system of indirect rule into Northern Nigeria in 1900, the shortage of trained officials and of money, Sir Arthur Gordon was compelled to use the chiefs in the administration of Fiji when he assumed the government of the colony after the Cession of 1874. It is, however, wrong to think that the Fijian Administration, as now organized, bears much resemblance to the Native Administrations set up in Nigeria. There the emirates and other Native Authorities were governed by their chiefs under the supervision of the Residents and District Officers.

For the purposes of the Fijian Administration the colony is divided into fourteen provinces, based on old tribal territories, and each province includes a number of *tikina*, which comprise groups of villages. In direct charge of each province there is a *Roko Tui* and at the head of each *tikina* is a *Buli*, all salaried officers of the Fijian Administration, appointed by the Governor on the recommendation of the Administration. These are not necessarily persons of hereditary rank although at the time of writing eleven of the thirteen *Roko* are of chiefly status, but not invariably the hereditary chiefs of the provinces they control as *Roko*. They are, in fact, salaried officials paid, not from their own tribal or provincial treasuries, but from Fijian Administration funds, a large proportion of which is provided by a subvention from the central government. Some of the *Roko* are seconded from substantive posts as Administrative Officers of the central government. The *Roko* and *Buli*, with their respective councils, are not therefore Native Authorities in the African sense, but paid officials of the government dealing, under the Fijian Administration, with one section of the population. In some areas, therefore, the Fijian Administration is responsible for only a fraction of the local population: side by side with it there is a District Administration which deals with those of other races. The four Divisions into which the colony is divided are each under a Commissioner responsible to the Governor. The Commissioners exercise a general supervision over all the activities of government within their Division and have accordingly general supervisory responsibilities towards the Fijian Administration officials there. It is obviously difficult for these four officers to exercise effective personal control over large areas. The role of their subordinates, the District Officers, is to some extent determined by the instructions the Commissioners give them, but also depends on their own personalities and their relationships with the Fijians amongst whom they work. In some areas they take no direct part in the affairs of the Fijian Administration except for periodic checking of cash, inspection of Fijian magistrates' books and the management of Fijian schools. In others they help the people to help themselves. There are, however, two administrations in each area of this small colony, one dealing with Fijians and one with all other races.

At the apex of the Fijian Administration is the Council of Chiefs which has existed since the time of Sir Arthur Gordon. It consists of the Secretary for Fijian Affairs (a post once filled by Sir Lala Sukuna but at present by a European), the *Roko Tui* of all provinces, one representative from each province selected by the Provincial Council of that province, one Fijian magistrate, one Fijian school teacher, and such other chiefs, not exceeding six, as the Governor may appoint. The Council meets, except in special cases, only once in two years, as the cost of bringing the members together more often would be very great. It is the duty of the Council of Chiefs 'to submit to the Governor such recommendations and proposals as it may deem to be for the benefit of the Fijian people, and in particular to consider such questions relating to the good government and well-being of the Fijian people' as may be submitted to the Council by the Governor or the Fijian Affairs Board.

This Board consists of the Secretary for Fijian Affairs, the five Fijian members of the Legislative Council, a legal adviser, and a financial adviser. Its main duties, as the executive arm of the Council, are to make appointments, to make regulations binding on the Fijians, to control the provincial budgets, and to make such recommendations to the Governor as may be thought fit for the benefit of the Fijian people.

As has been mentioned, the 'unofficial' Fijian members of the Legislative Council are all salaried officials, and these five are also members of the Fijian Affairs Board. Three of them, in addition, are members of the Native Land Trust Board, referred to on page 208, which controls the establishment of land reserves for Fijians and the leasing of other Fijian land. Some of them fill other posts or are members of other boards. Professor Spate referred to the manifold duties of one *Roko*, a man of enormous energy and great ability, who, in spite of his obvious desire to cope fully with all these duties, would himself admit that it is impossible. The fact unfortunately is that the limited number of suitable Fijians results in too many tasks being imposed upon too few, while the concentration of duties and responsibilities on the shoulders of a handful of chiefs or their nominees leaves too much power in the hands of a very small group.

More than half a century ago, in 1903, Mr. Joseph Chamberlain, then Secretary of State for the Colonies, wrote to the Governor regarding the aims of the British Government in their dealings with the Fijians. 'The first and most important', he said, 'is the encouragement among them of a spirit of individual effort and self-reliance. . . . The communal system must continue for the present in its essential features, while at the same time everything possible should be done to ensure that it shall not be worked exclusively for the benefit of the ruling class but with the steady intention of using it to educate the natives so that it shall become less and less necessary to them.' He anticipated opposition from the chiefs and emphasized the need for 'constant and vigilant supervision in order that the commoners may be protected in the possession of a reasonable amount of time and liberty'.

A former Governor, Sir Everard Im Thurn, in the Introduction to a book written by A. G. King, published in 1920, wrote that the Fijians were 'prevented by the Native Regulations from developing even along the lines which would have been followed by their forefathers, had they been left to their own devices, and prevented by the "privileges" secured to them by British law from sharing whatever may be the real advantages of full British citizenship'.

Many witnesses, including a number of Fijians, recommended to the 1959 Commission of Enquiry that the Fijian Administration should be abolished, as inefficient and unduly expensive. Some others were of the opinion that the absorption of the Fijian Administration into a multi-racial local government organization would involve the loss of racial identity, culture and custom to the Fijians, but customs and culture are of their essence changeable and those which are worth while would surely survive.

In view of the representations made, and more particularly on account of what the members of the Commission observed for themselves, the Commission of Enquiry recommended that the Fijian Administration should gradually be replaced by multi-racial local governments set up, area by area, throughout the colony. The Commission felt that, apart from other considerations, the Fijian Administration was an unnecessary expense which Fiji could not afford. In so small a colony a double administration is wasteful of man-power and money, and in rural areas the well-being of the Fijians could safely be left in the care of the District Officers. The Commission recommended that the elected members of the local government councils should consist, where the population was mixed, of three members of each race, Fijian, Indian and European, in accordance with the principle established in the constitution of the Legislative Council. In areas where the Fijian race predominated the number of Indian and European representatives should be reduced, and in such areas where practically none but Fijians live, the representation would be entirely Fijian.

This recommendation, not unnaturally, is difficult for many Fijians to accept. But the Commission themselves agreed that the change should be made gradually, and it is to be hoped that the Fijian leaders will come to realize that in their own best interests it is inevitable in modern conditions. As long ago as 1937 the Public Services Re-organization Committee invited attention to the growing separation of the Native Affairs Department (now exalted as the Fijian Administration) from the central government, warned against the separatist tendency 'of the present system', and advised 'the abolition of the Native Affairs Department'. Even longer ago, in 1913, the late Sir Henry Scott expressed the opinion that 'the continued separate existence of the Native Office is no longer necessary or desirable. . . . The Native Office has had a fair trial and I do not think that even the adherents to the system of that department can suggest its administration has been a success. To my mind efficiency and control is sadly wanting—more effective local administration in the provinces is what is required. It would lead to expedition of work instead of as at present the constant reference to the Native Department in Suva of minute detail. ... To perpetuate the present Native Department and its method of administration would in my opinion be a grave mistake.' Sir Henry, who was the father of the present Speaker of the Legislative Council, was born in Fiji and lived there all his life. He was one of the most highly respected Europeans in the colony and, like his son, a good friend of the Fijians. In his condemnation of the Native Department he was undoubtedly expressing views which he felt were in the best interests of their race. His criticisms could fairly be applied today to the Fijian Administration, the lineal descendant of the Native Department.

Before leaving the subject of the Fijian Administration it is worth considering the situation caused by the dual position of the man who is both a chief and an official. One chief told the Commission that 'only hereditary chiefs should be officials of the various districts in which they claim land ownership for this will strengthen their chiefly status in their own areas'. A commoner, on the other hand, said that chiefs should not be appointed *Roko*, 'for through custom they are unapproachable', and another, speaking of the *Buli* who are chiefs, said: 'This is one of the causes of the failure of the Fijians. These chiefs understand that no one would talk openly to them if they commit anything wrong. ... We cannot complain openly to them for they are both our chiefs and *Buli*.' Another serious disadvantage of the dual position lies in the virtual obligation of the people of a village to give a ceremonial reception to a *Roko* who is also a chief whenever he visits them, a reception which may be costly as well as wasteful of time. It is true that chiefly status adds to the authority of an official and that, to a certain degree, the position is acceptable to the people as well as to the chiefs, but on balance it seems to be undesirable.

The position of the chiefs is a peculiar one. For the most part they still command the respect of the people and generally they deserve it, but, as Sir Lala Sukuna once said in an address to the Council of Chiefs:

'We need clearly to understand, and be always conscious of, the fact that we can only be sure of our people continuing to follow us provided they appreciate that our authority is better than that of anyone else, that as a result of our forethought and

energy they prosper—that is, when we cease to rely on status to
see us through, and when we prove once more that we possess
both the qualification and the authority to rise to the occasion
such as our ancestors possessed. If we confine ourselves to
pleasure-seeking only, no useful purpose will be served in maintaining our claim to chiefly status. If we are merely decorative
our position is finished for ever, or will soon be tossed aside
when some other race rises to the fore. . . . There is an insufficient number of men at present available who are either
capable of, or who possess sufficient initiative effectively to carry
out the responsibilities of leadership.'

Sir Lala Sukuna himself represented all that was best in the
Fijian tradition. Born in 1888, of aristocratic lineage, he was
educated at Wanganui Grammar School, in New Zealand, and
at Wadham College, Oxford, taking his degree in 1921 and
being called to the Bar by the Middle Temple the same year.
His studies at Oxford were interrupted by the first world war.
When war broke out he at once made strenuous efforts to join
the British army, but, strange as this may seem to us now, he
could get no British regiment to accept his services. He therefore went to France and joined the Foreign Legion, being decorated for his services with the French Military Medal. While at
the front with the Legion he was severely wounded and, after
a period in hospital, went back to Fiji. Soon afterwards he
was attached to the Fiji Labour Company and returned to
Europe as an officer in this Company. When he was demobilized
he returned to Oxford.

After he left Oxford, Sukuna was appointed to the Administrative Service of Fiji and rose to the positions of Secretary for
Fijian Affairs and Chairman of the Lands Commission. His last
public office was that of Speaker of the Legislative Council. He
represented Fiji at the coronation ceremonies of 1937 and 1953
and led the Fiji contingent in the Victory March in London in
1946. In 1950 he was a member of the United Kingdom dele-
gation to the General Assembly of the United Nations, where
he created a great impression. He died in 1958 on his way to
the United Kingdom on holiday and his body was brought back
to Fiji for burial at Lakemba after lying in state in his residence
at Suva. At the military funeral in Suva people of all races
attended, many of the Fijians wearing the traditional sign of

mourning, a grass mat tied round the waist. The funeral procession passed between lines of kneeling Fijian women.

He was a man of outstanding ability and integrity, coupled with great personal charm, and was regarded with affection and respect by all who knew him. In his obituary notice in *The Times* it was said that 'his happy blend of western culture and of pride in his own national heritage found expression in his custom of wearing, even with formal European dress, the kilt and sandals of his native land'. I well remember him, so attired, dining with me one evening in the Athenaeum.

With his passing Fiji lost the services of a wise and experienced elder statesman whose influence was always exerted for the public good, and the Fijian people in particular lost a great leader and one who always stood up for the interests of his race. Sukuna was awarded the C.B.E. in 1939, the K.B.E. in 1946, and the K.C.M.G. in 1953.

In 1885 the European settlers in Fiji, dissatisfied with Crown Colony rule and the protection by the government of the Fijians' ownership of their land, sent a petition to the New Zealand legislature praying that the colony should be incorporated in New Zealand. This led to no result but in 1900, with some encouragement from Mr. R. J. Seddon, the Prime Minister of New Zealand, the European residents made a similar request, saying that 'not only are the native inhabitants governed under a system of personal government which retards the moral and injures the physical development of the race, but the white inhabitants of the colony, who are for the most part New Zealanders and Australians, and their descendants, are also subjected to personal government, are entirely deprived of all voice in the making of the laws under which they have to live, and are altogether unrepresented in the legislature which levies the taxes which they have to pay.' They sent in support of their petition a memorandum by a Wesleyan missionary, the Reverend W. Slade, who, referring to the method of governing the Fijians, said that its effect was to 'herd men together like sheep, take away from them all incentive and ambition, impose on them a legal code that stops all outlet for individual effort, stifle all expressions of individual opinion, and the result most assuredly will be the annihilation of all character and the production of a placid race of mental and moral invertebrates.'

This petition also led to no result, other than a somewhat unusual exchange of opinions, in speeches and published letters, between the Governor of Fiji and the Prime Minister of New Zealand. The Governor, Sir George O'Brien, warned the Fijians that the Europeans wanted their land and that amalgamation with New Zealand might cause them to lose their land as the Maoris had lost theirs. The Prime Minister said that he had read the speech with 'surprise and amazement'.

Disappointed by this failure, the Europeans then petitioned the United Kingdom Government for the right to elect members to the Legislative Council, and for representation on the Executive Council, stressing particularly the disabilities of the indigenous Fijians under the existing Crown Colony administration. The Fijians, they said, were heavily and unfairly taxed in comparison with the Europeans, and stated 'in the most emphatic manner that His Majesty's native Fijian subjects are cruelly misgoverned under the present extraordinary system causing them to be *de facto* slaves of the government; that they suffer under a perpetual tyranny and are deprived of personal liberty and individuality, and consequently are demoralized.' As we have seen, the constitution was changed in 1904 so as to provide for elected European Members and Native Members of the Legislative Council.

In the meantime interested parties had raised questions regarding the ownership and use of the land in Fiji, especially what was called 'waste land', which was not occupied or used by its reputed Fijian owners. The Europeans would have liked the Crown to take over this vacant land and sell it to those who were prepared to develop it. Up to this time the general official policy in respect of land had remained unchanged from that laid down by Sir Arthur Gordon after the Cession, but in 1903 the Governor, Sir Henry Jackson, in a message to the Legislative Council, said that 'the most important factor as regards the expansion of the colony and the growth of its prosperity is the improvement of the facilities for offering to settlers the opportunity of opening up the vast resources of the waste lands which are now of no use or benefit to the owners'. This indication of a change of policy received the blessing of the Secretary of State for the Colonies, and Fijian opinion was favourable.

The next Governor, Sir Everard Im Thurn, 'being convinced that the natives were willing that sales should be permitted', enacted an Ordinance in 1905 by which the sale of Fijian land was made legal for the first time since Fiji had become a British colony. Following this enactment, and until 1909 when further sales were prohibited except to the government, some 20,000 acres of Fijian land were sold to settlers, in addition to a larger area leased.

The government had always had power to acquire Fijian (and other) land for public purposes, and in 1905 another Ordinance was enacted which allowed the acquisition of any land which the Governor-in-Council thought could be used for a purpose 'desirable as directly benefiting the colony'. The immediate purpose of this Ordinance, against which the unofficial members of the Legislative Council protested, was to provide land over which the Colonial Sugar Refining Company wished to build a railway for the conveyance of sugar-cane to its mills. The Secretary of State allowed this Ordinance to stand but was obviously disturbed by its implications and urged the Governor to be careful in its application.

In 1907 yet another Ordinance was enacted which permitted the sale or lease of communally owned Fijian land to individual Fijians, a policy which the Secretary of State (and others) thought might be 'a device under which land held individually by a native Fijian may be disposed of to a non-native'. The danger of this was, in fact, obvious.

Sir Arthur Gordon, then Lord Stanmore, had, as stated on page 107, protested vigorously in the House of Lords against the change in Fijian land policy, and protests had also come from another former Governor, Sir William des Voeux. The Colonial Office was itself disturbed by these drastic changes and in July 1908 the Secretary of State informed the Governor that, 'without discussing the precise legal position, I am inclined to think that the course of events during the last thirty years has rendered it impossible for the Government of Fiji to adopt any position other than that the waste lands of Fiji must continue to be regarded as the property of the natives as much as the occupied lands. . . . I fully recognize the importance of developing the waste lands of Fiji, and I should be glad to see adopted any plan which would secure that they should be made available for settlement, on terms fair alike to the natives and to the settlers.'

The tide had now turned again, and the stoppage of all sales of Fijian land (except to the government) in 1909, and the repeal of the Ordinances which had permitted these sales, brought to an end an unfortunate period in Fijian history. Short-sighted Fijians might have been willing to sell their land for immediate profit, as they had done before the Cession, but this could not justify the colonial government, as trustee, in condoning such transactions. On the other hand, there could be no objection to the leasing, under proper safeguards, of unused and unwanted Fijian lands, and this has been made easier, though not yet easy enough, by the institution in 1940 of a Native Land Trust Board, which is referred to on page 208.

The next important decision regarding land was taken not by the government but by the Colonial Sugar Refining Company. The ending of the indenture system in 1916 and the reluctance of the former indentured labourers to work for wages, coupled with the fact that many of the 'free' Indians were already working as independent farmers on land leased from Fijians, led to a labour shortage which threatened the existence of the sugar industry. In these circumstances the company decided (as mentioned on page 113) to abandon the idea of plantation cultivation with hired labour and to lease its land, in plots of about ten acres each, to Indian farmers who would undertake to grow cane and supply it on agreed terms to the company's mills for processing. This has been described by an authority on the subject as 'the boldest experiment in colonial agriculture during the present century', and the experiment must be regarded as successful in spite of the disputes between the company and Indian farmers which are referred to on page 177.

11. FIJI AT WAR

T HE Fijians were noted, when they first became known to Europeans, as cannibals and warriors. They have long renounced cannibalism but the warrior instinct is still strong and this was amply proved during the last war.

The first disciplined Fijian force was that raised by Cakobau when he was recognized as King of Fiji in 1871. It was armed with modern weapons and trained and commanded by British officers, who found it comparatively easy to teach infantry drill to men accustomed to the precision of their old war dances. It is said that this force was well disciplined and steady on parade and it saw service against the hill tribes of Viti Levu who were responsible for the murder of Mr. Baker in 1867.

At the Cession the troops of the Cakobau government were taken over by the colonial administration and styled the Armed Native Constabulary of Fiji. They were soon again in action against the hill tribes who revolted in 1876. During this 'Little War', as it was called, the Constabulary was the only regular force employed by the government, although local levies under their own chiefs gave useful support. These levies were armed with spears and with old 'Tower' muskets, as well as with old muskets from America and Russia, the same as had been used, not many years earlier, in some of their tribal wars. Three of the chiefs were presented by Queen Victoria with Swords of Honour, in recognition of their loyal behaviour.

The Constabulary was last employed in military operations in 1894 when it suppressed without difficulty a rising in the Mathuata area of Vanua Levu. The rebels were hill-men from some of the small villages of the interior, who defied their chief and attacked other villages, killing and eating (the last known case of cannibalism in Fiji) some of the inhabitants. They then retired to a strongly entrenched hill fortress and, armed only with spears, refused to surrender to the Constabulary who carried Martini-Henry rifles. The issue was not long in doubt but the rebels fought with great gallantry until they were overwhelmed. Ten were killed and two were executed after trial.

In 1902 a contingent of the Fiji Constabulary proceeded to England for the coronation of King Edward VII. They were reported to be smart on parade and cheerful and willing at all times. Their uniforms and war dances, and above all their singing, made a great impression. They sang hymns in Fijian in St. George's Chapel, Windsor, and under the bedroom windows of the King during his illness.

Fiji was not greatly affected by the first world war. Half a dozen German officers and men under the command of Commander Graf von Luckner, from the wrecked raider *See Adler*, landed from a launch on the small island of Wakaya in September 1917, but surrendered to an unarmed party of Fijian police. Three contingents of Europeans and Part-Europeans, all volunteers, joined the armed forces, and a Fijian Labour Company rendered good service in France and Italy. When volunteers were sought for this Company the response was so great that selection was the only difficulty, and the Governor reported that there would have been no difficulty in raising either a labour battalion or a fighting battalion had the services of either been required. According to the military authorities under whom the Fijian Labour Company served, they were not only the best workers from any colonial territory but also the best behaved and the most amenable to discipline. Throughout the war, according to an official report, 'the loyalty of the (Fijians) generally has been, as always, most marked. They contributed liberally to war funds.' Reference has been made on page 135 to the part played in the war by that distinguished Fijian, *Ratu* Sir Lala Sukuna.

In the second world war Fiji's contribution was greater and more direct. Military training began as early as August 1939, and Home Guards, the 2nd (Territorial) Battalion of the Fiji Infantry Regiment, Fiji Artillery, and supporting units, as well as the Fiji Royal Naval Volunteer Reserve, played a useful part in the protection of Fiji and as training cadres for the units serving overseas. Dummy guns brought from New Zealand in September 1939 were replaced three months later with real weapons in a battery prepared for the protection of Suva harbour, and batteries were afterwards installed at other points. Many

European and Part-European residents in Fiji joined the Fijian armed forces or went overseas to serve in other British units. In September 1939 Fiji was selected as an advance base for New Zealand forces, and numbers of their men arrived in the colony, a New Zealand officer taking command of all troops in Fiji. Further reinforcements of New Zealand troops arrived from time to time and many New Zealanders served as officers and non-commissioned officers with the Fiji Commandos and the Fiji Infantry Regiment. In 1942 the first United States troops arrived to assist in garrisoning the colony and to train there for service in other Pacific islands. The New Zealand troops were then withdrawn and the Fijian forces came under American command. A large number of American soldiers passed through Fiji on their way to operations elsewhere, and a strong force was employed, in the words of an official United States history of the war, in 'holding the strategically important Fiji Islands'.

The first troops raised for service overseas were the Fiji Commando units. The Fijians were found to be particularly well adapted to commando work. Of excellent physique, they could endure cheerfully the tough training and exhausting marches over the roughest country. They were skilful scouts, able to conceal themselves from observation while getting close enough to the enemy to observe his position and numbers, and were well suited to patrol work in the thickly-forested areas of the Solomon Islands. There is a story that during their training in Fiji they were required to make a night 'attack' on a camp of European soldiers and to mark with chalk crosses the positions they had reached unobserved. No Fijians were seen or heard by the European sentries during the night, but next morning chalk crosses were found almost everywhere in the camp. In action they were just as efficient. During the Solomon Islands campaign an American officer sent forward a Fijian to reconnoitre an enemy position and asked, when the Fijian returned, 'How many Japs are there?' The Fijian smilingly replied that 'there *were* six of them'.

The first encounter of Fijian forces with the Japanese took place on the 28th December 1942, when a Commando patrol killed some of the enemy. The first unofficial report on their activities to reach Fiji stated that 'our score so far is twenty-six for no wicket', a message easily understood by the cricket-loving Fijians. Their later score was much more impressive, and it should be remembered that these were not trained soldiers turned into commandos, but men brought straight from their villages and hurried through a strenuous training before being launched against the Japanese in the thick jungle of the Solomon Islands. For some of the time these Fijian Commando troops were joined with men from Tonga and the Solomons to form the South Pacific Scouts. Under their gallant New Zealand officers, several of whom were killed, the Fijian Commandos won the respect of their American comrades for their skill and bravery.

Meanwhile, battalions of infantry were being raised and trained for service overseas. The 1st Battalion of the Fiji Infantry Regiment left Fiji in April 1943, for Guadacanal and Bougainville, and a year later the 3rd Battalion also arrived in the Solomon Islands. A Docks Company served in the Solomon Islands and received the following commendation from the officer commanding the American forces:

'It is desired to commend Company No. 1, Fiji Docks Company, for its superior service, efficiency, and devotion to duty under arduous conditions on Bougainville, Solomon Islands.

Our records show that your organization arrived 21st March, 1944, during an enemy attack on the Torokina area, and that under the leadership of its officers worked aggressively and enthusiastically while subject to enemy artillery fire. For a period of eleven months your men worked efficiently and untiringly with little time for sports and recreation.

During its service at this base the superior appearance of the personnel, equipment and installations of your Company was outstanding. The prompt and cheerful manner in which your officers and men executed orders under all conditions was noted by all who observed their work.

The excellent service of your Company contributed greatly to the success of supply and port activities at Bougainville, and thereby to the success of our campaign against Japan.'

As regards the fighting men of the Fiji Infantry Regiment, apart from ordinary patrol work, always carried out with skill and courage, the troops were engaged in an important operation in the interior of Bougainville, within the enemy's lines, which was afterwards described by the American general in command of the Allied forces as 'a minor tactical classic'. After five days' march through the roughest type of country, a base was established by the 1st Battalion in January 1944, at a place called Ibu, some 1,700 feet up on the slopes of a mountain range, and a small air strip was prepared to facilitate the evacuation of wounded and the supply of stores. From this base, for six weeks, patrols harried the Japanese and inflicted heavy casualties, including at least 183 killed, while the Fijians themselves lost only one man killed and four wounded. At last the Japanese attacked in such force that it became necessary to withdraw from Ibu and a fighting retreat was made to the coast, the Japanese losing heavily in their attacks on the Fijian rearguards, which were handled with great skill by their Fijian noncommissioned officers. Sections and individual Fijians, cut off by Japanese outflanking movements and reported as missing, invariably rejoined their units a day or two later.

As an example of the 'toughness' of the Fijian soldier, the case of Private Esivoresi Kete of the 1st Battalion is of interest. This man was severely wounded in an engagement, a bullet entering his head behind the right ear and making its exit under the left eye. He was discovered later by the Japanese who bayoneted him twice through the chest and through the arm, leaving him, as they thought, dead. He managed however, to crawl into a foxhole and lay there for three days while shells from an artillery barrage fell around him. He was then found and brought into hospital, where, contrary to medical expectation, he recovered from his injuries.

Less fortunate was that very brave soldier, Corporal Sefanaia Sukanaivalu, of the 3rd Battalion, who won a posthumous Victoria Cross for his conduct during an engagement in June 1944. The official citation is a record of which every Fijian can be proud:

'On 23rd of June, 1944, at Mawaraka, Bougainville, in the Solomon Islands, Corporal Sefanaia Sukanaivalu crawled forward to rescue men who had been wounded when their platoon was ambushed and some leading elements had become casualties. After two wounded men had been successfully recovered, this N.C.O., who was in command of the rear section, volunteered to go on further along and try to rescue another man in spite of the mortar and machine gun fire, but on the way back he himself was seriously wounded in the groin and thigh and fell to the ground unable to move.

Several attempts were made to rescue Corporal Sefanaia but with-

A botany class at the Government Agricultural Department

Above: Future teachers watch how a class is taught arithmetic
Below: Adi Cakobau school near Suva for 180 girls. 'The school choir
has been on a very successful tour of New Zealand cities'

Above: The Anglican Cathedral

Below: The Catholic Cathedral

Above: Girls at an Indian school who have just taken part in an entertainment. 'In the mission schools children of all races are admitted but few of the other schools are multi-racial'
Below: Indians in the marketplace. *Left:* Indian girls

Above: Indian smallholding. 'Homesteads are not clustered together but dotted here and there.' *Below:* Modern Indian house. *Above, left:* Building a *bure* from timber lashed together with plaited coconut rope. *Below, left:* Modern Fijian house

Above: The children's ward in the Colonial War Memorial Hospital in Suva. This hospital has 330 beds and takes patients from other islands in the Pacific. *Below:* Medical students in the same hospital

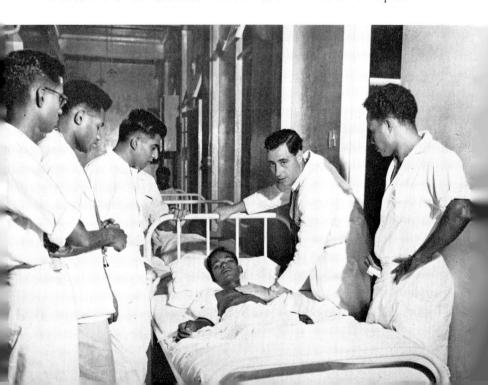

out success owing to heavy firing encountered on each occasion and further casualties were caused. This gallant N.C.O. then called to his men not to try to get him as he was in a very exposed position, but they replied they would never leave him to fall alive into the hands of the enemy. Realizing his men would not leave him as long as they could see he was alive and knowing that they were all in danger of being killed or captured as long as they remained where they were, Corporal Sefanaia, well aware of the consequences, raised himself up in front of the Japanese machine guns and was riddled with bullets.

This brave Fiji soldier, after rescuing two wounded men and being gravely wounded himself, deliberately sacrificed his life because he knew it was the only way in which the remainder of his platoon could be induced to retire from a situation in which, had they remained, they must have been annihilated.'

Some months later the body of Corporal Sefanaia was found by Australian troops and taken to the British cemetery at Cape Moeltke, where it was buried with full military honours in the presence of the representatives of the Fiji, Australian, New Zealand and United States armed forces.

In all some thirty Fijians were killed in action or died of wounds and a large number were wounded. Another dozen were accidentally killed or died of sickness overseas. Two of the descendants of King Cakobau, *Ratu* George and *Ratu* Edward Cakobau, served as Captains in the 3rd Battalion. Three Fijian officers won the Military Cross and of Other Ranks four won the Distinguished Conduct Medal and nineteen the Military Medal. Casualties among the European officers were also heavy.

Commendations from the United States Army commanders paid tribute to the Fijian troops. The commendation to the 1st Battalion stated that

'. . . On Bougainville the actions of your battalion were characterized by aggressive and spirited patrolling into distant areas beyond the established perimeter. In every action in which your battalion engaged, comparatively heavy casualties were levied on the enemy and valuable intelligence was secured. The success of your battalion at the Ibu outpost was one of the finest examples of troop leading that has ever come to my attention. The battle discipline of your battalion in the field and the soldierly bearing and sportsmanship of its individual members in camp has earned for you the highest esteem among the American Forces.'

To the 3rd Battalion the following commendation was issued:

'Arriving at Bougainville during the height of the desperate Japanese attack on the Allied beachhead, your battalion immediately prepared for combat operations and went on its first combat mission within ten days of its arrival. Shortly thereafter, you were engaged in the pursuit of Japanese forces. On 14th April a company of your battalion carried out a bayonet assault against two platoons of Japanese killing a number of enemy and securing a flank of the Allied positions. From 30th May to 23rd June your battalion conducted reconnaissance missions, sweeping the Augusta Bay shore . . . destroying many enemy fortifications and capturing six artillery field pieces. The excellent combat spirit, discipline, soldierly bearing, and sportsmanship of every member of the 3rd Battalion has earned the Fijians the highest esteem among the American Forces.'

In 1946 a contingent of Fijian troops, under the command of Lieutenant-Colonel *Ratu* Sir Lala Sukuna, went to England for the Victory Parade in London.

During the war over 11,000 men passed through the Fiji military forces and in August 1943 the peak strength was reached of 8,513. Of these, 6,371 were Fijians; 1,878 (including 808 from the New Zealand forces) were Europeans; and 264 were Indians. The poor showing of the Indian population of Fiji, as compared with the record of the Fijians, is striking and it undoubtedly added to the feeling of 'difference' between the two races. Persuaded by some of their political leaders that they should not serve in the army except on 'European' rates of pay, all members of the Indian platoon of the 2nd (Territorial) Battalion of the Fijian Infantry Regiment were discharged at their request in 1941. A few remained in other units and an Indian Company of the Fijian Labour Corps was formed in 1943 for service in Fiji. The 'strike' of Indian cane farmers, already referred to, accentuated the anti-Indian feeling. A large number of Fijian witnesses drew the attention of the Commission of Enquiry of 1959 to the behaviour of the Indians during the war as compared with the loyal and gallant conduct of the Fijians. It is a comparison which cannot, unfortunately, be easily forgotten.

The account of Fiji's part in the second world war can be closed on a happier note by quoting from the official history of the Fiji Military Forces:

'From a mere handful of enthusiastic territorials at the outbreak of war, the force had grown to a formidable size. The flower of the country's manhood was assembled and trained and then sent into conflict against a cunning and vigorous foe. They took their place and were not found wanting. They fought valiantly and met success with equanimity, adversity with fortitude, and death with honour. They lived up to the proud traditions of a warrior race and by their deeds left a heritage for the generations yet to come.'

The Battle Honours approved by Her Majesty the Queen for the Fiji Infantry Regiment are: South Pacific, 1942–4; Solomons; Bougainville. The Fiji Infantry Regiment is now an allied regiment of the King's Royal Rifle Corps.

The end of the war against Japan was not to be the end of active military service for the Fijians. The struggle against communist terrorists in Malaya gave them another opportunity to prove their efficiency as soldiers and their gallantry as individuals. In 1951 it was decided to raise again the 1st Battalion of the Fiji Infantry Regiment for service in Malaya, and the volunteers who answered the call far exceeded the number required. The officers were mostly Fijians or Europeans resident in Fiji, and a number of non-commissioned officers were seconded from the New Zealand Army.

The Battalion served in Malaya from January 1952 to June 1956, when it was relieved by a British regiment, and during this period 1,650 Fijians passed through its ranks. The Battalion operated for most of the time in the areas most threatened by the terrorists and proved again the skill of the Fijians in jungle fighting. They were responsible for the elimination of more than two hundred terrorists, and were referred to by the Press as 'the Fighting Fijians' and 'the Terror of Malaya's Communist Terrorists'. It was said that their military prowess, together with their athletic achievements and friendly good nature, endeared them to the Malayan peoples.

Of the Fijians, nine were killed in action and four died of wounds, in addition to eleven deaths by accident or disease. Twenty-eight were wounded. The decorations won by the officers and men of the Battalion included the award to one of the Distinguished Service Order, to four of the Military Cross, to two of the Distinguished Conduct Medal, and to eight of the Military Medal. Thirty-three were mentioned in despatches. Lieutenant-Colonel *Ratu* Edward Cakobau, O.B.E., M.C., and Lieutenant-Colonel *Ratu* Penaia Ganilau, D.S.O., commanded the Battalion for some months at different times.

On the return of the Battalion to Fiji a message was sent by the Secretary of State for the Colonies on behalf of Her Majesty's Government in the United Kingdom. 'Your Battalion', he said, 'has served abroad for four years with great distinction and can look back with pride on a record of achievement that has enhanced the high reputation of the Fiji military forces.'

In 1960 a Colour Party from the Fiji Infantry Regiment attended the celebrations in Malaya which marked the end of the emergency there. The Fijians were warmly cheered.

If, unhappily, the need should again arise, there can be little doubt that the Fijians' loyalty and warrior spirit would respond as before to any call for their services.

The close co-operation achieved between New Zealand and Fiji during the war still continues. At Lauthala Bay, near Suva, there is a flying-boat base of the Royal New Zealand Air Force.

Two shells. The large Triton shell is used as a trumpet

INTERLUDE

by

R. T. SANDERS

O N the island of Mbau, hereditary home of the supreme chiefly family of Fiji, coconuts are scarce in all their stages, including the green nut (*bu*) which yields the cool, faintly effervescent draught so refreshing to the tropical traveller. Sometimes, therefore, on Mbau a nut has to be used for drinking which is not exactly right—hence the phrase 'a Mbauan drinking nut' used of a man not ideally fitted to a task which must nevertheless be done. In this spirit I assume the task of writing this chapter. But there is another Fijian proverb 'Like pulling mature *dalo*' used, for example, when a person has been longing to go to a place and then finds himself despatched there on an errand. And the country districts of Fiji and their peoples have given me such happiness that an invitation to share them is irresistible.[1]

Fiji boasts one city and a number of growing towns and townships but the vast majority of her peoples lives in villages and settlements. While on the smaller islands the villages are coastal, set on the golden palm-fringed beaches of the tourist photographs, on the main islands many villages are inland, hugging the foot of the hill or clinging to slopes. This hill country, though less well-known, is just as much the real Fiji, and one can travel many miles and many days through rugged country which can rise to 4,000 feet. Muddy rain-soaked journeys they can be, but the rigours of such tramping are soon forgotten in the warmth of welcome offered by a Fijian village.

Apart from Fijians themselves, only a limited number of people visit these areas. A District Officer on a tour of village inspection through hill country is likely to be accompanied by the *Roko* or the *Buli* with whom he works closely and they will send word ahead to the villages. He travels light, but carriers take gear from village to village, often on horseback. Luggage

---

[1] The Fijian sayings quoted in this paragraph are taken from *Na i Vosavosa Vaka-Viti e so: A Collection of Fijian Idioms*, by Anare K. Raiwalui, Oxford University Press, 1954.

is handled as on a seven-day coach tour, in that it is never seen during the day but is in the house when wanted at night throughout the tour. The younger men perform this duty and, tutored by their occasional visits to the cinema, they are bold and fast riders, with a folded sack and a piece of rope as their only saddlery. Often there are streams, and the terrain varies considerably from wide flats to steep rocky slopes. But tracks are well defined, and regular use and weeding keeps them clear, though the muddy ones sometimes become what the Fijians call 'railways' with deep transverse furrows made by horses.

When the District Officer arrives at a Fijian village during daytime, he is likely to be offered the ceremonial *yaqona* root, which is then pounded, mixed with water and drunk; if a tour is streamlined and the people know his wishes, a bowl of *yaqona* will be already prepared. However it is done, the *yaqona* ceremony means that the guest has time to regain his breath and collect his thoughts before starting on business. *Yaqona*, particularly the green variety, has a pleasant astringent taste and provided it is not drunk to excess is an excellent ice-breaker and tongue-loosener. Amongst Europeans, the best speakers of Fijian tend to be those who have drunk most *yaqona*. There is certainly much truth in the affirmation that you cannot hate with *yaqona* in you, and many an awkward moment in conversation or in Council has been overcome with the word '*talo*' or 'pass round the *yaqona*'.

Probably a plate of ripe bananas or fresh sliced pineapple will be shyly placed before the guest by one of the ladies of the village, and often a pillow or two will be brought to provide comfort for those who either cannot achieve the cross-legged posture or maintain it for any period. The guest will be set in the place of vantage between two doors where he can get the maximum benefit of a through draught.

The guest will probably find himself in a Fijian house or *bure* strongly built from good native materials. Massive hardwood pillars support the roof, which often has bamboo rafters, and huge beams serve the dual purpose of connecting the pillars and also holding the house down in the event of a hurricane. The bamboos are often smoke-blackened even though there may be no fires in the house, since the smoking of the thatched roof prior to occupation prolongs the life of the roofing by killing destructive insects. Where this precaution has not been taken, one can wake in the morning to find tables and chairs flecked as though with fine sand from the insects' supernal activity. The floor, constantly swept either with a broom made from the 'backbones' of coconut leaves or sometimes a fan, has usually a base of large stones to raise it from ground level—a chief's house can have a foundation six feet high or more. The stones are covered with deep yielding layers of fern, then large *pandanus* mats and often small mats on the top of these. Little wonder that many a European guest will prefer supine relaxation to a proffered chair. The beams may be decorated with coconut coir twine, the natural red ochre colour intermingled with black to form an intricate mosaic pattern. Photographs of the Royal Family, past and present, look down benignly on the scene together with the usual college and sporting groups. Many houses have a table, probably covered with patterned *masi*, and at least one bed piled high with mats whose edges, garishly decorated with bright wools, however they may revolt the aesthete, give a dash of colour to the somewhat sombre interior of the house. Pillows too are gaily embroidered and captions range from the rather prosaic 'Bless this house' through a faintly poignant 'Remember me' to the frankly inviting 'Love me to-night'.

In some areas a shallow pit is dug in one corner of the house, and wire and a couple of iron bars provide an admirable fire-place—the numerous doors and windows and the high vaulted roof preventing concentrations of smoke. Trochus and other shells provide ash trays, and empty bully beef tins, carefully opened with the lids folded back to form handles, are Fijian spittoons, though they are used mainly for cigarette-ends and the dregs of over-thick *yaqona*. When they are washed and gleaming bright they are often festooned on a small tree at the door of a house, which then looks for all the world like a Christmas tree decked with silver baubles.

With their thick thatch, high roofs and numerous apertures, Fijian houses are admirably cool in hot weather while, with all the doors and windows closed, there are few snugger places to spend a stormy night. Their design of a large single room, with possibly a curtained annexe for sleeping, is ideally suited to Fijian communal gatherings both formal and informal. But their construction, however fascinating a study for the anthropologist, is very expensive not only in man-hours but also in the food which must be provided for the workers and the ceremonies which attend house-building. Nowadays even in inland villages, modern materials are making their appearance. Often a complete wooden and iron house is beyond the means of a villager but he will start with a corrugated iron roof and bamboo-plaited walls, replacing the latter with timber as often as funds permit.

The house is greatly respected in Fijian culture and Fijians will invariably discard any footwear before entering. If someone of rank is in the house, they will not walk upright but either stoop or even crawl; and on entering a house and sitting down they will give a respectful clap with cupped hands. Similarly the Fijian equivalent of 'excuse me' is always uttered when anything from a high shelf or recess is brought down and the fetcher, his mission achieved, will again sit down and clap.

But while we have been studying the house, drinking *yaqona*, and discussing subjects ranging from copra driers to votes for women, the carriers have gone ahead and we must move on. A quick *bili ni mua* (the Fijian equivalent of doch-an-doris—it really means a push on the stem of a canoe) and a rapid check round the village. Yes, with forewarning it is likely that all the latrines will have covers over the holes. Even in the most remote villages many of the latrines have cement slabs which are known as 'Misi Kendricks' after a notable public health enthusiast of many years ago, who has thus gained a sort of immortality among the Fijians. Many men leave less lasting and less useful memorials. The people can be assumed to grow sufficient food for their own needs—basically *dalo*, yam and tapioca with different strains of sweet potato and green vegetables for variety —and the District Officer and the *Roko* will be more interested in cash crops, like bananas for export to New Zealand. They may also enquire about the *dalo* cultivation to supply the workers at the Vatukoula gold mines under a scheme run by the Fijian Economic Development staff. Perhaps there will be a word with an independent farmer wanting a loan to buy oxen and a plough, then an absolutely final *titoko* (stirrup-cup—the Fijian word means a walking-stick) and away.

Off on the track again the Fijians' bush lore comes to the

fore. Fruits will be found for the traveller in the most unlikely places, and he will be given a leaf to chew with a most refreshing bitter sweet flavour; the right jungle vine when cut will yield him a cooling draught; if the sun is too strong, a hat is quickly woven for him from a coconut frond; if it pours with rain, a large lily leaf is found to make an umbrella. A picnic lunch puts the boys on their mettle. They chop up wild or the domestic variety of yams, mix them with water and press them down into sections of bamboo. The same type of receptacle takes rolled-up balls of green leaves and another may have a cargo of prawns. All are put in a fire which will be lit with matches, though the Fijians have not lost the art of fire-making. They do not rub two sticks together but rapidly push a small, sharp-pointed, hard stick backwards and forwards on a large piece of soft inflammable wood till it begins to smoke and the spark appears from which the wispy inner leaf of a coconut frond can be ignited. In competitions this has been done in under a minute.

But to return to our victuals, the cooked food is delicious. Bamboo will form the goblets for draughts of crystal spring water, for a stream is the normal venue for such a meal, and if one has brought *yaqona*, the bush yields a *yaqona* bowl in the shape of a banana leaf rendered pliable by fire, the *yaqona* being strained through another banana leaf with a filter of fern. Small wonder that the Fijian took so happily to guerilla warfare and living off the country, when called to serve in the jungles of the Solomons or Malaya.

In the late afternoon we arrive at the village where we are to spend the night. As this is the leading town of the district, there will be rather more ceremony. But first a bath. Despite the fact that they are often seen in old and dirty clothes (and, after all, agriculturists the world over are not conspicuous for their sartorial elegance) the Fijians are a very clean people and morning and evening baths are the rule. So much so that when a village group which gained some publicity for a somewhat authoritarian regime laid down such baths as an order, Fijians were surprised. It was like telling people to eat. Going to bathe the men wear only a Tongan *sulu*—a plain strip of cloth wrapped round them—and there is no bath robe more convenient to discard and resume. As with so many Fijian activities, bathing is communal, and is the occasion for much fun and laughter particularly among the young. Distinct areas of river, usually hidden from each other by a bend, are allocated to men and women.

On their return to the village the men rub themselves with coconut oil pleasantly scented with sandalwood and other agents, getting the last traces of oil off their hands by rubbing it through their hair and giving it a black glossy gleam. It is by no means unusual for men as well as women to put flowers in their hair, and a comely youth with a flaming hibiscus behind his ear is more likely to attract admiration than to incur the charge of effeminacy.

The group sense and the sex division apparent in bathing permeate village life. In church, men and women do not sit as a family with their children but on opposite sides of the aisle. Apart from great fish drives in which an island's whole population may join, fishing parties tend to be either groups of women going fishing with nets in shallow water over the reefs, or bands of men going out in boats. Men go off to the food gardens to plant and nowadays one can see groups of Fijian women weeding and hoeing in the canefields. In the evening the men tend to gather in one house to discuss village affairs, tell stories and drink *yaqona* whilst the women are probably elsewhere, weaving mats, dress-making or ironing. As with women the world over, their talk is of babies and clothes and men. This is not to say there cannot be real affection between husband and wife, and they are united in their love of their children, but the Fijians seem most at their ease in their separate groups. This traditional division is beginning to break down, largely through the creation of women's clubs in the villages, and there have been a number of joint meetings at provincial centres on such subjects as village hygiene (environmental sanitation to the specialist) and child welfare where men's and women's interests converge. It usually takes some time at such gatherings before the women will venture to speak in front of the men but it is beginning to happen, and as men see the difference the progress of the women is making to the villages and their own lives (even at its lowest level of flowered sports shirts made by their wives for Christmas presents) they are recognizing the right of women to have a say in affairs. At least one all male Provincial Council has voted funds for its women's clubs and the proposal of votes for women was raised by the Fijian chiefs themselves.

On return to the house from bathing there may be a full welcome ceremony. This has been so often described that it will suffice to glance at one or two side-lights. When a whale's tooth is offered, no matter how large, it will be described by the donor as 'tiny', and this will immediately evoke from the recipient the response *levu* (great) no matter how small it is. This self-depreciation and often mock deprecation runs through Fijian life and may well be one of the reasons for the close feeling that exists between the Fijians and the British.

It can of course be carried to extremes. An invitation to drink a cup of hot water can mean a full-scale afternoon tea. And on a classic occasion when the wood-carvers of Kabara, the master craftsmen of Fiji, presented the Governor with a magnificent set of *yaqona* bowls—the very pinnacle of their art—they described them as 'just a few chippings'. On at least one occasion an unfortunate man has found himself in the invidious position of making a presentation of a 'small bite of food' and then, in absence of any alternative interpreter, also having to make the speech of thanks for the Gargantuan repast on behalf of the visitor. If he felt any incongruity he certainly did not show it and delivered both speeches with aplomb and every evidence of apparent sincerity. It is all part of traditional Fijian courtesy, one of their most unfailing characteristics. Nor is the courtesy merely verbal. An enthusiastic European lady, seeing large numbers of oranges going to waste, thought that a class in marmalade-making would be useful. All the women nearby came, were most interested in the preparations and most appreciative when given a pot of marmalade each to take home. A fortnight later when the lady asked her house-girl why she had not opened her own jar, the girl, caught in an unguarded moment, said, 'Oh, we don't like marmalade jam.'

On another occasion a lady shopping in the local market saw a Fijian with a small supply of rather rare grape-fruit. She hastened to buy them, only to learn he was himself a purchaser and not a vendor. But as soon as he knew she wanted them, she had the greatest difficulty in deterring him from pressing them on her. A sewing class in simple stitching included an earnest young woman who attended all the lessons with assiduity, coming some ten miles to do so. Later she was employed by the teacher as a wash-girl. One day, having an attractive piece of material, the teacher asked her house-girl, 'Who can make this up for me?' The house-girl said, 'Oh, Uqea is a good dressmaker.' Needless to say, Uqea was the wash-girl. She had been making dresses for years. A final notable verbal example. A church was started on a Government station and at the inaugural service the Government speaker referred to the establishment of the church 'in the Government compound'; the reply founded the church 'on the seat of leadership'.

The whale's tooth ceremony over and also the presentation of a *yaqona* root, *yaqona* is mixed in the bowl and strained through hibiscus fibres, and a cup brought to the chief guest. Fijians serving *yaqona* seem able to judge to a nicety the capacity of a drinker's cup, and even if the serving cup is of widely disparate size, the amount dispensed usually tallies with the size of the drinker's cup. In at least one province the ceremonial cup of *yaqona* is followed by a cup bearer carrying a 'chaser' of cold water. After the first ceremonial round limited to a small number of drinkers, the visitor will speak, sure of attentive listeners for any important matter he may wish to raise. Thereafter drinking becomes general, and in the relaxed atmosphere of tobacco smoke the affairs of the village, the district, the province, Fiji, and the world for that matter, are reviewed, plans made and stories told.

Just about dusk the voice of the village headman will be heard shouting out the allocation of duties for the following day; men to carry the visitor's baggage to the next village, women to go fishing to provide for a feast for a visiting preacher next day, men to work on building a house for the school teacher and so on. In the past the authoritarian system even used to lay down the amount of food crops a man should plant to maintain himself but now 'Programmes of work' as they are called are founded on more realistic lines.

As will be gathered, life in a Fijian village is not lived at a fast tempo, and custom and manners militate against any display of undue haste, but the *canard* that Fijians are a lazy people can be dispelled by moving through the country districts. There is much to be done in the normal daily routine and it is usually all accomplished in good time. Witness the effort made by inland people growing bananas for the export market. After the work of growing good fruit, the bunches are cut and transported by hand or horse to the nearest head-waters of a river leading to the main road. There bamboo rafts are constructed and the bananas floated miles downstream, past long deep stretches which need hard poling, through bubbling rapids calling for skilled watermanship and occasionally over shallow reaches where the rafts must be dragged by sheer man-power. When the crating point is reached, the bananas are unloaded and packed into cases and the rafts abandoned to drift downstream—the next trip will call for fresh rafts. The cases will then be manhandled to the main road to be loaded on to lorries for Suva. Then, after this the villagers make the long trip back overland to the village.

Bamboo raft

But the expedition has not been a doleful procession. Somewhere downstream there will have been a picnic break—wild yams baked in the fire, and, if they are lucky, the succulent white flesh of Malayan fish speared in the river as the men cool off. After a meal and a smoke, with no dishes to wash, back to the rafts, often with a song and always with stories and jokes. Moreover the men will be paid at the roadside for their former consignment and will be able to buy some of the simple extras for their village life—tea, sugar, soap and kerosene, and possibly a shirt or material for their wives. Nevertheless this is not a lazy man's way of earning money.

Some of them also work at pit sawing, surely one of the heaviest jobs done under the tropical sun. A huge log is balanced over a pit and one man stands above on a frame wielding one end of a long hand saw. His companion works in the pit below, and despite a wetted handkerchief tied over nose and mouth against the clouds of sawdust, he has constantly to blink and rub specks from his eyes into which salt sweat also trickles. Nor does he know when some flaw in the pit and frame construction may not send the log crashing down on top of him. A lazy man could earn money in easier ways.

Fijians have also taken to cane farming—and not just yesterday. It is a measure of their adaptability and willingness to work that about thirty years ago the people of the island of Malake, traditional fishermen, took up cane farming areas in Tavua on the mainland and worked them for nearly twenty years. What tends to hold a Fijian back is the lack even of that minimum capital for basic equipment—oxen, plough and harrow. This is now being remedied in various ways. But even before, there were men who made their way, like the one who came from what is perhaps the most inaccessible village in the Province of Ra, far away from the main road in difficult country. He grew *yaqona* on his home slopes and saved his money till he could come down to the valleys and lease cane land. He now produces over 200 tons of sugar-cane annually and is planning a beef cattle farm. But it is in the use of money, when acquired by their industry, that the Fijians require most guidance, and advance in this cuts across their custom. When any money or goods which you may possess are likely to be begged from you, saving or investment in permanent things loses its attraction. As the late *Ratu* Sir Lala Sukuna put it in a memorable phrase 'The Fijian is apt to fritter away his substance on evanescent trifles.' Fijians are commonly seen enjoying the luxury and comfort of taxi rides where there is a perfectly adequate bus service. But then someone may beg your wages, someone may beg a shirt you have bought, but no one can beg a taxi ride you have already enjoyed.

Expenditure over weddings has been catechized often enough and at a Fijian wedding in the country I have seen *fakawela* or exchange rivalry carried to extremes. It all began when one member of the groom's party gave a cigarette to a member of the bride's party. The return was a packet of cigarettes. The groom's party responded with a shirt to be trumped by a wristlet watch. The performance only came to my notice when I saw the gaol warder, who was one of the bride's party, removing a chair and two tables from his house to take to the groom's side, and I feared that prestige was to be maintained at the expense of the government's list of non-expendable equipment!

In the more remote villages, the supply of what might be called basic extras—tea, sugar, kerosene, soap, cigarettes, etc.—is a constant problem, met in various ways. Sometimes there is a Chinese store on a lease just outside the village. The Chinese fit well into the community and many take Fijian wives. Some are accused of sharp practice but an examination of their books would show that they often carried villages through depression years with debts that they will never recover. The Chinese is a shrewd business man who usually has the requisite capital to make his business succeed. Not so successful are many Fijian ventures. A man will return to his village after a year or two's work in Suva, Lautoka or the gold-mines in Vatukoula with his small savings which he will sink in a store and a supply of goods. 'Sink' is unhappily only too often the appropriate word. The spasmodic nature of the villagers' earnings, combined with their traditional custom, may lead them to request and expect credit. Before the storekeeper realizes it, he has disposed of all his goods but has only been paid for half. His next stock replenishment is therefore on a smaller scale and so on, until the law of diminishing returns inexorably reaches its inevitable conclusion. Village stores often meet the same fate. They belong to everyone and so they belong to no one, and their end can be quicker than an individual enterprise. Some co-operative stores succeed, but here again, despite rigid rules prohibiting credit, too often the rot sets in and the store folds up. Yet the extraordinary thing is the resilience with which such individuals and groups will rise Phoenix-like from the ashes and start all over again; and though in some spheres it is true that Fijians can be easily discouraged, they seem determined to be worthy partners of the Nation of Shopkeepers.

But despite the hard work, life is not an unrelieved tedium of toil in a Fijian village and the following experience of the writer[1] shows how villagers can enjoy themselves in their own environment while shrewdly making money at the same time.

I had spent a long and weary day holding Provincial Court in a Fijian village, and even the lightest linen jacket—the minimum

---

[1] Reprinted, by permission, from *The Times* of 9th June 1960.

requirement for decorum—had seemed a burden. Moreover, one of the cases which involved a new regulation about the sale of copra had attracted widespread interest, and the result had been an unusually packed and stuffy Court house. I was therefore looking forward to a swim, a meal and then a quiet yarn around a *yaqona* bowl before turning in.

The programme I had mapped out for myself proceeded smoothly till I sat back from my evening meal with a repletion which comes from Fijian hospitality. My pipe was barely lit when, instead of a man carrying a *yaqona* bowl, the village schoolmaster entered. Quietly sitting down and clapping his cupped hands he gave the customary prefatory cough for which numerous district officers over the years, including myself, must take the blame. 'We are holding a small *gunu peni* in the village tonight in aid of the school funds and I wondered if you would like to open it since you are the manager of the school.'

This triple-pronged approach left me defenceless. It was to be a small affair, I was to have the honour of opening it, and finally I was Manager of the school. In any case I had seen so often in my Fijian school accounts 'To proceeds from *gunu peni* £5 16s. 4d.' that I was keen to see how such funds were raised. My schoolmaster mentor instructed me to the extent that I should put a piece of money in the bowl after I had drunk the *yaqona* and with this scanty fore-knowledge I stepped out into the dark. I was conducted round behind the biggest house in the village where, presumably during our judicial deliberations, a large temporary shelter of palm leaves had been built, gaily decorated with hibiscus blossoms and brightly lit with hurricane lamps. It is perhaps needless to say that the occasion was not a small one and people were there from all the other villages which sent children to the school. At the far end, full to the brim, was the largest *yaqona* bowl I have ever seen. I seated myself where I was told and a cup bearer brought me the first half coconut shell full, amid a hush that had fallen on the buzz of conversation. I drained it and put a ten shilling note in the bowl—grossly excessive but occasioned by the everlasting fear of seeming mean. Moreover it was worth that to open such an affair without speech. A guitar and ukelele band were playing a gay little tune from Raratonga and my feet had just begun to tap when the music stopped in the middle of a bar. I must have made a gesture of disappointment for I was asked 'Do you like that tune?'

'Yes I do.'

'Well Jone over there has paid sixpence to have it stopped but you can have it started again for a shilling.'

I parted with a shilling. The drift of the evening was beginning to make itself plain. However, the strains of my tune beginning again reconciled me and my foot resumed its tapping. But in less than a minute it stopped again. Jone had paid four shillings for its curtailment. At this stage I thought discretion the better part of valour and resigned myself to silence, and another bowl of *yaqona* at the advertised rate of one penny. But this did not content the Fijian Magistrate. If I had no pride, no shame, someone had to take my part, and eight shillings tinkled into the bowl to save my honour and to provide new desks for the school. Whether Jone had reached his limit or the Fijian Magistrate's prestige made him pause, my tune was strummed through to a triumphant conclusion.

Thereafter I refrained from comment on the band's performance and allowed others to contest to the limit of their financial ability the repertoire available. When dancing commenced and the company began to bid for their favourite performances the money really began to flow into the bowl. The actions of the dancers in starting and stopping became almost a dance in themselves. And all the while *yaqona* flowed.

During a pause in the music a cup bearer approached me with a bowl of Gargantuan dimensions brimful of *yaqona*. There are people who prefer the breadth and depth of the ocean to the shallows of a tiny tarn but I am not of their number. Little and often is my motto for *yaqona* drinking. Dismay must therefore have been writ large on my face at the advent of the Homeric potation, and I noticed quiet smiles on the faces round me, and on the face of the local teacher a look of devilish glee.

'I can't drink this,' I murmured to my earlier champion, the Fijian Magistrate.

'Well,' he said, 'the schoolmaster has paid sixpence for the pleasure of seeing you drink it, but you can send it back to him for a shilling.' I did so, but the pledging of a florin by the teacher brought the bowl swimming towards me once more.

At this point a sudden flash of reminiscence brought to my mind an old problem which started by placing a farthing on one corner of a chess board and then doubling the amount for each square. I had a dim memory that Rockefeller himself could not have afforded to fill the board. Being no Rockefeller and mentally squaring my cowardice with the reflection that I should not beggar the school-master, I swallowed my pride and the brimming bowl. This brought the *yaqona* up to my ears and I thought it was perhaps time to be leaving. When I heard someone mutter something that sounded remarkably like 'Sixpence to hear the District Officer sing a song' I knew it was time to leave. The band struck up my tune and stopped suddenly, but I was not to be tempted. I had already learned enough and more than enough for my purpose. I took the proceeds off next morning for safe deposit. At the stated price it represented one thousand eight hundred and seventy three bowls of *yaqona*.

A special paragraph should be devoted to Fijian women, who must surely rank as the kindest of their sex to be found anywhere. Their life is a hard one, finding food, fishing, fetching firewood, cooking, washing up, washing—the list of their occupations is interminable, and if to some extent it sounds not unlike that of a housewife anywhere, do not forget that fishing may involve a whole day in the water on a cold day (there are such in Fiji), firewood may have to be carried by back a couple of miles, cooking is on smoky wood fires and washing is done in a creek. But the women are not only uncomplaining, they never seem to let work seem a burden. They always have a smile and a thought for others, so that though they return drenched from the reef they will be overcome with pity for a traveller who arrives in a light shower. Actions and burdens which are their daily accepted lot are regarded as feats when performed by others. Their normal garb about the village is an old European style dress, often with a *sulu* as well to save the dress a little. And the dress normally stays on for swimming and fishing. But when they go to church, town or even for a dance in the village, none is smarter than the Fijian women with their erect carriage and a dress with a swaggering dip in the full skirt at the back, sometimes with a plain silk *sulu*-like garment underneath reaching down to their ankles.

There remains so much of Fijian life in the country to describe: the days and nights on the deck of an auxiliary cutter butting through the Koro sea on its way to the Lau islands; the long wade ashore if the vessel arrives at low tide; the dignity, vigour or humour of the Fijian dances with fan, club or spear; *yaqona* plantations on steep mist-clad hills; the excitement of inter-district rugby; the long horse trips to market along rugged trails with copra or *yaqona*, to return with a drum of kerosene or a sack of sugar; the thrill of the wild pig chase with dogs and spears; the clamour, splashing and shimmering haul from a fish drive; men away for whole days weeding tracks and picnicking on the roadside; housebuilding where apparent confusion disguises the remarkable control of the master builder; feasts with all the wealth of sea and reef, shore and river; school-children walking up to ten miles on a Sunday afternoon to village boarding-school to return the same distance home on a Friday; the pulsing throb of the *lali's* beat summoning the people to church; the fragrance of a *lei* of frangipani; the rhythmic clack as the women beat out *masi* cloth, and their concentration as they apply the stencilled patterns—all these and many more sights and sounds, smells and tastes make up village life in Fiji. It is an unsophisticated life and admittedly has its frustrations, particularly for the younger people. Few villages have electric light (though some have) and distance often means that a visit to the cinema is a rare occasion. But it is a life with a tradition and a closely knit pattern which encourages a man to help his neighbour, since he himself is so dependent on his neighbour. The village, too, offers a secure base from which the more venturesome can branch out on their own, and now that funds for agricultural development are becoming more readily available, many of the obstacles to Fijian economic advancement in the country will be removed. And this is as it should be, for it is in the rural areas that the main scope for development lies, and it is the rural areas which represent the real Fiji.

The Indian people should be described separately because, although the country districts provide some of the best examples of inter-racial co-operation when some project of joint benefit such as a feeder road is contemplated, and although Fijians and Indians will take advantage of the skills and strength of each other to achieve some end, there is little purely social contact between the races. They have, of course, inevitably adopted various habits from each other. For example, Indians are firm converts to *yaqona* (and some are very heavy drinkers) but they tend to drink it stronger than the Fijians. Conversely the Fijians have taken kindly to curry but they eat it milder than the Indians.

Generally speaking the Indian in the country is a confirmed individualist, whether he is a taxi-owner, storekeeper or farmer, and a glance at his settlements will bear this out. Homesteads are not clustered together but dotted here and there over the fields and the hills and as close to his crops as the farmer can be. For the vast majority of the Indians in the countryside are farmers, and sugar-cane farmers at that, which is natural as this was the purpose for which they were introduced into Fiji.

The first sign that one is approaching an Indian settlement in Fiji will probably be the barking of dogs, and one will be greeted by a pack of them, snapping and snarling until they are driven off by their owner with a shout or a well-directed stone. The dogs are kept, partly for protection—particularly of their families when the men are off in the fields—and partly for hunting wild pigs which abound in the bush and can do extensive damage to crops.

The Indians' individualistic style of living needs a smaller house which nevertheless follows Fijian pattern. They have, however, acquired considerable skill in building and the best built Indian houses can rival many Fijian ones. They also tend to have more refinements in the shape of shutters and glass windows since, unlike Fijian villages, they are subject to the Public Health and Building Regulations. They have brought with them from India the style of flooring with clay and cow dung which gives a smooth cool surface. Large families are the rule (and ten children is by no means unusual or the limit) so living is sometimes very cramped, and a sack with rope tied at the four corners suspended from a convenient bough makes a good cradle and when the wind blows the cradle rocks.

Some of the houses have a bamboo partition to allow some privacy to the husband and wife at night, and refinements like curtains and pictures of scenes from the *Ramayana* brighten up the house, and show the people are trying hard to maintain and improve their standard within the limitations of their pockets. In the corner of the house will be a sack or two of rice, probably harvested from the farmer's own land—a family of six will live for well over a month on two sacks of *padi*. Diet is predominantly vegetarian (*baigans* or egg plants are extensively eaten) flavoured with curry, but celebrations will see the immolation of one of the fowls which peck around the yard and have constantly to be driven out of the house. A big occasion may mean the last day for one of the goats which many Indians keep. These are a sound commercial proposition in Fiji where many of the population do not eat beef. Goat's milk and cheese, however, do not seem to be used as in other countries.

Few farms are without at least one pair of bullocks, sometimes of vast size, and it is like looking at a Van Gogh impression to see a lone farmer ploughing a slope of patterned fields of green, yellow and brown in heat that shimmers like the Midi. Even on farms where tractors do the bulk of the work—and their numbers are increasing either on an ownership or a hire basis—the bullocks remain, for there is still much work they can do best; and from time to time with a creditable lack of rancour or superiority they rescue the noisy, spluttering usurpers from the thick mud. Many a motorist too has reason to be grateful to these strong beasts and their helpful owner, particularly if he ventures off the beaten track in the wet season. Like as not the farm will have a pair of young bullocks being trained to replace the older ones as they pass their peak, and a cow will provide milk for the household and *ghee* for cooking with possibly a small surplus to sell.

Beside the main house may stand a small thatched shelter with no sides, though the posts are sometimes connected by planks to form seats. In the hot season this is the lounge and the nearest approach to air conditioning in the country districts. In its shade may also be a small wooden rice pounder. Nowadays, however, rice mills with small diesel engines are common throughout the colony and perhaps twice a week one can see groups of people bringing in their sacks of *padi* to be milled at a small charge per tin.

Local subsidiaries of the large tobacco concerns are now using some Fiji leaf in their products and are encouraging Fijians to grow it under supervision to supply their factories. In the old days a number of provinces paid their taxes in tobacco. But for many years tobacco growing and curing was an Indian monopoly and even today most of the Fiji tobacco smoked in leaf form or rolled up in a banana leaf into a rough cigarette is produced by Indians. The Indian hawker, with his rolls of dark twist tied in long rolls of sacking and trussed up with string like a long ham, is a familiar figure, trudging the countryside and selling in Fijian village and Indian settlement alike.

While a few fortunate large farmers have freeholds, the majority of Indian farmers are tenants, either on freehold from the sugar milling company, on sub-lease from a company head lease, or on leases from the Crown or the Native Land Trust Board acting on behalf of the Fijian owners. Leases tend to be of about ten acres which can provide a good living for one family, but not also for grown up sons and their wives and families. As the latter arrangement is common, many of the farmers have a real struggle. But they are hard workers. It is normal for them to rise at daybreak and work two or three hours before eating and when they eat it is often just a snack brought to them in the fields by their wives. There will be another meal at midday, leaving the main meal for the evening. During school holidays whole families are to be seen in the fields, hoeing and weeding the cane, or deep in mud transplanting rice seedlings. Another busy time for the whole family is the rice harvest; reaping, gathering, threshing in the time honoured way with trampling oxen, then winnowing in the breeze.

The phrase 'during the school holidays' is used advisedly, for the Indian people in Fiji would do nothing to interfere with their children's education by which they set very high store, though they have a tendency to place too high a premium on examinations and certificates. But it is a daily miracle to see emerging from poor houses little girls in crisp freshly laundered dresses of white, blue, green, mauve or pink, their pigtails neatly tied with ribbons, and the boys in spotless shirts and khaki shorts.

But the Indians' life is not one of unremitting drudgery. They too have festivals when the rumble of cane lorries is stilled and the cane cutter's knife is at rest. Although the great festival of *Ram Lila* with its dramatization of the *Ramayana* has become very commercialized—as Christmas has in the Christian world —it can be a most colourful occasion, particularly at night, when the image of the mighty demon, king Ravana of Ceylon, towers up to forty feet on a wooden framework covered with bright cloth or paper and casts great shadows across a ground ablaze with benzine lights. Stalls glitter with silver filigree work and a riot of sweetmeats attract their customary crowd of youthful buyers or gazers. The evocative twang of Indian instruments and high pitched intoning blend with the thrilling beat of the *tabla* (drum); exciting smells of savoury curries and exotic chutneys permeate the air. The combined assault on all the senses leaves the visitor slightly dazed but yet with the sense of having to some small degree and for one night at any rate shared in the spirit of the East. But even as the ages are rolling back to the springtime of the world and Rama Chandra's wanderings in the jungle, an ear catches the rhythm of modern Indian dance music played over a loudspeaker, and an eye sights the stream of taxis speeding through the swirling dust, and once more there is the clash of old and new which is so typical of Fiji and so symbolic.

Dipawali or the Festival of Lights in November marks the Indian New Year which is also the time when merchants close their books. Then all along the verandahs of the little Indian stores guttering wicks floating in tiny clay bowls filled with *ghee* make chains of yellow light, while green coconut fronds on the verandah posts give the festival a Fiji flavour. On the stone pavements the womenfolk trace with infinite care age-old patterns in coloured powdered chalks, keeping alive in a new land the stories and beliefs of their forebears from India.

The Moslems too maintain their festivals, and though the rigid discipline of the fast of *Ramadan* is far from universal, the feast of *Id* to mark the end of the fast is widely celebrated in the country when neighbours gather to feast and make merry together. They also remember their poorer neighbours and almsgiving is an important part of the celebration. In the old days gifts in food and kind were the rule, but nowadays a gift of money is common. On such an occasion the scene at a small Indian hill farm by a stream recreates Horace's picture of the rural festival by the spring of Bandusia, even to the sacrifice of the goat.

Historically, psychologically and now as a result of his environment in Fiji, the Indian farmer is closely attached to his land—the only closer link possibly being that which may attach his crop to his creditor. But he jealously guards his rights and neither Fijian nor brother Indian can expect to encroach with impunity. Rights of way and boundary disputes always require careful handling and some go on for years. By far the most satisfactory settlement is reached when one of the old original survey pegs can be found in its original site (new pegs are not uncommon and adjustments are not unknown) and to see two angry old men furiously digging on either side of a disputed boundary in search of a true peg whose location each is convinced he knows is to realize the strength of feeling such matters evoke. It is, however, fair to add that there is another side of the coin where farmers give areas of land for schools or temples.

Hospitality seems the mark of country people everywhere and the Indians in Fiji are no exception. A visitor to an Indian settlement will find the farmer plying him with *yaqona* from little enamel bowls, tea—hot, sweet and laced with *massala* (spices)—and if the stay is longer a savoury curry of chopped up chicken and the flat round *chapatis* well known to the partaker of Indian food. Even if a traveller cannot stay, the farmer will try to think of something to refresh him on his trek, such as a couple of lemons or a cucumber from his little vegetable garden to eat on the way.

In addition to his industry, the average farmer is a law-abiding man of good sense who still tends to regard Government as his father and mother. He himself, however, is usually not well educated and therefore tends to lack confidence in his own sound judgement. He is therefore fruitful soil for agitators whose superior education and qualifications overawe him. His isolated life also makes him particularly vulnerable to intimidation and twice in the last twenty years he has been led into strike action which many admitted they did not support. Precariously balancing his budget as so many other farmers do, he can ill afford to be thrown off balance, with a result that he ends up further in the hands of the moneylenders.

The spread out nature of Indian homesteads and the size of the houses means that somewhere else must normally be found for a forum or meeting place. This is usually the verandah of the local Indian store where men gather to smoke, drink *yaqona* and discuss local affairs. It has even been known for meetings of a co-operative group aiming to run its own store to be held at this universal centre. It is in a very real sense the economic hub of an Indian farming area and, in the absence of rural banking facilities, plays an important part in its financial life. Before looking at some of the defects of the system, it should be remembered that if these stores and merchants did not provide facilities they would not exist at all. Farmers everywhere, and particularly small farmers with a seasonal crop, find themselves compelled to live on credit, and to a large extent this credit is supplied by the local storekeeper. Not only will he supply goods on credit, but, usually being a moneylender also, he will advance money to enable such charges as school fees to be met on time. At his best therefore, a good merchant is doing something for the farmer that no one else will do, and one should beware of sweeping generalizations and universal condemnation. But the system is, of course, open to abuse where one party is a shrewd business man with perhaps not too many scruples and the other is a simple farmer who may not even be able to read and write. Only recently has consideration been given to a move to oblige shopkeepers to give dockets for sales and the only record tends to be in the merchant's book, kept possibly even in a language unknown to the farmer. Unfortunately sometimes both parties are only too ready to let a debt reach a level quite out of relation to the farmer's income. This tends to be the turning point when the merchant calls the tune. He will refuse the farmer further credit until the latter executes a crop lien attaching the proceeds from his cane farm to the merchant. As the crop lien meets only his current debts, and he continues to draw credit and add to his debts, he is running up debts against his crop two years ahead and certain it is that his crop lien will have to be renewed. And it is at this stage that an unscrupulous merchant will turn the screw, so that the farmer will be too frightened even to ask to see details of his account. In this state, life and work lose their purpose and he can become little more than a worker for the merchant, constantly afraid that even more rigorous measures will be taken against him. Nor, in the traditional pattern of tragedy, does he fail to contribute himself to his own fall; for he will burden himself with more debt over his daughters' marriages in the age-old way of the East.

'Saxon, Norman and Dane are we', and the Indians in Fiji are by no means a homogeneous mass. In the market on a Saturday bearded Sikhs from the Punjab jostle with dark Madrassis, pale Gujarati storekeepers, and here and there a descendant of the Mopla people from the Malabar coast. Nor are these all, for among the Indian languages spoken in Fiji are Hindi, Urdu, Tamil, Telegu, Gurmukhi, and Malayalam. Fortunately a *lingua franca* masquerading under the name of Hindustani has evolved which is widely used and understood throughout the colony. Masquerading is perhaps a rather derogatory expression as the grammar is a charming simplification of tense, number, mood and person into the singular imperative of the verb. This offends the purists but many a schoolboy faced with conjugating the future perfect tense of *amo* must wish the practical Romans had shown the same refreshing disregard for grammar in the interests of simplicity. One explanation, probably apocryphal, is that the version of the language which the original indentured labourers brought with them to Fiji was not of the highest. This was learned by the overseers and the like who did not improve the style and then the children of the immigrants had to learn the language of the overseers. Whatever its origin the resultant tongue is admirably suited for its purpose in the country and its use the 'open sesame' to the countryman's understanding. Indian women in the country seem to be even less emancipated than in the towns. Their lot is one of hard work in house and field punctuated by frequent pregnancies. They are commonly seen beating the dirt out of clothes at a creek, or drawing water from a well, or milking a cow, or bearing heavy burdens on their heads, or joining in all the heavy work of the field. And to cook for their large families is a job in itself. They have little if any say in the finances of the household—indeed many of them have had no say in their choice of husband. Indian girls are very closely watched and have little opportunity for mixing with young men and gaining confidence. Small wonder then that they are so submissive as wives and that they usually keep well in the background when guests are present. But they have their moments, and on high days and holidays they can bloom forth in gorgeous saris of saffron, emerald, ivory, turquoise and other brilliant colours, often shot with threads of silver and gold. In general however, it would appear that Pericles' ideal of womanhood—she who is least spoken of for good or evil—holds true for Indian women in the country.

Apart from the staff of the sugar mills, the banks and the large firms, which are usually located in the townships, the Europeans in the country are predominantly owners or managers of copra plantations or cattle farms. And some of them set a fine example of estate management, both in pasture control and improvement, and in plantation work. Well-spaced trees, cleared underfoot and with good roads running through, show what can be done by hard work, organization and capital. And many started off without the latter asset and built up their properties by heartbreaking toil, weathering periods of depression and keeping going in spite of everything. These men were tough—they had to be—and still today they have much of the independent spirit of the frontiersman and the pioneer. That they drove their labour hard is illustrated by the story of the plantation owner who frustrated the normal Fijian method of having a short break—sitting down to sharpen a cane knife—by constantly whetting a cane knife as he stood over them and always having a sharp one ready to hand over to the would-be laggard. However, they did make themselves familiar with the languages of their labour force and it is a tribute to them that third generations of workers can be found on their estates.

As they have prospered, the planters have built themselves spacious homes and their wives, after years when they cheerfully put up with the lack of many amenities which their city counterparts would consider essential, have now evolved a gracious design for living where the produce of the country combines happily with the comforts and luxuries which many can now afford. Plantation hospitality is a byword, and a visitor to one plantation will find it hard to keep up with the invitations which will bombard him from every side. Nor have the workers been forgotten and there have been improvements in their living conditions too. Individual family houses are replacing the old unsightly labour lines, some have electric light, and amenities such as a cinema and a restaurant. There are, of course, unyielding traditionalists, unresponsive to change, but the majority are always ready to experiment with new methods—weedicides, bulldozers, and original types of copra driers, even to the extent of a drier based on solar energy. They work laborious days; up at daybreak to start the labour off, then back for a bite of breakfast with their families, then off on a round of the property, often on horseback, supervising fencing, cattle musters, weeding, copra cutting and drying and all the multifarious jobs on an estate. Lunch will be at eleven o'clock by which time they will have earned it. Then an afternoon similarly employed with possibly, in addition, a coastal vessel to load with copra or cattle. The evening may see the planter working on his accounts. Many wives are unofficial nurses and dispensers for the workers and their families and win their esteem and affection. It is one of the disadvantages of this type of life that even if it is no farther than Suva, children have to be sent away to school and are separated from their parents. But what a wonderful place to come home for holidays with tramping and riding over hill tracks and sailing or fishing round the island reefs.

These men combine a watchful critical attitude towards the central government of Fiji with a deep and lasting loyalty to the British Crown. They have also a strong local patriotism and any public or charitable cause in their own district is sure of their warm and generous support.

And what, briefly, of the vantage point from which all these scenes are viewed—the position of a District Officer in Fiji? He has still to a great extent the same varied, exciting and rewarding life as his predecessors. He may travel by car on metalled roads through his district but much of his journeying is still on foot or horseback or by sea in boats large and small. He still finds himself Magistrate, Deputy Sheriff, Gaol Superintendent, District Registrar, Marriage Officer, Market Superintendent, Commissioner for Oaths, Chairman of the Rural Local Authority, Administrator of Estates, Fisheries Inspector, Road Builder, Lease Inspector, Development Officer, Marketing Adviser, Manager of Schools, Trustee, Recruiting Agent, etc. But his primary task is, as ever, to know his people. There is a fund of goodwill towards the District Administration in Fiji which is a humbling experience for the young officer and at the same time a tribute to his predecessors. He is still something of a father-figure—which has been defined as meaning that the people ignore his advice but come to him when they are in trouble. The latter is certainly true and to judge by some of the requests he receives country people believe the age of miracles is not yet past, with the District Officer as its high priest. In a single morning he may be expected to conjure up non-existent land, to sell peanuts at a higher price than has been prevailing for months, to arrange all the formalities of a marriage in one day, to amend the laws of the Colony for a special case or to build a road through manifestly impossible country. He is constantly moving through his district and from time to time his wife and family join him on tour. Thereby his wife too comes to know the appeal and problems of the people. Cooking and sewing classes evoke an enthusiastic response and women will come long distances to attend, but it is her experience of country conditions in the women's own homes that enables the teaching to be geared to their requirements and environment. There is nothing like slowly submerging in a leaking dinghy and having to swim for it to impress on her the difficulties women face in travelling to classes. And a night spent by the whole family on an Indian farm or in a Fijian village makes friendships at all levels, none warmer than among the children who find each other filling in the gaps in their education. Booklearning and European card games are exchanged for bareback riding lessons and all the young countryman's lore of beasts and crops. And how many other chances would a European boy of eight have to milk a cow or even take a turn with a plough in Fiji? It is to be hoped that the reading of *Alice in Wonderland* and an introduction to the intricacies of 'knock-out whist' and 'beggar-my-neighbour' arc considered adequate recompense.

This short outline is not designed to show the work of a District Officer but rather the climate in which he lives. Despite all the strains and stresses of recent years, his lot is still a most favoured one, the days are never long enough, and the intangible rewards that come his way far outnumber the frustrations. In the words of Robert Louis Stevenson:

> 'There's the life for a man like me,
> There's the life for ever.'

Beating a *lali*

PART TWO

Problems, Present and Future

1. INDUSTRIAL TROUBLES

IN the past the population of Fiji has been generally orderly and well behaved, and such few labour disputes as did occur were settled fairly easily and without violence. The position during and since the last war has been less satisfactory. As mentioned in the chapter 'Fiji at War', while Fijians flocked to the colours to serve against the Japanese, the Indian section of the population were advised by some of their political leaders not to enlist in the army except on 'European' terms of pay, and few of them actually joined the armed forces. Further, at a critical period of the war, the Indian cane farmers were persuaded to 'strike' for better terms from the Colonial Sugar Refining Company, and this strike, which caused serious loss to the public revenue and the community generally, is estimated to have cost the farmers themselves over £1,000,000. This was not the worst. Disorders and arson made it necessary to divert troops who should have been otherwise employed to maintain order in the cane areas where most of the Indians lived.

For a time after the end of the war there was little further trouble and even in 1955 it was possible to write, in *South Pacific Enterprise*, a book published on behalf of the Colonial Sugar Refining Company, of 'the good working basis which has been evolved by solving industrial problems (in Fiji) by collective bargaining between the company and the Sugar Workers' Union. This has worked so well that neither side avails itself of arbitration. These are achievements of which a company and a people may well be proud.'

The later situation has not been so happy, but probably no worse than in other parts of the world. After several disputes and strikes which began in 1957 a Board of Enquiry was set up in 1959, under the chairmanship of Mr. G. G. Honeyman, Q.C., who has had long experience on Industrial Disputes Tribunals in England, 'to enquire into the causes and circumstances of a dispute which is apprehended between the Colonial Sugar Refining Company, Limited, and the Fiji Sugar Industry

Employees' Association and to make recommendations for the maintenance of industrial peace in the sugar milling industry'. The other members of the Board were a European, a Fijian and an Indian. The report of the Board was not unanimous as the Indian member signed a dissenting memorandum, but the opinion of the majority was clear. This opinion was that the company had contributed to the general industrial unrest through an attitude of paternalism and the effect of remote control from its head office in Australia, and the report recommended an increase of wages of about 17 per cent. At the same time the majority expressed strong views regarding the activities of one of the Indian leaders. 'We are satisfied that one of the main causes was the deliberate misrepresentation of the industrial situation by some officers of the Association,' ran the report.

Following the settlement of the wages dispute there was another strike of the Indian cane farmers. It was particularly unfortunate that in 1960, when other problems, such as the closing of the Nausori sugar mill and the report of the Commission of Enquiry, were causing some emotional repercussions in the population, that the long-term contracts between the Colonial Sugar Refining Company and the farmers came to an end and were due for renewal. The farmers refused to sign the new contracts offered them by the company as they wanted the company to buy a greater supply of cane than it was prepared to do, or, alternatively, to pay compensation for unbought cane. For several weeks the Indian planters refused to cut their cane and it was uneconomic for the mills to start work on the small amount of cane that could be supplied by Fijian growers. Some of the Indians, on the advice of their leaders, also declined to plant cane for future crops. The losses caused by this stoppage have been considerable, and but for the stockpile left over from the previous year's crop it is doubtful whether Fiji would have filled its sugar export quota for 1960, which would have seriously affected the possibility of any increase in the quota in future years.

Once again there was need to send troops of the regular army and of the territorial force to the cane centres, where police and special constables guarded cane-fields, mills, water pipe-lines and bridges, and once again the conduct of the Fijians was in marked contrast to that of the Indians. The colony was shocked by a cowardly attack made on Mr. H. G. R. McAlpine, the Commissioner of the Western Division, who was shot and seriously wounded, outside his own house, on the night of the 12th July 1960, by an unknown assailant.

It is said that the dispute was not due so much to economic reasons as to 'personal antagonisms and a struggle for supremacy by the competing leaders of the farmers' group and thus for top leadership of the community', and this allegation is supported by assertions of Indian politicians themselves. One Indian member of the Legislative Council went so far as to accuse two other Indians of being leaders of a group which was deliberately trying to get the farmers into debt so that they would become 'the vassals of the business community'.

It must be remembered that many of the farmers are poorly educated and unable to judge the position for themselves. They are therefore easily swayed by the oratory of political aspirants for power (who are not themselves cane farmers) and the orator who will promise more, and be more vehement in his denunciation of the milling company, is the more likely to secure a following. It is almost inevitable that the company should be mistrusted and criticized, as the fact that it exercises a practical monopoly creates a feeling of helplessness among those who have to deal with it. It is said that the company's senior European officials are lacking in a proper human approach to the problems affecting the sugar industry and that the public relations of the company are archaic.

After some months a temporary truce was arrived at and cane was cut and supplied to the mills. A Commission of Enquiry, under the chairmanship of Sir Malcolm Trustram Eve, was set up to examine and report on the organization, operation and prospects of the sugar industry, and this Commission's report was published in September 1961. The Commission recommended the appointment of an independent chairman of the sugar industry in Fiji, with an advisory council and a statutory sugar board, which, it is hoped, would have the confidence of all concerned; other recommendations affecting the future of the industry were made, and the Commission dealt briefly with the dispute which led to its own appointment.

The Commission considered that the Colonial Sugar Refining Company were 'entitled to be proud of the part they have played in developing the sugar industry in Fiji during the past eighty years', but criticized them 'severely for their handling of the growers in 1959 and 1960'. They placed the main blame on the board of directors in Australia, who gave no real authority to their local representatives to negotiate or to give information regarding the finances of the industry.

The Commission 'equally severely' criticized the cane-growers for their attitude during the negotiations in 1959 and 1960, and considered that 'particular blame attaches to the leaders of one group of growers who advised that the cane crop for 1960 should not be cut. This advice was followed for a time by nearly half of the growers and regrettably their leaders persisted in this policy after the offer to appoint a commission of enquiry. We were unable to discover how many growers followed of their own free will and how many from fear of reprisals such as burning cane or beating up. We can only believe that it was the deliberate intention of these leaders to cause disruption to the largest industry in Fiji in the hope of gaining advantages for themselves and of trying to drive the (Company) out of Fiji.' Of one leader, the Commission said that his conduct was 'obviously against the interests of the growers'. The sugar workers' union, the Commission thought, 'has been run on lines of extreme hostility to the (Company), and to increase the popularity of its president', who is one of the Indian members of the Legislative Council.

The Commission estimated 'that the growers have lost (through the dispute) between £850,000 and £900,000 and the millers nearly £600,000. The government have lost large sums in taxation, and mill and farm workers in wages. . . . We cannot see that the quarrels have gained anybody anything.' Perhaps more important than the financial losses is the damage done in Fiji to relations between the main races of the population.

Meanwhile a wage dispute with even more serious consequences had arisen between two oil distribution companies, Shell and Vacuum Oil, and their employees. According to the report of Mr. (now Sir George) Lowe, Chief Justice, who was appointed to hold a Commission of Enquiry into the disturbances which followed, 'many lower paid workers . . . found difficulty in making ends meet on the wages they received', and the companies had aggravated the issue by delaying negotiations with their employees, whose union had been trying for four months to bring about these negotiations without getting any further ahead.

The men went on strike on the 7th December 1959, and efforts made by the government to ensure the supply of petrol for essential services, for the bus companies, and for private motorists, irritated the strikers and their sympathizers. On the 9th December rioting began in Suva and the police had great difficulty in controlling the situation as the strikers by now were supported by a number of hooligans who joined in attacks on European-owned business houses and cars driven by Europeans. During the riot there were only three casualties, none of which was fatal.

Mr. Lowe in his report states that 'the police were stoned and abused time and time again but, in spite of injuries to some of them, they could not be subdued, small though their numbers were. This angered the criminal elements who, as an act of retaliation against the police in particular and lawful authority in general, led others in the destruction of shop premises in the vicinity. . . . The Police Force, which proved itself to be of very high calibre, carried out an extremely difficult duty with considerable fortitude and, indeed, the riot squads did so with bravery. . . . There can be no doubt that officers and men maintained the highest possible discipline and acted in a most exemplary manner. So did the Special Constabularly and the Fiji Military Forces (who were called in to aid the police) on their guard and patrol duties.' It is pleasing to be able to record these tributes to the police who are so often and so unjustly criticized by those who should know better.

Mr. Lowe further reported that 'there was a very pronounced anti-European feeling throughout the disturbances. . . . This manifested itself by anti-European abuse hurled at Europeans and by the stoning of European driven cars. The few other cars which were slightly damaged by stones would appear to have been accidentally struck. . . . Both Fijians and Indians were responsible for the abuse and the stone throwing. . . . The expressed anti-European feeling and actions, however, were confined to the criminal elements and their supporters.'

Of the sixty-four rioters arrested, thirty-two had previously been convicted, sixteen of them of serious offences. A police witness described some of the men who took part in the rioting as having distinctive haircuts and a special type of beard similar to that worn by Fidel Castro of Cuba! The value of European property damaged, destroyed or stolen during the rioting was £14,304 out of a total of £16,610.

On the 12th December the Fiji Industrial Workers' Congress agreed to mediate in the strike and the success of their mediation was made possible by the temporary incapacity of the principal strike leader, James Anthony. As Mr. Lowe amusingly puts it, 'the success of the negotiations, and so the end of the strike, owed a great debt to medical science. . . . By the time matters had settled down in the city, Mr. Anthony was feeling the strain and realized that human endurance has its limits. He then found it necessary to consult the Physician Specialist at the Colonial War Memorial Hospital who prescribed two tablets as a "sleeping draught".' While Anthony was sleeping a more moderate leader took charge of the union's affairs.

The riots came as a great shock to everyone in Fiji. As the Governor said, 'Never before has the colony's capital seen such wanton hooliganism, with gangs of roughs, some of them mere children, running around the city, looting and throwing stones.' The Fijian leaders realized with horror that some of their own people had been among the rioters. They blamed Indian agitators for misleading the guilty Fijians and publicly deplored that these should have joined in demonstrations against Europeans. A typical speech was that made at Suva, immediately after the rioting, by Semesa Sikivou, one of the Fijian members of the Legislative Council, who said:

'I am ashamed to see what we Fijians have done. We have a reputation in sport, in games and in war, but what has happened now has brought about a black mark which will stand for ever. I am sad to see that some Fijians have fought the very ones they have given their protection to. I never dreamt that I would live to see the day on which a Fijian would stone the white men, to whom the Fijians' forefathers ceded this country. Let me make it clear to you. Those people of Britain are your best friends. They are your best neighbours. They are the ones closest to us and the ones who stand to help us. I warn you: be very, very careful. Do not accept any advice that comes to you from foreign people.

'Never will we part from Britain, and when I say Britain I mean the British Empire. We are not here to stop the strikers. We support their claim. We agree they need more pay. We all realize that, but the things that have been done are not the methods to gain what they want.

'We Fijians are physically strong. Clever people will do all they can to use our physical strength to ride on us so that they become our drivers. Beware of them. Do not take their advice. We have our Fijian customs and our Fijian leaders and our own way of expressing our wishes to our chiefs. Use your Fijian leaders. Follow them. Be wise and unite. Do not accept advice from any foreigners around you who wish to use you as tools for their own benefit. Remember my appeal to you: love your real friends and neighbours and do not offend them.'

Another member of Legislative Council, Ravuama Vunivalu, agreed with what Semesa Sikivou had said, and added: 'Although violence was done by Fijian hooligans, it was not their real feelings. It was the effect of influence from outside. Be very careful of the people around you who are foreigners. Do not accept any advice except from your leaders.' *Ratu* Penaia Ganilau said that 'we are ashamed of what has happened, but we must realize that most hooligans are ignorant. . . . Like our other speakers, I warn you to beware of the foreigner.' *Ratu* George Cakobau struck a good note when he said: 'Whatever you do, remember the name of Fiji. The reputation of the Fijians is up to you.'

To the Europeans in Fiji, also, the fact that Fijians joined in the riot and demonstrated against them came as a painful surprise. From the beginning of the colonial administration, and even before, the two races had got on well together, and the most pleasing impression made on a visitor who was in Fiji only three months before the riot was the obvious friendliness between individual Fijians and Europeans. Everywhere that one went there were smiles and friendly greetings, and particularly striking was the fact that so many Europeans spoke Fijian. (Perhaps too few speak the Indian languages.) Notwithstanding the unhappy events of December 1959, I do not believe that the mutual regard of Europeans and Fijians has been seriously affected.

The Fijians have, in fact, been generally law-abiding and

have given little trouble to the colonial administration in political matters. However, Sir Harry Luke relates in his *South Seas Diary*, published in 1945, the story of a Fijian carpenter, Apolosi Nawai, who became a notorious agitator and was three times banished to Rotuma, in 1917, 1930 and 1940, on account of his mischievous activities. He indulged in semi-religious anti-white and anti-Indian propaganda, promising a new era of prosperity for the Fijians, with himself as their Messiah, and combined this with fraudulent commercial activities, extortion and debauchery. The reasons given for his banishment were curiously mixed:

(a) claiming to have supernatural power derived from ancestral gods and thereby falsely leading the natives to do his bidding;

(b) claiming for himself a high chiefly status and accepting ceremonial homage to which he was not by birth entitled, thereby causing discontent amongst the natives;

(c) claiming for himself powers vested only in the Government and acting in a manner detrimental to Government authority;

(d) preaching against the European and Indian communities and leading the Fijians to believe that the other races would be driven out of Fiji;

(e) spreading abroad false reports, thereby causing alarm and disorder amongst the native community;

(f) systematically robbing the natives and seducing their women.

Sir Harry Luke says that 'this man, by reason of his genius for subversive intrigue, his quasi-religious influence over his dupes, his utter lack of scruple, his abnormally developed and sustained sexual appetite and the ease with which he secures the victims of his lust, his real eloquence, his faith in himself, and his irrepressible persistence in all sorts of evil-doing, may well be described as the Rasputin of the Pacific.'

2. SUGAR

THE principal export crop of Fiji is sugar, which in 1960 was valued at £8,705,656 out of a total value for all domestic exports of £12,780,486—(owing to the disputes in the industry referred to in the previous chapter, there was a serious fall in the amount and value of the sugar exported in 1961). In addition, the export of molasses, which is a by-product of the sugar-cane, was valued in 1961 at £100,702. A certain amount of sugar is also sold for local use. Sugar-cane is therefore most important in the economy of Fiji.

Although the varieties of cane now planted have all been imported from other countries, certain kinds appear to have been indigenous and to have been grown by the Fijians from early times for use as food. In 1862 David Whippy, an American, set up a small mill on Wakaya island and produced sugar for local use. A large mill was built at Suva in 1872 and by the following year there were about twenty sugar plantations on the banks of the Rewa river. Other mills were built during the 'seventies and 'eighties as the growing of cane increased in various parts of Fiji, but most of these went out of business when the price of sugar fell towards the end of the 'eighties. The survivors were the Fiji Sugar Company, whose mill at Navua, on the south coast of Viti Levu, subsequently changed hands and was finally closed in 1922; the Penang Company which had a mill, built in 1878, near Vaileka on the north coast; and the Australian-owned Colonial Sugar Refining Company.

As already mentioned, this company bought land on the Rewa river in 1880 and began to clear it for sugar cultivation with Polynesian labour, changing over later to Indian indentured labour. A large mill was erected at Nausori to crush the cane produced in this area, and this mill continued in operation until the end of 1959. The company later installed other mills at Rarawai, near Mba in the north-west of Viti Levu, in 1886; and at Lambasa (Labasa), in Vanua Levu, in 1903. The company's mill at Lautoka, which is one of the largest in the southern hemisphere, started operations in 1906, and in 1926 the company bought the Penang mill referred to above. These four mills are still in operation, and it is significant that they are all in the dry zones of the main islands. The cultivation of cane on the south and east of Viti Levu, which are included in the wet zone, has been found by experience to be unremunerative.

Professor C. Y. Shephard, who reported on the sugar industry of Fiji in 1944, pointed out that, at that date, 'the mill at Nausori is exceptional in that it is the only one which has survived on the windward or wet side of Viti Levu, and its results are consistently inferior to those obtained at the other mills' which 'draw their cane supply from the leeward or dry zones'. As stated above the Nausori mill was closed down at the end of 1959 after ample warning to the cane growers in the area. This caused considerable resentment among the Indian farmers although it was obvious that production in this part of Viti Levu had ceased to be a commercial proposition; it has been pointed out that over the past ten years the yield of sugar in the Nausori-Rewa area had averaged about two tons per acre whereas over all other areas the average yield had been 2·77 tons per acre, a difference of 38 per cent.

It will be seen from the above that the Colonial Sugar Refining Company, generally referred to as the CSR, was since 1926 the only manufacturer of sugar in Fiji. The company acquired at different times, from the original European freeholders, 75,091 acres of land, of which about one-third are probably suitable for the production of sugar-cane. It was estimated that in 1961 more than 160,000 acres were devoted to this crop, so that a considerable amount of cane is grown on land which does not belong to the milling company. Most of this land is owned communally by Fijians and leased to Indian cultivators.

When it first began work in Fiji and until about 1909 the CSR itself produced practically all the cane crushed in its mills, with the aid of wage-paid labour, mostly Indians on indenture. (In this connection it should be pointed out that Indian labour was first imported before the CSR had any investment in the colony.) Between 1909 and 1920 the CSR endeavoured to divest itself of responsibility for the growing of cane by leasing its estates to independent farmers, most of whom were former senior employees of the company. These planters were dependent on labour and when the indenture system was abolished in 1916 it became increasingly difficult to obtain an adequate supply of workers. As a result most of the planters found it impossible to carry on and handed back the estates to the CSR.

The company then tried to establish Indian planters on smaller blocks of land but this scheme also failed for the same reason, the difficulty of obtaining labour. A settlement scheme proved unworkable and the CSR then made the bold decision to divide their estates into small holdings, each of about ten acres, on which the tenant (generally an Indian) could grow cane which the company would buy at agreed prices. This arrangement proved a success and has been in operation for about forty years. When the scheme was initiated it was considered that from ten to twelve acres of cane land could be cultivated by an Indian family without additional labour, and provide the family with an adequate livelihood. Today, with increased production from the land, due to the introduction of higher yielding varieties of cane, the financial return is better than was anticipated and it is significant that many tenant farmers employ wage labour. On the other hand, there are on the average more Indians living on each farm than the single family originally envisaged.

Before going any further it may be useful to explain, for the benefit of the uninitiated, how sugar-cane is grown and how the sugar is made from it. The land is cultivated by ploughs, scarifiers and harrows, drawn by tractors, horses or bullocks. Nearly all the Indian planters own draught animals and those who own tractors do the ploughing on a contract basis for their neighbours. The use of fertilizers has been encouraged by the CSR, which supplies them to the farmers at cost price. Coral sand is used instead of lime on the lands that need it. The 'seed' cane is then planted during the rainy season, between February and May, in drills or deep furrows, and nearly eighteen months later is ready for harvesting. A second growth from the same root, the first 'ratoon', now develops and can be harvested in another twelve months.

In other countries a second, third, and even further ratoons are grown, but this is not usual in Fiji where the roots are ploughed out after the first ratoon is harvested. The crop from the first ratoon yields less than that from the plant cane and the yield decreases with each later ratoon; the loss from this decrease has to be considered in relation to the cost of replanting seed cane. In British Honduras I was shown a field of sugarcane which was said to have been ratooned for over forty years!

In Fiji, after the first ratoon is harvested, a rotation crop of some type of legume is grown and ploughed in, and the land is then allowed to lie fallow for a period before seed cane is replanted. This rotation allows one-third or one-quarter of any farm to be under cane at all times.

Harvesting in Fiji generally takes place between June and December. The cutting of the cane is done by gangs of men composed of the farmers or their paid substitutes. Each farmer agrees to join in the cutting of cane on all the farms, including his own, within a certain area, or to provide a substitute, the amount of work involved for the farmer being roughly equivalent to what he would have to do if he cut the cane on his own farm single-handed. The gang, which may include Fijians as well as Indians, elects a sirdar, or foreman, who directs operations under the general supervision of the field officers of the milling company. This co-operative effort not only saves time— an important matter during the harvesting season—but allows of a mingling of races and religions which has its social value. Professor Shephard in his report says that 'the intricate but highly efficient system employed in the harvesting of cane is one of the most interesting features of the industry' in Fiji and 'both the company and the farmers are to be congratulated' on this arrangement. He points out that the orderly co-operative harvesting system enables the Indian family in Fiji to cultivate larger areas of cane than, for example, in Trinidad, where each farmer cuts and carts his own cane to the purchasing centres.

After the cane is cut it is loaded on trucks which are hauled into the fields on portable lines; the trucks are then hauled to the main railway line for conveyance to the mill. The CSR has constructed and maintained over 400 miles of permanent railway lines, with more than 150 miles of portable lines which can be laid quickly into the areas where cane is being cut. Some of the cane grown in remote areas is delivered to the mill by lorry. At the mill the cane is crushed between heavy rollers, the juice expressed being clarified and concentrated by evaporation of water under vacuum. The resulting sucrose is then crystallized and separated from the molasses (the principal by-product) by centrifugal force and the raw sugar remains to be dried and bagged, or stored in bulk, for shipment to refineries overseas.

Most of the cultivation of sugar-cane in Fiji is carried out by Indians. Of the 128,000 acres devoted to this crop in 1958 over 118,000 were worked by Indians and rather more than 8,000 acres by Fijians. The milling company itself works only a small area and that mainly for experimental purposes. On the other hand, the company supplies the capital required for the industry and is entirely responsible for the milling and the marketing of the sugar and molasses produced. The CSR, which has had extensive experience of cane-growing in Australia and has carried out much research there (it began work in Australia as long ago as 1855), has made this experience and research available to Fiji. Most of the varieties of cane grown in Fiji have been bred by the company either in Queensland or in Fiji, and all have been introduced into Fiji by it. New hybrid varieties recently introduced are increasing the yield of cane per acre by about 25 per cent. Research has also been carried out on means to combat the plant diseases which affect the cane, and a soil testing and advisory service to assist farmers on their soil and fertilizing problems has been established.

Professor Shephard reported in 1944 that 'the geographical distribution and varied nature of its enterprises have endowed the company with a measure of financial stability which has been of the utmost importance in the development and maintenance of the sugar industry in Fiji. The strength of its technical sections has enabled the company to attain a high standard of efficiency at its sugar mills in Fiji.' This efficiency is important to the cane farmers as well as to the company itself since the price paid for the cane depends partly on the amount of sugar extracted from the cane.

The company's experienced field officers give valuable assistance to the farmers. They advise cane growers on all matters of cane culture and make available to them the results of experiments. They also organize the cane harvest to ensure that it yields its maximum and generally act as the farmers' 'guide, philosopher and friend'.

Not only does the company provide fertilizers for the farmer at cost price, but the amount charged is not recovered until months later by deduction from the payments for cane. Cash advances are also made at a low rate of interest for normal living and farming needs.

The CSR has built a railway and bridges over rivers and gullies which are used by road as well as rail traffic. It reclaimed mangrove swamps and protected the reclaimed area by miles of sea-walls near Lambasa. No reasonable man can doubt that the CSR has made a large and valuable contribution to the economic development of Fiji, and also, by its policy of purchasing cane from small farmers, to its social development. The Commission of Enquiry of 1959 regarded this 'as one of the most interesting and successful large-scale development projects which has taken place in any colony and we consider the achievement of the Colonial Sugar Refining Company in establishing former indentured labourers as farmers in their own right to be most praiseworthy'. In view of all this it may be wondered why the company has been troubled in recent years by the organized discontent of the farmers.

One of the latest causes of this discontent was the inability of the company to purchase all the cane that the Indian farmers wished to sell. The amount of sugar which may be exported from Fiji is limited, as in the case of other sugar-producing countries, by International and Commonwealth Sugar Agreements, and the annual quota (184,000 tons in 1960) had already been reached. In 1959 when 2,447,251 tons of cane were crushed, yielding 283,005 tons of sugar, more sugar was produced than could be exported and there was a considerable stockpile at the end of the year. The company obviously cannot continue to buy more cane than is required to produce the export quota of sugar and the amount (about 15,000 tons a year) which can be consumed locally, but this plain economic fact is not understood by the unsophisticated farmer. He was, indeed, encouraged by others to believe that the Colonial Sugar Refining Company was responsible for a situation which it was powerless to control.

The reason for the restrictions of the Sugar Agreements should perhaps be explained. They are not arbitrary limitations on development imposed by governments but the result of long negotiations aimed at the regulation of the sugar industry for the benefit of all concerned. In past years sugar production had greatly exceeded the demand, with the result that the price had fallen to an extent that was disastrous to those territories (such as certain West Indian islands, Mauritius and Fiji) where sugar is practically the only crop. Such over-production could easily occur again, as sugar-cane and sugar-beet cultivation can rapidly be expanded, and this would drive out of business the weaker producers and throw thousands of workers out of employment. For this reason it was decided, by the International Sugar Agreement between all the sugar-producing countries of the world, to limit the amount of sugar which each may export annually. In this Agreement the British Commonwealth is treated as a unit and a separate Commonwealth Sugar Agreement divides the amount allotted to the whole Commonwealth between its various component countries. This is the export quota allowed to each, which must not be exceeded.

The export quota allowed to Fiji for 1961 was 170,000 tons, and the first recommendation of the Sugar Inquiry Commission of 1961 (referred to on page 179) was that this quota should be increased by 50,000 tons, 'so small in relation to the world, but very important to these small islands'. This would, the Commission says, 'in the long run make more people happy with a worth-while job and at a cheaper cost than probably in any other island country in the world'.

To assist the sugar producing colonies the United Kingdom Government undertakes to buy at a guaranteed price, which is higher than the normal market price, a proportion of the sugar exported from each colony, and this is known as the Negotiated Price Quota. Of the sugar which Fiji was allowed to export in 1961 under the Commonwealth Sugar Agreement, 126,000 tons were bought by the United Kingdom Government at the negotiated price of £45 2s. a ton, leaving 44,000 tons for sale in the open market. It is therefore a fact, not always appreciated in Fiji (and elsewhere), that the United Kingdom taxpayer for the last twelve years has generally been paying a higher price for colonial sugar than would have been necessary if he had bought in the world market, and he has been doing this to assist the primary producers in territories not so well developed as his own. The Sugar Inquiry Commission, in its report, wrote: 'We cannot stress too strongly how grateful all should be for the Commonwealth Sugar Agreement. It is the very life stream of the industry and of Fiji.'

It is clear from the above that the Colonial Sugar Refining Company cannot be blamed for the limitation imposed on sugar exports from Fiji. The only blame that could perhaps be attached to the company is that it failed to foresee the success of its own efforts to improve cane cultivation and the remarkable increase in production which resulted from the introduction into Fiji of new varieties of cane. In past years, when the crops were insufficient to produce enough sugar to fill the export quota, the company encouraged farmers to cultivate additional land and today, with the quota easily filled and each acre producing more cane than it did formerly, it is necessary to limit the cultivation. This means that the additional land latterly placed under cane cultivation and, indeed, some parts of the older cane farms, should be planted with other crops, a step which the Indian farmer is most reluctant to take.

It is an indication of the improved production resulting from the recently introduced varieties of cane that the export quota, seldom attained in the past, can now be easily reached without any of the cane formerly grown in the Rewa area and crushed at the Nausori mill which was closed at the end of 1959. As mentioned earlier, the closing of this mill was greatly resented by the Indians in spite of the fact that the Colonial Sugar Refining Company gave long notice of its intentions and has done a great deal to encourage farmers to grow other crops, including the erection of a modern rice mill at Nausori and a guarantee to purchase *padi* grown in the area at a reasonable price. An effort was made by a group of Indians to float a new company which could erect another sugar mill at Nausori and so permit cane cultivation to continue in this district, but there was not sufficient support for the scheme. In view of the climatic handicaps to cane cultivation on the windward side of Viti Levu, and the experience of the Colonial Sugar Refining Company in that area, it is almost certain that a new company could not have made its mill a financial proposition. The Sugar Inquiry Commission dismissed the scheme, calling it 'a political stunt with no commercial sense behind it'.

The Colonial Sugar Refining Company, Ltd., has recently formed a wholly owned subsidiary company, the South Pacific Sugar Mills, Ltd., with a nominal capital of £15,000,000, to take over all the parent company's sugar milling assets and activities in Fiji.

Mangrove tree

3. TRADE AND PRODUCTION

IN the preceding chapter the importance of sugar to the economy of Fiji has been pointed out. Both as to quantity and value it is the principal export and the cultivation and processing of the sugar-cane provides more employment than any other industry. There are, however, other valuable exports and there is no reason why these should not be increased in the future. The production and trade of the colony have increased steadily in the past. In 1884, ten years after the Cession, the total exports of Fiji were valued at £345,344, which included the value of the 8,729 tons of sugar shipped during the year. In 1960 domestic exports were valued at £12,780,486, but largely as the result of the disputes in the sugar industry these exports fell in value to £9,400,482 in 1961. The quantities and values of the main domestic exports during these two years were:

	1960		*1961*	
	Quantity	*Value* £	*Quantity*	*Value* £
Sugar	217,833 tons	8,705,656	132,006 tons	5,354,731
Coconut Products	28,852 tons	2,396,982	41,170 tons	2,323,757
Gold	71,676 ozs.	1,002,655	95,349 ozs.	1,082,883
Bananas	13½ m. lbs.	206,518	15 m. lbs.	215,795
Molasses	54,517 tons	61,336	57,414 tons	100,702
Manganese	1,788 tons	24,932	2,265 tons	14,363

The total exports, domestic and re-exports, were valued in 1961 at £11,826,127, as against imports valued at £15,483,785, the adverse trade balance being only partly covered by receipts from the tourist industry.

It will be seen that after sugar the products of the coconut palm are the second most important export crop. These products include a certain amount of coconut meal and a little copra, but the principal coconut product exported is now coconut oil, expressed from copra in two mills at Suva. Copra is the dried 'meat' of the coconut, and is generally prepared at or near

194

the place where the palm is grown. The nuts that fall from the trees are split open and the meat extracted; this meat is then dried in the sun or in hot air or smoke driers. The copra, after preparation, is taken to the mills at Suva, where payment is made for it at a price which varies according to the quality.

The quality of the copra depends a great deal on its preparation. Inefficient drying of the green copra causes deterioration and damage and results in a lower price. A very much larger percentage of high grade copra is produced on plantations under the supervision of European owners or managers than is produced from Fijian-owned groves. In 1958, 65 per cent of plantation copra was of good quality as against 36 per cent of the Fijian-produced copra.

It is not only in quality that the Fijian plantations fail. The average production of copra from Fijian groves is estimated at four hundredweight per acre as against five hundredweight per acre from plantations, and eight to ten hundredweight per acre from the few well-run estates. These last show, to European and Part-European planters as well as to Fijians, what can be done by proper cultivation and care.

Of the 168,000 acres planted with coconuts, 84,000 acres are owned by Fijians, 76,000 by Europeans and Part-Europeans, and 3,000 by Chinese. Long before copra or coconut oil was exported from Fiji, the coconut palm was of value to the Fijians. Milk from the young nuts provided a pleasant drink; the flesh of the nut was an ingredient in many dishes; the dried flesh produced an oil used to anoint the body; the leaves were used for thatching, basket-making, and rough matting. From the husk of the nut was made a cord known as sinnet; the husks were first steeped in pools of water for about a fortnight, weighted with stones to keep them below the surface; the outer skin was then removed and the short innermost fibres thrown away, the remainder being beaten out with a short club till the fibres separated and became straight and fine; the fibres were then dried and plaited by the men as they sat around the fire in the evenings telling stories. The timber of the coconut tree was used for house-building and the trunks are often used as bridges across creeks and streams; these bridges, round and slippery, are easily crossed by the experienced Fijian, who is often barefooted, but are hazards to the unpractised European wearing shoes. The coconut palms, sometimes a hundred feet high, grow from sprouting nuts, either fallen from the parent trees and left to take root where they fell, or planted deliberately by man in groves or on estates. The trees begin to bear after about five years and may continue to produce nuts for as much as a hundred years, although the yield begins to decline after about fifty or sixty years even with careful cultivation.

In many cases the coconut groves owned by Fijians or Part-Europeans receive little care. There is a story in Fiji that the coconut trees say to those who plant them: 'If you will look after us for the first four years of our lives we will look after you and your family for four generations', and this is roughly what happens in many cases. For the first four years the young coconut shoots must be protected from animals and weeds but after this period care is not essential, although the production of nuts is much greater if the land below the trees is kept clear of weeds and overcrowded groves are judiciously thinned. Too often, however, the land is covered with dense undergrowth and, apart from the loss of production, many of the nuts that fall cannot be found in the tangle of weeds that germinate there.

Over much of Fiji the coconut groves and plantations have an uncared-for appearance. In many cases, also, the palms are old, probably more than 65 per cent of them having been planted at least half a century ago. On one estate on Taveuni I saw some very tall palms which I was told, by the European owner, were more than a hundred years old. It is, I think, essential that a coconut replanting scheme should be started at once, and the Commission of Enquiry of 1959 recommended that financial assistance should be given to those wishing to replant. Unless replanting is undertaken on a large scale the colony's second largest export crop (the most important crop produced by the indigenous Fijians) will rapidly decline. The Coconut Rhinoceros Beetle, which has done so much damage to the palms in other island groups of the Pacific, is unfortunately established in Viti Levu, but in consequence of precautions taken has not spread to other islands of the colony.

The third most important crop grown for export is the banana, grown exclusively by Fijians and shipped mainly to New Zealand, where there is a limited market. The bananas grown in Fiji are of excellent quality and flavour (I have never tasted better) and it is a great pity that the export cannot be increased. There is no demand for Fiji bananas in Australia owing to local production, and preference is naturally given by New Zealand to bananas shipped from territories which are, or were, under New Zealand administration, such as Western Samoa. It is possible that the export trade to Japan may be developed.

Bananas are produced in Fiji very largely under a system of 'shifting cultivation', farms being abandoned after three or four years as the soil becomes exhausted, while the farmers move to another site on the communally-owned lands. The best and most accessible land was naturally used first and each successive shift inevitably takes the banana farms to less fertile land and further from Suva, where the crop is carried for export.

From the upper reaches of the Rewa river, where quantities of bananas are grown, much of the fruit is taken to market on rafts. These are constructed of bamboo poles lashed together, with a rough shelter for the crew, and the rafts drift downstream with the current, skilfully steered through rapids and past rocks, until they reach their destination near the coast. Here the bananas are unloaded and taken to Suva for disposal, the rafts being abandoned, while the crews return overland to their villages.

A strict system of inspection by the Agricultural Department ensures the quality of the bananas exported and protects the long-term interest of the industry. This inspection was not at first popular with the growers, but they are beginning to appreciate its value and the proportion of rejected bananas is steadily falling. The production of bananas could probably be increased by the use of fertilizers and by better attention to weeding (which would reduce the need for shifting cultivation). Leaf-spot disease, which affects bananas in various parts of the world, is often referred to as Singatoka Disease because it was first identified in the Singatoka area of Viti Levu.

In addition to those exported, a large number of bananas are consumed locally and bananas are a common sight on stalls in roadside villages.

As regards mineral exports, the most important is gold. The only mine operating is that owned by the Emperor Gold Mining Company, on the Vatukoula goldfields in the north of Viti Levu. This mine is most picturesquely situated in hilly country.

Here live, in a well-laid-out township, some sixteen hundred labourers with their dependants, in all about five thousand persons. Housing, schools and hospital services are provided by the company, and here, at a delightful dinner party given by the Australian manager and his wife, I met the Fijian Assistant Medical Officer who was responsible for the medical care of the mine employees. It was obvious that he was held in high regard by the Europeans present, and I was impressed by the interest he took in his work and his general approach to the problems of the colony. This was one of the most interesting parties I attended in Fiji.

Unfortunately, owing to the rising costs of production and heavy expenses incurred in the exploration and development of the goldfield, the company has found it difficult to carry on, and it became necessary for the Government to subsidize its operations in order to avoid the serious unemployment which would have followed the closing of the mine.

Gold was first reported in Viti Levu in 1868, but the first find of any importance was in Vanua Levu. Here a plant was installed, near Savusavu, in 1931 but was closed in 1943. In 1932 important finds were made near Tavua, in Viti Levu, and numbers of companies were formed as a result of the boom that followed. By 1936, however, the boom had collapsed and most of the smaller companies went out of business. The larger companies were later compelled to close down and the Emperor Gold Mining Company is now the only survivor. During 1960, however, another company has shown interest in a gold deposit at Waimanu, near Suva, which was first discovered more than sixty years ago. It is possible that this may lead to a development of the industry.

The other mineral export of value is manganese, which is quarried by small local companies in the mountains. The roads by which the ore is transported to Lautoka for shipment are steep and rough, and the lorries used for this work must have a short life. My own visit by Land-Rover to one of the manganese quarries in Viti Levu left painful reminders.

There is no doubt that further prospecting for gold and base metals would be well worth while, and the Chief Geologist of the colony considers that the possibilities should attract the attention of mining companies. New discoveries have recently been made of copper, zinc and other metals in the south-east of Viti Levu.

The exports of less importance are hides (valued in 1961 at £16,740) and Trochus shell (£18,530 in 1961), which yields the mother-of-pearl of trade. Bakery products, chiefly biscuits (valued in 1961 at £69,732), wearing apparel (£95,345) and laundry soap, made in Suva factories, are also exported to neighbouring groups of islands. The principal re-exports are aviation spirit and various manufactured articles.

In 1961, 43·18 per cent of the total exports went to the United Kingdom, 12·93 per cent to Canada, 11·92 per cent to Australia and 9·76 per cent to New Zealand. Of the imports, 28·26 per cent came from the United Kingdom, 26·64 per cent from Australia, 7·70 per cent from New Zealand, and 5·40 per cent from Indonesia.

This chapter has dealt, so far, only with crops grown for export and with the external trade of the colony, but there are also many crops grown for local consumption and a few non-agricultural industries which provide work for the inhabitants. The Fijians produce, besides coconuts and bananas, a large quantity of food crops, which include *dalo*, *kumala* (or sweet potato), yams, and cassava, and do a certain amount of fishing within the reefs and in the rivers. The Indians, in addition to sugar-cane, grow rice and other vegetables. European and Part-European farmers, besides growing coconuts, are engaged in dairying. The Chinese are mainly employed in market gardening.

While the foodstuffs produced by some of the above-mentioned industries are considerable, and go some way towards satisfying demand, it is surprising how much is imported from abroad which could be provided by local effort. Rice, for example, is an important article of diet, especially among the Indians, and can easily be grown in Fiji, yet in 1961, 4,119 tons of rice, valued at £259,398, were imported into the colony. The limitation to the growing of sugar-cane, imposed by the need to keep within the export quota for sugar, may lead to a considerable increase in rice cultivation, and this will be encouraged by Government protection and by the offer of the Colonial Sugar Refining Company to buy *padi* for processing in the new rice mill at Nausori.

Many other foodstuffs now imported could be produced in Fiji. Meat and poultry, dairy produce, potatoes and various vegetables imported in 1958 cost nearly £1,000,000. In his *South Seas Diary*, published in 1945, Sir Harry Luke, who was himself a knowledgeable fisherman, wrote that 'it is absurd that an island colony like Fiji should spend over £20,000 a year on imported tinned fish when its own seas teem with good, edible fresh fish'. In 1961 the value of imported fish, mostly tinned, was £242,158, which makes the situation look even more absurd. The shelves of shops, even in small villages close to the sea, are stacked with tins of fish.

Japanese vessels are regularly fishing for tuna near Fiji waters, sending their catch by a mother ship to Japan for processing and canning, and it is strange that Fiji has so far been unable to take any share of this lucrative business. An attempt is being made to promote a company which would set up, in co-operation with Japanese interests, a fish canning factory at Levuka. Apart from the profits and employment such a factory would provide, it would restore a measure of prosperity to the town of Levuka, which today has little left but a remembrance of its past history.

During the past twenty years, four fishery experts have visited Fiji and made recommendations designed to develop the fishery resources of the colony, the principal recommendation in each case being that a Fisheries Officer should be appointed. This recommendation has not been carried out.

The production of beef and dairy cattle could certainly be increased and improved in quality. At Yangara, in Viti Levu, the Colonial Sugar Refining Company for years maintained a beef ranch, which showed how much of the dry grassland country could be used to advantage, and there is no reason why the example set there should not be followed, perhaps by co-operatively run ranches. Apart from tuberculosis, Fiji is particularly fortunate in being free from serious cattle diseases. There is no rinderpest, pleuropneumonia or foot and mouth disease, or those diseases caused by blood parasites transmitted by ticks and flies, and it should, in these circumstances, be possible to build up a large and flourishing cattle industry.

Apart from those mentioned, there are other foodstuffs now imported which could be produced in the colony. The principal obstacle to this is the inflated ideas that farmers and fishermen have as to the prices they should receive for their produce. The good returns on the sale of sugar-cane, at today's prices, have set a standard which the farmers believe should apply to everything and led them to consider that no other crop is worth while. The price which they ask for groundnuts, for example, is double that paid in other countries, while 'English' potatoes can be imported at half the price demanded for an equal quantity of locally grown *dalo*. *Yaqona* powder, from which the popular drink is made, can be imported from other Pacific territories at a lower price than is asked for the Fijian product.

It is true that the consumer generally prefers the imported article, but this is due very largely to inefficiency in local production and irregularity of supply. For instance, in the case of poultry, some 20,000 dressed table-birds were imported in 1958 because hotels and other purchasers often found the local poultry inferior in quality. One large industrial organization, which has to ensure that its labourers can buy sufficient food in the market near their work, has had the greatest difficulty in getting regular supplies of *dalo* and other foodstuffs from Fijian contractors. These things should not be. Excellent meat and poultry are actually produced in some places in Fiji and could be produced elsewhere if care were taken, and a reputation for reliability can be regained by regular work and a proper regard for obligations.

Besides the desirable increase in the production of established crops and industries, and the improvement of quality, there is undoubtedly opportunity for new developments. In particular, tree crops such as cocoa, coffee and tea could be grown in some of the hilly areas for which other crops might not be suitable. A start has already been made with cocoa, and coffee and tea have been grown in the past. Pineapples used to be grown and exported tinned but the industry has been abandoned as it was found unremunerative.

One of the greatest opportunities for development in Fiji must surely lie in the utilization of the extensive forests which clothe the mountain sides in all the larger islands. It is estimated that more than half of the total land area of the colony is under forest, which includes both hard and soft woods, yet in the past the use and development of this valuable property have been largely neglected. It was not until 1940 that a small Forestry Department was instituted, and owing to the war nothing much could be done for five or six years. However, in recent years a considerable advance has been made, and it was interesting to one who has served in British Honduras to find that mahogany and pine trees, of Honduras origin, are growing well in the Forestry Department plantations. A sound forest policy has been promulgated, but the implementation of this policy still depends on the co-operation of the indigenous landowners.

In the meantime, the annual imports of timber, valued at £223,228 in 1961, are about equal to the local output of the sawmills operating in Fiji, and Oregon pine from North America is being used instead of woods which could easily be found locally. In this case, as in others, consumers often prefer the imported timber, which is seasoned and cut to standard sizes that can be depended on, to the local wood which is often unseasoned and badly sawn. These difficulties could be overcome, but a considerable change will be necessary in the attitude of landowners before the sawmilling industry can be improved and full value obtained for the valuable forest asset.

At present, timber-cutting licences are only valid for twelve months, with no guarantee of renewal, and no sawmill owner is willing to invest much money in machinery and development for so short a period. This is only one example of the handicaps imposed on industry by the system of land tenure and the attitude of landowners, referred to in the next chapter.

The most important factories in the colony are those processing sugar-cane and coconuts. Some of the products of one of the copra mills in Suva are used for making soap. There are also biscuit, cigarette, clothing and furniture factories and a brewery, and some of these export their products to neighbouring groups of islands. A cement factory, using local raw materials, has recently been opened near Suva; besides providing employment for about eighty persons, it will save expenditure on imported cement which in 1961 amounted to £222,161.

In addition to the government savings bank, four banks have branches and agencies in the colony: the Bank of New South Wales; the Bank of New Zealand; the Australia and New Zeaand Bank; and the Bank of Baroda.

Fiji has its own currency which is linked to sterling at the rate of £111 Fijian to £100 sterling. Fiji currency notes and coins are in circulation.

Fiji is well served by ships and aircraft. In 1961, 363 vessels, of a total of 1,202,536 tons, and 2,204 aircraft arrived in the colony from overseas. The principal port of entry is Suva, which has a fine harbour capable of accommodating almost any vessel afloat; the King's Wharf, at which large vessels berth, is now being rebuilt. A new government wharf at Lautoka, the second port of entry, has just been completed; previously the only wharf at this port was owned by the Colonial Sugar Refining Company. The third port of entry, Levuka, is seldom used by ships from overseas.

The international airport at Nandi, recently reconstructed at a cost of about £4,000,000, is used by aircraft operating the main services between North America and Australia and New Zealand. The airport is managed by the Government of New Zealand, and is a good example of Commonwealth co-operation, Australia, Canada, New Zealand and the United Kingdom, as well as Fiji, having contributed to its cost.

Reef heron

4. LAND PROBLEMS

ON page 107 reference has been made to the circumstances in which, both in the Deed of Cession and subsequently, through repeated pledges given by government representatives, the Fijian people were assured of the ownership of their ancestral lands, in so far as they had not already been alienated before Fiji became a British colony. It is true that when the Deed of Cession was signed nearly all the inhabitants of Fiji were Fijians, and that even later, when the first verbal pledges were given, very few Indians had yet arrived in the colony. No one at that time could have foreseen that within eighty years the Fijians would be outnumbered in their own islands by immigrants of another race, and no one can be blamed for giving assurances that under British rule the Fijians would not be dispossessed.

Several Indian witnesses maintained in the evidence presented to the Commission of Enquiry of 1959 that circumstances had changed so greatly since those assurances were given that they should no longer be held binding, and that there should be a fair distribution of the land among all the races in Fiji. Whether or not these assurances should have been given (and I, for one, think they were properly given) there is no gainsaying the fact that the British Government gave solemn written and verbal promises which cannot in honour be repudiated. In the words of the Commission of Enquiry, it is now 'quite impossible to ignore the Fijians' right to the ownership of all the land in the colony, other than Crown Land and land under freehold'. But, the Commission went on, 'we do not consider that this implies the right of the Fijians to use (or neglect) all this land without regard to the other sections of the population, and, indeed, to the long-term interests of the Fijian people themselves'.

So important does the land question appear to the Fijians that they are often unnecessarily anxious on the subject, and easily alarmed by rumours that their land may be taken from them. One such absurd rumour which I heard of while in Fiji was that the Indians, when they came to power as the result of the Commission's report, intended to remove all the Fijians from Viti Levu to Vanua Levu, and to keep the former island for themselves. This was perhaps no more absurd than the representation made to the Commission by a number of Fijian witnesses that all the Indians should be deported from Fiji. It was, however, because of the stories that were circulating, that at the formal opening of the Commission of Enquiry in Suva it was necessary for me to say that 'my colleagues and I have learned with regret of a rumour that the Commission propose to disregard the assurances frequently made in the past to the Fijians regarding their land. The Commission has no such intention. We will make no recommendation which does not take into consideration these assurances. This does not mean that we may not find it necessary to recommend measures which would result in better use being made of the land in the interest of the colony as a whole.' Without in any way impugning the *ownership* of Fijian land, the Commission considered that the *use* of this land should be made available for rent to those able and willing to make use of it. It must be remembered that today the Fijians are not using their land fully, and that, apart from the indirect benefits which will flow from the economic development of the land, the Fijians will receive the rents accruing from the tenants.

The total land area of Fiji is estimated to be 4,541,274 acres, of which the Crown holds, for public purposes, some 294,000 acres which have been purchased, or have reverted to the Crown because they were unclaimed at the time of the Cession or because the owning families have died out. Some of the rents from these lands are paid to the Fijians and the rest goes to the general colonial revenue.

Europeans and Part-Europeans own as freehold some 330,515 acres (7·3 per cent of the total acreage), of which 75,091 acres belong to the sugar-milling company. Indians own 74,458 acres (1·6 per cent) and Chinese own 5,086 acres (0·1 per cent). The Fijians and Rotumans hold, under customary tenure, 3,787,000 acres, or 83·4 per cent of the total. The land tenure maps of the main islands show graphically how the land is held and it will be seen that most of the freehold is on the coast where the land is reasonably flat and generally very fertile. The interior, most of which is owned by the Fijians, is mountainous and large areas are completely useless for agricultural purposes. Nevertheless, a considerable amount of land remains which could be developed.

Although the Indian section of the population owns such a trifling portion of the land, they occupy and farm a much larger

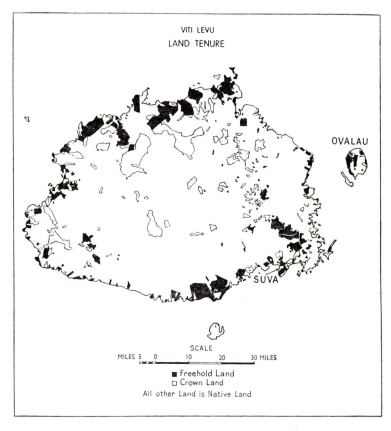

proportion of the total cultivable acreage, some 350,000 acres in all, including much of the best and most fertile land in the colony, where sugar-cane, the most remunerative crop, can be grown. Included in this figure are 230,000 acres leased to Indians by Fijians and 50,000 acres leased by the sugar-milling company.

The Fijians do, therefore, lease a considerable amount of land to the Indians and they would undoubtedly be prepared to lease more if the Indians were prepared to use some of the rough land of the interior, away from the good level land where sugar-cane is best grown. This the Indians are reluctant to do. They are accustomed to cane cultivation which gives them a good return, and, although there are, of course, exceptions, as a rule they have no wish to experiment with new crops on land which is not of the highest quality. When the Indians complain that

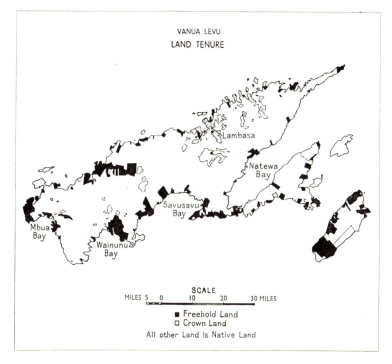

VANUA LEVU
LAND TENURE

Lambasa

Natewa
Bay

Savusavu
Bay

Mbua
Bay

Wainunu
Bay

SCALE
MILES 5   0   10   20   30 MILES

■ Freehold Land
□ Crown Land
All other Land is Native Land

they cannot obtain enough land, what they often mean is that they cannot get the best fertile land on which sugar-cane can be grown. At the same time, the Indians undoubtedly have grounds for complaint relating to land. The preliminaries to obtaining a lease are tedious and expensive and the leases are not for long enough periods. Moreover, the delays connected with the establishment of reserves (which will be referred to later) have led to uncertainty and frustration of which the Indians have been the principal victims.

Most of the freehold land owned by the sugar-milling

company is leased to Indian cane farmers. Other European and Part-European freeholders for the most part lease their land to Indians, or themselves grow coconuts or raise cattle on their land. There is, however, a certain amount of freehold land which is put to little or no use and this causes resentment among the landless Indians.

Lastly, and most important of all, there is the Fijian-owned land which is more than four-fifths of the total area of the colony, although, as pointed out above, much of this land is mountainous and unsuited for agriculture. Fijian land is held under customary tenure on a family basis. The direct descendants of the legendary founder of a family form a *yavusa*, which includes a number of *mataqali*, descended from the senior male relatives of the ancestor. The *mataqali* is a recognized land-owning unit and some *mataqali* hold large areas while others hold very little. There are also considerable differences in the quality of the land owned by the various *mataqali*, some owning rich cane land for which high rents are paid while others hold land in the mountainous interior which is of considerably less value. Professor Spate estimated the annual individual share in a cane area at £4·5 and in a poor area at £0·04.

Every member of a *mataqali* (and every Fijian is a member of one) is entitled to a share in any rents received for leased land belonging to that *mataqali* and to an adequate area of the *mataqali* land which he can cultivate himself for his own benefit. He is, however, in addition to other communal obligations, liable to be called on to work on the communal lands, planting and reaping crops in accordance with the directions of his chief, and sharing in the proceeds.

The established policy of protecting the Fijians in the possession of their lands was further strengthened in 1940 by the establishment of a Native Land Trust Board and the decision 'to set aside and proclaim as a native reserve' some of the land belonging to the Fijian people. The Board, of which the Governor is President, includes three *ex-officio* members (usually Europeans) and seven other members, of whom five are selected from a panel presented by the Fijian Council of Chiefs. The principal functions of the Board are to issue leases of Fijian lands, to collect the rents, and to distribute the amounts collected after deducting its own charge of 25 per cent.

'The *yaqona* ritual, which is almost sacramental, is still faithfully observed. The dried root is cut into small pieces and pounded or grated into a powder. . . . Those taking part in the ceremony wear the traditional skirts of grass or leaves, with the upper part of their bodies bare'

Above left: Fijian fire-walking. 'The performers, dressed largely in leaves but with bare feet and legs, enter the pit and walk in a circle, in single file on the hot stones.' *Below, left:* Indian fire-walking

Above and below: 'The best of the men's *meke* are the wild war dances with clubs or spears, while the women's *meke* are quieter and more graceful'

The feast when *Ratu* George Cakobau (inset) was installed as *Vunivalu* at Mbau, the first such ceremony to be held since 1853

Above: 'Rugger was introduced after the first world war and quickly became popular with the Fijians to whose temperament and physique it appears particularly well suited.' *Below:* 'At cricket also the physique of the Fijians stands them in good stead, particularly as hitters'

Above: The Fijians have always been good canoeists and last century were known as the best canoe builders in the Pacific. Model canoes and two of the actual oars from those days are in Suva museum. *Below:* Local steamer off Taveuni

Two views of the international airport at Nandi

From the balance, 5 per cent goes to the chief who is the head of the *vanua*, or confederation of *yavusa*, 10 per cent to the chief of the *yavusa*, and yet another 15 per cent to the head of the *mataqali*. This leaves no more than 52½ per cent of the rents collected for distribution among the other members of the *mataqali*, and if there are many of them the individual share is small. Professor Spate has pointed out that the head of the *vanua*, who may receive as his share from £200 to £300 a year as an unearned income, has his normal needs met within the village and his house built as part of the personal service due to him as chief. The Commission of Enquiry recommended that no share of the rent due to a *mataqali* should be paid to the heads of the *vanua* or *yavusa*, leaving a larger amount for the members of the *mataqali*. Perhaps not unnaturally, this recommendation was found unacceptable to the Provincial Councils and the Council of Chiefs, and the Fijian Government has decided that it should not be proceeded with, unless the landowners themselves wish it!

In the past the usual length of a lease of Fijian land was thirty years, but it is hoped that this will be extended to up to sixty years, or ninety-nine years where tree crops are to be planted. This will undoubtedly help development, as will proposed changes in the rules regarding the survey of land to be leased. Anything that would tend to reduce vexatious delays in the finalizing of leases would encourage agricultural enterprise and mitigate the grievances of would-be tenants.

The greatest cause of frustration and grievance has been the inordinate delays in the implementation of the policy on reserves. This policy, of setting aside and proclaiming as a 'native reserve' some of the land belonging to the Fijian people, is, as pointed out above, in accord with the general policy of protecting the Fijians from outside danger—and from themselves. They were not to be allowed to sell their land, as so many did before the Cession and again for a few years after 1905, nor were they to be allowed to lease land which might be required in the future for the use of members of their own race. There was, however, a second purpose in this policy, which was clearly stated, and accepted, when the law which provided for the establishment of reserves was promulgated and discussed in the legislature in 1940. This was to make available for leasing to persons of any race those native lands outside the reserves, a purpose which was entirely reasonable in view of the racial composition of the population. Two years earlier, in 1938, the Governor, Sir Arthur Richards (now Lord Milverton), an administrator of considerable experience, had expressed the view that the work of demarcating and proclaiming the reserves would be completed in about two years, and, if this had in fact been achieved, the scheme might have proved successful. As it is, after more than twenty years, the work was less than half completed.

In those areas where the position has not been finalized, renewals of leases as they fall due are being refused and former holders are only allowed to remain at will on yearly tenancies. In some cases Indians who had previously held leases have been kept in suspense, as tenants at will, for periods of several years, uncertain of their future occupation of the lands they had previously farmed. In these circumstances, as might be expected, the tenant does nothing to improve the land and generally exploits it mercilessly. In other cases, or when land has been definitely 'reserved', the former tenant is forced to leave and, as the Fijians sometimes do not use the land, it quickly reverts to bush. There can be no doubt that the spectacle of Fijian land, which was previously cultivated, lying waste and neglected, must be galling to would-be Indian farmers and leads to a cry of 'dog in the manger'.

It is to be hoped that the work on the demarcation and proclamation of reserves will quickly be completed if the policy is to be maintained. It is extremely doubtful whether this policy, in present circumstances, is a good one, but owing to Fijian sensitivity on the land question it would be unwise to attempt to vary it at present, or until the Fijians themselves realize its disadvantages. One of these disadvantages lies in the virtual sterilization of valuable and much needed land which could otherwise be developed in the general interests of the colony, and the loss to the Fijians of the rent that would be paid to them if it were leased. This latter point has not escaped the notice of some Fijians who are secretly and illegally allowing Indians to use land in reserves and receiving direct payment for this concession. (Thereby avoiding the loss of percentages which in other cases go to the Native Land Trust Board and the chiefs!) Another disadvantage lies in the setting up of two classes of

Fijian land, reserved and non-reserved, which may lead to a distinction in the public mind in the future and weaken recognition of the Fijian claim to the non-reserved land.

The anxiety of the Fijians regarding their land is reflected in the policy of the Native Land Trust Board, on which there is a majority of Fijian members. It is doubtful whether the Board's excessive caution is in the best interests of those it is supposed to protect; it is certainly not in the best interests of the colony. The rents demanded, for example, are not always related to the comparative value of the land. The Agricultural Department, for instance, is willing and able to regenerate some badly eroded land, which is now useless, by controlled pasture work and management, but is not allowed to take over the land temporarily for such a purpose without paying an 'economic' rent. For the use of useless land, in order to improve it for the benefit of its owners, it is difficult to understand why anything but a peppercorn rent should be charged. Again, the Forestry Department could do much to preserve for future generations the valuable asset which now exists in the forests of the colony, were it not for the policy of the Board which demands from the department an economic rent for the forest areas to be improved, based on the capital value in addition to royalties on timber cut.

The explanation usually given by the Fijians for their economic backwardness is the lack of capital with which to develop their lands, as, owing to the communal holding of land, they are unable to offer it as security for loans. This is true enough, if it is also remembered that the reputation of the Fijians for financial irresponsibility makes borrowing without adequate security almost impossible for them. It would help if the *mataqali* could be empowered to offer their land as security with safeguards to prevent its permanent alienation. This could be arranged through the Native Land Trust Board which, if the borrowers failed to meet their obligations, could lease the land and pay the creditor from the proceeds until the debt was paid off, when the land would be restored to the *mataqali*. Whether this or some alternative scheme enabling the Fijians to pledge their lands as security for loans can be arranged remains to be seen. Apart from the risk involved to the creditor, it would be harmful to the future economic and educational development of the Fijians themselves if they were allowed to borrow without full security, whether from private sources (which is unlikely) or from government or Fijian Administration funds.

It has been mentioned above that a certain amount of freehold land, as well as considerable areas of Fijian land, are put to little or no use. That great Fijian leader, Sir Lala Sukuna, foresaw the danger of this. As long ago as 1936, in a speech to the Council of Chiefs, he said:

> 'It is thoroughly understood that the control of our lands is in our hands, but the owner of property has an important duty to perform. . . . It is the bounden duty of landowners to utilize what they possess for the benefit of all. An idle landowner neglects his duty to his State. Should his holding be more than he can utilize, he should lease the surplus to those that can make use of it. . . . This is why I insist that as leaders of the Fijian people it is our duty to use our influence, our power, to open up waste *Mataqali* lands for agricultural purposes, whether they be taken up by Europeans, Indians or Fijians.'

So far as freehold land is concerned, the problem could be met by a penal land tax on unused, or inadequately used, land, and in a country where good land is at a premium such a tax would not be unreasonable. As regards the unused Fijian land the problem is more difficult, as much of the area involved is not suitable for any kind of cultivation and other parts are suitable only for pasture. Moreover, the failure to pay tax, which in the case of freeholds would result in the sale of the land, should not in the case of Fijian land be allowed to lead to the permanent loss of the land by the *mataqali* concerned, as this would be contrary to the approved policy of preserving the land for future generations of the Fijian people. Here again, however, it could pass for a period to the Native Land Trust Board which could hold it in trust for the owning *mataqali* until the tax had been paid off by rents collected.

It has been shown that such of the communally owned land of the Fijians as is not leased is mainly worked, if it is worked at all, by the common effort of the members of the *mataqali*, and that the individual Fijian is required by regulation, which has the force of law, to do his share in the planting and upkeep of food crops. It is, however, possible for a Fijian to commute his services by an annual payment and a number do this in order to become independent farmers or to take employment in the towns. They have to obtain permission from their *Roko* and the *Tikina* committee to take such an independent line and this permission is not always given and is liable to be withdrawn. It is clear that the best workers, who are the most likely to seek independent status, are the ones who can least be spared from the village work force, and for this reason there is unwillingness to let them go. On the other hand, the applicant for exemption may merely be trying to evade his communal duties and to lead an idle life, with little intention of farming seriously on his own account; in any case he still retains his right to a share in the communally owned land and to a house site in his village, while he escapes communal labour in return for a small commutation payment. It is true also that one whose application has been refused may appeal against the decision, but, as Professor Spate has said, 'it would be a very tough man, very sure of his ground', who would appeal, 'in view of the possibilities of harassment'.

The Government of Fiji has now decided that the independent farmer (known in Fiji as a *galala*) should be actively encouraged instead of, as in the past, merely tolerated. This is undoubtedly in accord with the wishes of the majority of the Fijian people and will almost certainly lead to a better use of the land. As Professor Spate has said, 'the natural direction of growth is towards individualism . . . and I feel assured that it is increasingly the direction desired by the people. . . . One cannot be sure of success with a policy of individualism; but I am as nearly certain as one can be in human affairs that one can be sure of failure on the opposite policy of communalism. Between a risk and a certainty of failure, there can be only one rational choice.' As long ago as 1880 Sir Arthur Gordon anticipated the existence of independent farmers, and provided by law for the continuance of the communal system only 'until the native race be ripe for a division of such community rights among individuals'.

Apart altogether from the better use of the land which should result from individual effort and ambition, it is surely wrong that the Fijian should not be free to live and work where he pleases for his own benefit and the benefit of his immediate family.

An important move to improve the economy of Fiji has been

the creation in 1961 of a Land Development Authority. The Authority will have the task of establishing resettlement schemes for the development of vacant land and the rehabilitation of settled agricultural areas whose present economy is stagnant, and will be able to assist primary producers through loans. On the results of this new scheme a great deal will depend.

Hibiscus

5. SOCIAL SERVICES

THE most striking social achievement in Fiji is in the medical and health services. Although fortunately free from most of the dangerous diseases which afflict tropical countries, such as malaria and yellow-fever, Fiji has nevertheless suffered much in the past from 'imported' diseases. The terrible epidemic of measles which in 1875 swept through the islands and killed about a quarter of the Fijian population was the worst, but at the end of the first world war the almost universal 'Spanish' influenza struck Fiji, killing over 5,000 Fijians and about half that number of Indians.

Today, although influenza is the most prevalent disease, the greatest menace to public health is tuberculosis, which is about four times more prevalent among Fijians than among Indians. There is a Tuberculosis Hospital in Suva with 362 beds, and in 1958 a massive campaign was launched against the disease by which it was planned to immunize with vaccine, by the end of 1961, the whole of the population under twenty years of age.

In 1911 a Leprosy Hospital was established on the island of Makongai to which patients from other territories, as well as from Fiji, are admitted for treatment. Numbers have been discharged as cured in recent years and, although it is estimated that there are still about three hundred cases of leprosy in the colony, Dr. Dill-Russell, lately Director of Medical Services, is optimistic for the future in view of the efficacy of modern forms of treatment. New drugs, he has pointed out, may be discovered which will be even more effective than those in present use, but even without this the need for the Makongai hospital will probably disappear as the disease is gradually eradicated.

Thanks to an efficient health service and well-run hospitals, the general health of the population is good. In the last ten years the crude death-rate has been falling and is now estimated to be less than 10·0 per thousand as compared with 9·0 per thousand in New Zealand and 11·7 per thousand in India. The birth-rate, roughly 40·0 per thousand, has not greatly changed during the same period, and it has been pointed out that the very success of the medical service in reducing the death-rate (but not the birth-rate) has been an important contributing factor to Fiji's present economic problems.

The Colonial War Memorial Hospital in Suva is a large and well-equipped institution, with 330 beds, to which patients from all parts of Fiji, and indeed from other islands in the Pacific, come for consultation and treatment. I can testify to the skill and kindness of the doctors and nurses of this hospital, and especially of Dr. C. H. Gurd and the Physiotherapist, Miss L. Owtram, who treated me after a slight accident I suffered while travelling with the Commission of Enquiry. Apart from my personal experience, I heard nothing but praise of Dr. Gurd while I was in Fiji, and I have seen Miss Owtram with some of her crippled patients, Indian and Fijian children; the obvious trust and affection with which they regard her told without words the story of what she does for them.

The Central Medical and Nursing School attached to the Suva hospital has done a great work, not only for Fiji but also, since 1926, for many other places in the Pacific. Started in 1884 as the Fiji Native Medical School, it was able to expand, partly through generous financial assistance from the Rockefeller Foundation. Students come there from other British and foreign territories, and in 1961 the territorial origin of the medical and dental scholars was as shown on the page opposite.

The course for an Assistant Medical Officer is one of five years and for an Assistant Dental Officer three years. These graduates of the Fiji Medical School are not fully qualified but there can be no doubt that most of the 107 Fijian and 24 Indian Assistant Medical Officers now in the government service in the colony are highly competent and have in fact a wide experience of work equivalent to that of the general practitioner in other countries. Many Europeans in Fiji have spoken to me of the admirable work done by these Assistant Medical Officers and those that I met greatly impressed me.

When in 1950 I visited the various Trust Territories in the Pacific with a United Nations mission, I met several of the men trained in Fiji and heard from Australian and American officials of the good work they did. Some of my colleagues on the mission were surprised by this example of British colonialism,

MEDICAL

AND

DENTAL

SCHOLARS

Fiji:	
Fijians	25
Indians	27
Gilbert and Ellice Islands	7
British Solomon Islands	6
Australian administered territories:	
Papua and New Guinea	15
Nauru	2
New Zealand administered territories:	
Cook Islands, Niue, and Tokelau	19
Anglo-French condominium of the	
New Hebrides	9
Kingdom of Tonga	7
United States administered territories:	
Caroline, Marshall and Mariana	
Islands	14
Western Samoa	13
American Samoa	5
Dutch New Guinea	6
British Honduras	1
	156

and it was with great pleasure, and some pride, that I went with them later, when we passed through Fiji, to see the Medical School.

In addition to the Suva Hospital there are three other main hospitals in the colony, at Lautoka, Lambasa and Levuka, and fourteen smaller rural hospitals. Altogether, including the Tuberculosis Hospital, but excluding the Leprosy and Mental Hospitals, there are 1,384 beds in the various hospitals. There are also 45 dispensaries and 4 mobile clinics. Women's committees in most of the Fijian villages keep a watch on the health of the young children, while Health Sisters travel through the districts, supervising the work of more than three hundred nurses, trained in the Central Nursing School, who are stationed in various parts of the colony.

Sir Alexander Wilson Rae, formerly Chief Medical Officer in the Colonial Office, has said that 'in no other territory is there such extensive medical coverage as in Fiji and I was deeply impressed with the work of Medical Officers, Assistant Medical Officers, Nursing Staff and ancillary staff. In tuberculosis work Fiji stands pre-eminent among colonial territories.'

With 62 fully qualified doctors and 131 Assistant Medical Officers in Fiji, there is one medical practitioner for every 2,111 persons in the population, a figure which compares very favourably with that in other countries. These figures should be kept in mind in view of the demand in Fiji for more extensive medical and hospital services.

There is also a demand, especially from the Indians, for free and compulsory education, with the suggestion that an education rate should be levied to pay for this. It is only on the island of Rotuma that education is compulsory, though the Fijian Administration regulations require that every Fijian child between the ages of six and fourteen should attend a school if one exists within a distance of three miles from its home. In the 1956 census it was shown that 92 per cent of Fijian children in this age-group have attended school at one time or another. The position regarding Indian children, and especially Indian girls, was not so good. Although the Fijians have a satisfactory proportion of literacy there are few with higher education, while the Indians, with a lower average of literacy, have a greater proportion of men who have qualified professionally.

There are 37 government schools and 514 schools which receive financial assistance from the government in the form of building grants and by the payment of three-quarters of the teachers' salaries. Of these schools all but 31 are primary schools. There are in addition some 50 schools which do not receive government assistance.

During the last few years government expenditure on education has risen rapidly, and in 1961 amounted to £1,346,469, or 18 per cent of the total annual expenditure. This was additional to expenditure on education met by the Fijian Administration, by the Christian missions, and by Indian and other communities, which, in the aggregate, amounted to a considerable sum.

The managing bodies of the existing non-government schools may be classified as follows:

	Schools
Fijian and Rotuman Committees	279
Indian Committees	175
Christian Missions	88
European Committees	6
Chinese Committees	2
Others	14
	564

Of the mission schools, thirty-nine are managed by Roman Catholics, twenty-six by Methodists, and six by Anglicans.

The fees charged in the government schools range from £3 to £7 16s. a year for a child in a primary school, and from £16 10s. to £21 18s. a year for one in a secondary school. Tuition fees in non-government schools are generally somewhat higher.

In the mission schools children of all races are admitted but few of the other schools are multi-racial, and the following table shows the racial distribution of existing schools in 1961:

	Government	Aided	Unaided	Total
Fijian	13	309	18	340
Indian	11	164	23	198
European	8	12	1	21
Chinese	—	2	—	2
Mixed	5	27	8	40
Total	37	514	50	601

There may be something to be said for racial segregation in the lower classes of primary schools on account of language difficulties, although these difficulties are sometimes exaggerated, but in general the existence of these 'racial' schools is unnecessary and harmful. Visitors are unfavourably impressed by the sight of two schools, within a short distance of one another, labelled respectively 'Indian School' and 'Fijian School'.

University entrance classes were held at 7 schools in 1961, and were attended by 25 Fijians, 24 Indians, 21 Europeans and 9 Chinese.

One of the most interesting visits I paid in Fiji was to the Adi Cakobau school near Suva. Here about 180 Fijian girls are educated under a remarkable headmistress, Miss F. L. Charlton, a New Zealander. Apart from academic studies, the girls receive a practical training which will be of use to them in later life and fit them for their destined position as leaders of Fijian womanhood in the future. It seemed to me that the morale of the school was particularly high. The singing of the girls (all

Fijians are musical) was excellent and they were taken later to Suva to sing to Princess Alexandra when she passed through Fiji on her way to Australia.

More recently, the school choir has been on a very successful tour of New Zealand cities; one of the newspapers there has said: 'These girls are completely charming, captivating and delightful in everything they do, be it a Christmas Carol or a Melanesian dance.'

At another Fijian school (for boys) I was surprised to find that the sons of chiefs were addressed by their companions, even by the prefects, as *Ratu*, the title given to all the male members of chiefly families.

At Ratu Kadavulevu school in Viti Levu, and at the Lambasa Secondary School, which was under an Indian headmaster, Fijian and Indian students were being effectively trained in agricultural and technical work, and excellent work is done at the Navuso Agricultural School, near Nausori, which is conducted by the Methodist Mission. Although this school would admit students of all races, no Indians have been there for the last thirty years, and the Drasa Training Farm, maintained by the Colonial Sugar Refining Company and specializing in instruction on sugar-cane cultivation, is for Fijian students only. No doubt the Indian youth who intends to be a cane farmer can learn a lot as an 'apprentice' on his father's farm, but these are further examples of the division, deliberate or incidental, between the two races.

In spite of the high percentage of literacy among the Fijians, few of them seem able to compete successfully against those of other races for overseas scholarships. Many of those who have received scholarships, whether through competition or otherwise, have failed to take advantage of their opportunities and neglected their studies. They are, in fact, too popular with their fellow students and others, as they are musical and good at games, while their good nature makes them welcome at social gatherings. It has been suggested that a number of scholarships should be reserved for Fijians and that a group should be sent to a university in the United Kingdom under the supervision of someone with experience of Fiji who, working with the university authorities, could keep a friendly eye on them.

In 1961 there were 126 overseas scholarship or bursary

holders: 53 Fijians and Rotumans, 52 Indians, 12 Chinese, and 9 Europeans or Part-Europeans. Of these, 60 were financed by the Fiji Government and 5 by the Fijian Provincial Councils, while others were financed by other overseas governments (including 16 by the Government of India) or by international organizations.

Most Indian peasant youths work with their fathers on their farms, but when Fijian youths leave school at the age of fourteen they are not required to take part in communal activities until the age of eighteen and most of them idle away these four years of 'freedom'. A few assist their parents, and one group of youths in Viti Levu has been organized into a work force which has built its own barracks and cultivated many acres of *yaqona* on the mountainside above their village. Such enterprise is, however, unusual, and many young men spend their days in complete idleness, the best form of training for 'teddy-boys'. It is a serious problem which demands early attention.

Considerable interest is taken in housing in Fiji. In the towns, Europeans and rich Indians live in large and well-built residences and even among those who are less wealthy the housing is not bad. Nevertheless, and especially in Suva, there is overcrowding, and serious if belated efforts are being made to get rid of the slums and provide better accommodation for persons with low incomes, a number of houses being built by the Housing Authority in a suburb of Suva.

An interesting experiment has recently been made in cheap house-building in concrete by what is known as the Ctesiphon method of construction, so called from the ancient town of Ctesiphon in Iraq, where it is believed that the first arched building was erected. The method is based on the principle that concrete is most efficiently used in the shape assumed by a chain which is suspended from each end, that corrugations increase the stiffness and strength of a thin plate, and that corrugated concrete shells can be cheaply produced on flexible moulds. The building is constructed by draping wooden forms with hessian and building up on the hessian successive layers of cement mortar. A cement shell of $1\frac{1}{4}$ inches in thickness is thus formed and when this has hardened the wooden forms are removed. By allowing the hessian to sag between the forms a 'corrugation' is formed and this adds greatly to the strength of the structure. One such house that I saw appeared thoroughly satisfactory and the cost was low for the result obtained.

The housing provided for their labourers by the Emperor Gold Mining Company is very good, and a recent Commission of Enquiry into the sugar industry has expressed the opinion that the accommodation provided by the Colonial Sugar Refining Company for their labourers was 'reasonably adequate but capable of improvement'. The houses of many of the Indian farmers on their own farms are certainly inferior to the housing provided by the company.

Among the Fijians in the villages the greatest importance is attached to housing and in the twelve months ending on the 31st July 1958, a sum of nearly £111,000 was spent on new houses and over £28,000 on repairs to existing houses. Most of these houses were in villages in the copra-producing areas, and the funds required were derived from a cess on copra sold. In addition, in other areas, houses have been built and repaired with funds derived from land rents. Some of the new houses have been built of permanent materials but many are still built in the traditional fashion, with wooden posts and rafters and thatched roofs and sides, which have to be frequently renewed. Fijian funds could no doubt be more profitably spent on development schemes to improve the economic condition of the people, but it is doubtful whether the Fijians would willingly abandon their ambitious plans for house-building. Apart from anything else, house-building in the villages is a communal undertaking which involves as much fun as work. There are frequent 'tea breaks' for the workers, during which much *yaqona* is consumed amid general conversation and laughter.

Co-operative societies have been established in various areas, with objects varying according to the racial composition of their membership. Of the 16 Indian societies, 3 are credit societies and the others are for the pooling of agricultural machinery and co-operative cattle-grazing. The 1 European, 10 Rotuman, and 8 multi-racial societies are all consumer societies. Of the 54 Fijian societies, most are producers' societies handling copra and other crops, and are engaged also in trading ventures such as village shops. There are in all 98 registered co-operative societies which are fairly efficient, and about a hundred others which have not been registered as they have not yet come up to

the standard required by the Registrar of Co-operative Societies. This officer has reported that 'the biggest single factor re-
tarding the growth of the societies is their inability to raise the
standard of membership by excluding over-conservative and
non-productive elements. Discrimination being socially unacceptable, most village societies become identical with the
villages or other social units they incorporate.'

Greater progress seems to have been made with credit unions.
Sir Ronald Garvey, who was Governor of Fiji from 1952 to
1958, had previously been Governor of British Honduras and
had been impressed by the credit unions operating in that
colony. In 1954 he was successful in persuading Father Marion
Ganey, a Jesuit priest who had experience of credit unions in
British Honduras, to come to Fiji and introduce them there.
There are now more than 250 unions with a total membership
of over 25,000. Their aim is the training of their members in
the use and control of money and the encouragement of regular
savings, a matter of particularly great importance in the case of
the Fijian people. The affairs of each union are controlled by a
Board of Directors from among the members, with general
supervision by the central office of the Fiji Credit Union
League. The success of each union depends upon the existence
of a common bond among the group of people it serves, and
village life provides that bond. The unions make loans to members in time of need or to enable them to finance approved pur-
chases. It is good to know that the officials of the unions have
no hesitation in taking legal proceedings against delinquent
debtors, with the result that there are comparatively few bad
debts. The educational value of this in Fiji can scarcely be over-
rated. Nearly all the members of the credit unions are Fijians,
but the Indian peasants are also in need of training in the use
of money and should be encouraged to save. It is to be hoped
that the credit union scheme will be developed among them.

6. PRESENT PROBLEMS

THE chief anxieties among the inhabitants of Fiji are caused by the alleged shortage of land and the too rapid growth of the population, and it was these anxieties which led, at the request of the Legislative Council, to the appointment of the Commission of Enquiry which visited the colony in 1959 and reported early the following year. It was believed that the land was already insufficient for the existing inhabitants and that the rising birth-rate would make a bad position worse and lead to disaster. There is no doubt that there is a shortage of high quality land as all the best areas are, as might be expected, already occupied, although not all of them are yet being used to full capacity. But there are still large areas which could be developed in one way or another if more enterprise were shown, sufficient in fact to absorb the increase of population for many years to come.

It has been suggested that birth control should be encouraged, and even enforced, as the only effective solution to the problem of over-population, and a majority of the members of the Commission of Enquiry did in fact recommend that contraceptives should be provided free of charge to married persons and that additional family planning clinics should be established to help and advise those parents desirous of limiting their families. For my part, and apart from the moral question, I do not believe that birth control would have much effect in dealing with the problem of land and population. What would be much more effective would be a greater degree of enterprise and hard work.

Although most of those who advocated birth control were Fijians, a surprising number of Indian witnesses agreed that it was desirable, and most of those who are attending the existing clinics are Indians. For example, at the Family Planning and Marriage Guidance Clinic at the Colonial War Memorial Hospital at Suva, attendances for the three years from June 1957 to May 1960 were 1,213 Indians, 132 Fijians, 10 Europeans, 9 Chinese, and 43 of various races.

One Fijian enthusiast wrote to the Commission at some length on the need for birth control and urged that it should be made compulsory—but, he added, such compulsion should apply only to the Indians and not to the Fijians. This is symptomatic of the general Fijian fear of Indian domination by sheer weight of numbers. The Indians today outnumber the Fijians by some 30,000 and represent nearly 50 per cent of the entire population. It is estimated that by 1971 they will be more than 53 per cent of the total.

The Fijian population is not increasing as fast as the Indian and in the past it has fluctuated greatly. At the time of the Cession it was thought that the Fijian population was between 150,000 and 200,000, but Miss Norma McArthur, who conducted the 1956 Census, thinks that in 1874 it was no more than 135,000. In any case, about a quarter of the population died during the measles epidemic of 1875, and in the 1881 Census the number of Fijians was reported to be 115,000. By 1905 the Fijian population had shrunk to 87,000 and for some years it remained stationary, beginning to increase again in 1917. Then came the world-wide epidemic of 'Spanish' influenza which caused great mortality in the colony and reduced the number of Fijians to 83,000. Since then their numbers have increased and the present Fijian population (excluding the Rotumans) is estimated at 172,455. However, the crude birth-rate of the Fijian section of the population in 1961 was only 36·89 per thousand as against the Indian rate of 44·75 per thousand.

A recent change in the marriage laws may have some effect in correcting this disparity in the birth-rate. From the 1st January 1961, the legal minimum marriage ages for all persons in the colony, irrespective of race, will be eighteen years for males and sixteen years for females. Previously there were different minimum ages for different races, and whereas Fijian girls were not allowed to marry until they were seventeen, it was legal for Indian girls to get married at fourteen years of age.

In the early days of Indian immigration, when the proportion of women among the immigrants was small, the natural increase was limited and not alarming, but as the balance of the sexes became more even the Indian birth-rate progressively and rapidly increased. The main reasons for the more rapid increase of the Indian population, as compared with the Fijian, are stated in the official annual report for 1960 to be:

(a) the fertility rate of the Indians is higher than that of the Fijians;

(b) Indian women bear children at an earlier age than Fijian women; and

(c) Indian women have apparently given birth to a high, and Fijian women to a low, proportion of female children.

Whatever the causes, the fact remains that from being a trifling fraction of the population the Indians have increased in numbers until they are nearly half, and shortly will be more than half, of the total. This is the principal cause of all the stresses and strains of life in Fiji today. While the Indian and Fijian peasants get on very well together, and in the Police Force constables of both races work side by side without friction, the leaders on both sides, and especially the Fijian chiefs, look anxiously to the future.

It is particularly in regard to their land that the Fijians are anxious, in spite of repeated assurances from the Government, the opinions expressed by the Commission of Enquiry, and the statements of Indian politicians. The Commission wrote in their report: 'We are convinced that the terms of the Deed of Cession, supplemented by the assurances given by Government spokesmen from time to time, make it quite impossible to ignore the Fijians' right to the ownership of all the land in the Colony, other than Crown Land and land under freehold'; as was to be expected, this was formally accepted by the Government.

Indian political leaders have been equally explicit. At a meeting of the Legislative Council in December 1960 Mr. A. I. N. Deoki declared that 'the Indian community recognize the fact that the Fijian people are the owners of the land and the Indian community does not wish in any way to disturb their ownership'. At the same meeting another Indian member, Mr. B. D. Lakshman, said that 'no responsible Indian had ever claimed that there was any doubt or any question about the ownership of the Fijian land'. All that Indian leaders have ever asked is that their people might be allowed to lease, and pay rent for, some of the land which is not now being used.

It does not seem possible to relieve Fijian anxieties regarding their land. They believe that if, through political changes in the future, the Indian majority gains control of the administration, all these promises and assurances will be ignored, and it is largely for this reason that they resist any material alteration in the existing constitution or the abolition of the Fijian Administration.

While Indian leaders deny any desire for Fijian land or for the setting aside of the Deed of Cession, which the Fijians regard as their Magna Carta, they repeatedly ask for equal treatment in other matters. They refer to the despatch sent in 1875 by the Marquess of Salisbury, then Secretary of State for India, to the Government of India, dealing with the terms on which indentured labourers should be employed in British colonies. Lord Salisbury considered that 'the colonial laws and their administration' should ensure that the Indians 'will be in all respects free men, with privileges no whit inferior to those of any other class of Her Majesty's subjects resident in the colonies'. Some Indian witnesses before the Commission stated, and others implied, that Indians in Fiji are discriminated against and unfairly treated, contrary to the policy laid down in Lord Salisbury's despatch. Some even suggested that the Government's recognition of Fijian land ownership was contrary to the spirit of this despatch. The present strong position of the Indians in the economy of Fiji seems a sufficient answer to complaints of unfair treatment.

It is only in the matter of political representation that the Indians might have cause for complaint, and then only if it is admitted that our idea of democracy in Britain, where every voter is equal, is necessarily the best thing for a territory like Fiji. The Indians have pressed in the past, and still press, for constitutional reform and elections to the legislature on a common roll. The Fijians prefer the existing equal distribution of seats on a racial basis, fearing that with a common roll the Indian majority would quickly get complete control. The Europeans, who today are over-represented in proportion to their numbers, but not in proportion to their contribution to and influence in the economy, would probably lose most, if not all, of their seats, if the common roll were introduced. In the circumstances, the continuation of the present constitution seems desirable, and almost inevitable.

The Commission of Enquiry of 1959 was not required by its terms of reference to comment on constitutional matters, but in the desire that the Fijians should be as well treated constitutionally as those of other races, and taught to stand on their own feet, they recommended that the Fijians should be allowed to elect directly, as the other races do, three out of their five representatives in the Legislative Council, all of whom were then appointed by the Governor on the recommendation of the Council of Chiefs. This very modest proposal led to a lengthy discussion in the Council of Chiefs and it was only by a majority of five that it was finally accepted, because it was felt that 'direct election was inevitable and it was better to make the change at this stage than have it possibly forced by circumstances at a later date'. This strange reluctance to allow the ordinary Fijians the same political privilege that is enjoyed by other races was typical in the past of the attitude of the Fijian leaders.

They adopted an even more cautious attitude towards a recommendation by the Commission that local government should be introduced in the towns and rural areas, and that the Fijian Administration should cease to operate in those areas as local government is established. Local government must be introduced sooner or later, if only to train the people, Indians and Fijians alike, in the working of representative government. The Indians would welcome such a development, but the Fijian leaders fear to be associated with the Indians in such a system and prefer to continue with the separate Fijian Administration by which their people are insulated from everybody who is alien and from everything that is new and strange.

The whole Fijian philosophy of life, as enshrined and enforced in the Fijian Administration and by its regulations, is inimical to the progress of the race and must handicap it in competition with others. The late Mr. G. K. Roth, at one time Secretary for Fijian Affairs and one of the most devoted friends of the Fijian people, refers in his book, *The Fijian Way of Life*, to the Fijian 'failure to accept routine as an element of any job of work, whether in employment away from the village or in such tasks as the feeding of an infant or the milking of a cow twice daily, high days and holidays not excepted'. He refers in this connection to the statement by Professor G. C. Henderson, made some twenty years earlier, that the salvation of the

Fijians 'must come eventually from the Fijians themselves and most of all by a recognition of the supreme importance of work . . . regular, responsible and efficient work. . . . Men and races who wish to survive must work hard enough to develop the powers that are latent in them and so enable them to compete successfully with others.' The Fijians will certainly not learn to compete successfully with anyone if they are screened from all contact with the cruel world.

Another writer, the American John Wesley Coulter, of the University of Hawaii, wrote in 1942 that 'the *malua*, or "wait awhile" attitude of Fijians towards many things which in western civilization must be done regularly is not conducive to the success of native people in individualistic enterprise. A Fijian said one morning in reply to a greeting, "This is a lovely day; why waste it working?" A Fijian would rather let his cow die of thirst than be bound by the necessity of giving her water at regular intervals.' The Fijian Administration which, in one form or another, has existed for many years has failed to teach the Fijian the necessity for regular work, and its policy seems to discourage initiative and enterprise.

Were the Fijians the only inhabitants of the colony this would not greatly matter, but the Indians are there also, working harder and more perseveringly than the Fijians, as they attach greater importance to the financial rewards of labour. The presence of this alien race in their islands presents the Fijians with a challenge which they appear reluctant to accept. It is merely dodging the issue to shelter behind the protection of the Fijian Administration and to take no steps to show themselves, by energy and initiative, to be the equals of any other people.

Their leaders are, however, against any mingling of the races, politically, socially, or in education. In his speech to the Legislative Council in June 1959, the Governor, Sir Kenneth Maddocks, while saying that he appreciated the language difficulty, pointed out that it was uneconomic and inconvenient for Fijian children to have to walk long distances to the nearest Fijian primary school when there was an Indian school near their homes, or for Indian children to travel equally far when a Fijian primary school was near at hand. He added that the fact that these children were attending different schools emphasized and consolidated differences and prevented the mutual understanding which would result from working and playing and growing up together.

This statement was welcomed by the Indians, but was referred to unfavourably by Fijian members, one of whom described the question under discussion as 'a rather unpleasant subject'. While he admitted that the Governor's suggestion was administratively attractive and Christian, he pointed out that 'the Fijian people are the minority race. If they should lose their culture, the sum total of things which make up their way of life, they will have nothing. The Fijian must keep his culture. The spiritual and social values that are inherent in it must be instilled in the children at their most formative stage of life. The Fijians want protection, not because other people are repugnant to them, but because they are weak. . . . While one part of me thinks it would be a good thing to support this Christian move, we must not be too hasty about mixing people up.' The Director of Education has recently said that as regards the mixing of children in the schools the position is much better than it was four or five years ago, and gave the following figures in support of his statement. Of 325 Fijian primary schools, 88 had non-Fijians on their rolls in 1960; of 166 Indian primary schools, 53 had non-Indians on their rolls; and of 20 European primary schools, 9 had non-Europeans on their rolls. He did not say, however, how many 'alien' children were in these racial schools.

The Fijian leaders are also against the admittance of Indians to the higher ranks of the Civil Service and have asked the Government to continue to fill the senior posts with men from the United Kingdom until such time as there are suitable Fijians available to fill them. There are, in fact, Fijians already serving in the Administrative Service and the Government is alive to the position. In a speech to the Legislative Council in November 1960, the Governor referred to the policy of appointing local residents to the Civil Service whenever possible. 'However,' he added, 'because of the small number of Fijians who have received higher education there is a danger that unless special measures are taken there will soon be an undesirable imbalance in the higher grades of the Civil Service as between the two major races in the colony. This imposes a responsibility on Government to do everything in its power to hasten the training of members of the Fijian community to enable them to take their rightful place in Government. To this end I propose that a number of overseas scholarships should be reserved for the Fijian people.'

It is in the suspicion and rivalry between the two major races of its population that the greatest danger lies for Fiji in the future, and the greatest cause for anxiety. Other problems, serious enough in themselves, are trivial in comparison, although anything which could improve conditions and lead to a more profitable use of the land would have its bearing on the main issue. It is important, therefore, that no opportunity for development should be neglected. The vast forestry potential of the colony should be exploited; existing crops should be improved and (except for sugar-cane which is limited by quota restrictions) increased; and new crops should be tried. A fisheries industry could be established and other industries developed. In this connection the recent stationing of a representative of the Colonial Development Corporation in Fiji and the setting up of the Fiji Development Company, a subsidiary of the Corporation, are to be welcomed. It should be possible to attract tourists to the islands in increasing numbers.

All these things would provide opportunities for the increasing population and improve the general standard of living, which is low in comparison with that of highly developed western countries but high as compared with that of the mass of the people in under-developed territories. Professor Spate, who knows Fiji well, has said that 'those Fijians and Indians who think they are sunk in abject poverty can be excused for thinking so when they look at Australia and New Zealand, but they are still on a much better standard than that of at least half of the world's people—the peasantry of Asia, Africa, South America, and many of the peasants of southern and eastern Europe.'

To allow of the developments suggested capital is required, and the United Kingdom Government has agreed to prime the pump by providing several millions for essential purposes. Private investment must also be attracted and in this connection it must be remembered that disorders and industrial disputes such as have recently occurred in the colony are not encouraging to potential investors.

When the Fijians ceded their islands to Britain in 1874, they sought peace and a stable administration in place of the constant wars and uncertainties of the Cakobau regime; these things, to a great measure, they have achieved. Of the Europeans who favoured cession some hoped that colonial administration would bring improved trade and greater prosperity to honest workers; the value of domestic exports in 1961 was £9,400,482 as against £345,344 in 1884, ten years after the Cession. Other Europeans who hoped that their legitimate titles to land bought from Fijian chiefs would be safeguarded were justified in their optimism. On the other hand, there was disappointment among those whose title was doubtful or who hoped that annexation would bring the solution of labour difficulties by putting the services of Fijians at their disposal. There were no Indians in Fiji in 1874 and those who came later as indentured labourers no doubt hoped to escape from the grinding poverty that was their lot in India; the fact that so few exercised the option to return home, and that so many, as shown on page 114, have prospered in Fiji, is sufficient proof that they have not been disappointed in their hopes.

There is no reason to despair of Fiji's future. It is inhabited by an industrious Indian population and a most attractive indigenous Fijian people. The latter are at the moment behind in the economic race, but they are quite capable of catching up and playing their part as men in a modern world. Professor Spate has referred to the 'curious blend of pride and self-pity' in the make-up of the Fijians. The pride is justified for they have much to be proud about; the self-pity is unnecessary.

Cakobau's war club, now the Mace in the Legislative Council

APPENDIX A

DEED OF CESSION

INSTRUMENT of CESSION of the Islands of Fiji by Thakombau, styled Tui Viti and Vuni Valu, and by the other high Chiefs of the said islands to Her Most Gracious Majesty Victoria, by the grace of God, of the United Kingdom of Great Britain and Ireland Queen, Defender of the Faith, &c &c &c:

WHEREAS divers of the subjects of Her Majesty the Queen of Great Britain and Ireland have from time to time settled in the Fijian group of islands and have acquired property or certain pecuniary interests therein; AND WHEREAS the Fijian Chief Thakombau styled Tui Viti and Vuni Valu and the other high native chiefs of the said islands are desirous of securing the promotion of civilization and Christianity and of increasing trade and industry within the said islands; AND WHEREAS it is obviously desirable, in the interests as well of the native as of the white population, that order and good government should be established therein; AND WHEREAS the said Tui Viti and other high chiefs have conjointly and severally requested Her Majesty the Queen of Great Britain and Ireland aforesaid to undertake the government of the said islands henceforth; AND WHEREAS in order to the establishment of British government within the said islands the said Tui Viti and other the several high chiefs thereof for themselves and their respective tribes have agreed to cede the possession of and the dominion and sovereignty over the whole of the said islands and over the inhabitants thereof and have requested Her said Majesty to accept such cession,—which cession the said Tui Viti and other high chiefs, relying upon the justice and generosity of Her said Majesty, have determined to tender unconditionally,— and which cession on the part of the said Tui Viti and other high chiefs is witnessed by their execution of these presents and by the formal surrender of the said territory to Her said Majesty; AND WHEREAS His Excellency Sir Hercules George Robert Robinson, Knight Commander of the most distinguished[1] order of Saint Michael and Saint George, Governor, Commander in Chief and Vice Admiral of the British Colony of New South Wales and its dependencies, and Governor of Norfolk Island, hath been authorized

[1] Interlineation referred to in the Interpreter's certificate, the word 'honourable' being altered to 'distinguished'.

233

and deputed by Her said Majesty to accept on Her behalf the said Cession:—

NOW THESE PRESENTS WITNESS,

1. THAT the possession of and full sovereignty and dominion over the whole of the group of islands in the South Pacific Ocean known as the Fijis (and lying between the parallels of latitude of fifteen degrees South and twenty two degrees South of the Equator and between the Meridians of longitude of one hundred and seventy seven degrees West and one hundred and seventy five degrees East of the meridian of Greenwich) and over the inhabitants thereof, together with the possession of and sovereignty over the waters adjacent thereto and of and over all ports harbours havens roadsteads rivers estuaries and other waters and all reefs and foreshores within or adjacent thereto, are hereby ceded to and accepted on behalf of Her said Majesty the Queen of Great Britain and Ireland her heirs and successors, to the intent that from this time forth the said islands and the waters reefs and other places as aforesaid lying within or adjacent thereto may be annexed to and be a possession and dependency of the British Crown.

2. THAT the form or constitution of government, the means of the maintenance thereof, and the laws[1] and regulations to be administered within the said islands shall be such as Her Majesty shall prescribe and determine.

3. THAT, pending the making by Her Majesty as aforesaid of some more permanent provision for the government of the said islands His Excellency Sir Hercules George Robert Robinson, in pursuance of the powers in him vested and with the consent and at the request of the said Tui Viti and other high Chiefs the ceding parties hereto, shall establish such temporary or provisional government as to him may seem meet.

4. THAT the absolute proprietorship of all lands not shown to be now alienated so as to have become bona fide the[2] property of Europeans or other foreigners or not now in the actual use or occupation of some Chief or tribe or not actually required for the probable future support and maintenance of some chief or tribe shall be and is hereby declared to be vested in Her said Majesty her heirs and successors.

5. THAT Her Majesty shall have power, whenever it shall be deemed necessary for public purposes, to take any lands upon pay-

---

[1] In the original the phrase 'and the laws' appears twice, the second being deleted.

[2] Interlineation referred to in the Interpreter's certificate, the word 'the' being transposed from a position before the words 'bona fide' to that shown above.

ment to the proprietor of a reasonable sum by way of compensation for the deprivation thereof.

6. THAT all now existing public buildings houses and offices, all enclosures and other pieces or parcels of land now set apart or being used for public purposes, and all stores fittings and other articles now being used in connection with such purposes are hereby assigned transferred and made over to Her said Majesty.

7. THAT on behalf of Her Majesty His Excellency Sir Hercules George Robert Robinson promises (1) that the rights and interests of the said Tui Viti and other high chiefs the ceding parties hereto shall be recognized so far as is and shall be consistent with British Sovereignty and Colonial form of government, (2) that all questions of financial liabilities and engagements shall be carefully scrutinized and dealt with upon principles of justice and sound public policy, (3) that all claims to title to land by whomsoever preferred and all claims to pensions or allowances whether on the part of the said Tui Viti and other high chiefs or of persons now holding office under them or any of them shall in due course be fully investigated and equitably adjusted.

IN WITNESS WHEREOF, the whole of the contents of this instrument of Cession having been, previously to the execution of the same, interpreted and explained to the ceding parties hereto by David Wilkinson, Esquire, the interpreter nominated by the said Tui Viti and the other high chiefs and accepted as such interpreter by the said Sir Hercules George Robert Robinson, the respective parties hereto have hereunto set their hands and seals.

DONE at LEVUKA this tenth day of October, in the year of Our Lord one thousand eight hundred and seventy four.

	CAKOBAU R. TUI VITI & VUNIVALU	(Seal)
	MAAFU	(Seal)
HERCULES	TUI CAKAU	(Seal)
ROBINSON	RATU EPELI	(Seal)
(Seal)	VAKAWALITABUA TUI BUA	(Seal)
	SAVENACA	(Seal)
	ESEKELE	(Seal)
	B. V. TUI DREKETI	(Seal)
	RITOVA	(Seal)
	KATO-NIVERE	(Seal)
	RATU KINI	(Seal)
	MATANITOBUA	(Seal)
	NACAGILEVU	(Seal)

I hereby certify that, prior to the execution of the above Instrument of Cession—which execution I do hereby attest—I fully and faithfully interpreted and explained to the ceding parties the whole of the contents of the said document, the interlineations appearing on line[1] 33 of page 1 and on line[2] 30 of page 2 having been first made, and that such contents were fully understood and assented to by the said ceding parties. Prior to the execution of the said instrument of Cession I wrote out an interpretation of the same in the Fijian language, which interpretation I read to the Tui Viti and other high chiefs the ceding parties, who one and all approved thereof. A copy of such interpretation is hereto annexed marked A. Dated this tenth day of October, A.D. 1874.

D. WILKINSON,
Chief Interpreter.
The interpreter named in the foregoing
instrument of Cession

[1] Line 32 of page 233 of this volume.
[2] Line 32 of page 234 of this volume.

APPENDIX B

SOME BOOKS OF FIJIAN INTEREST

(See note at end of Appendix)

CONSIDERING how little was known of Fiji until the beginning of the nineteenth century, there is a surprising number of books about the islands. All those quoted from or referred to in the text of this volume are mentioned below, as well as a selection of other books relating to Fiji. Also mentioned are certain official reports and documents of importance. For convenience they are placed in six groups.

I DISCOVERY

The first group of books are those relating to the discovery of the islands. The first European known to have sighted any part of Fiji was the Dutch navigator, Abel Tasman, in 1643. The most easily referred to account of his visit is contained in Professor G. C. Henderson's *The Discoverers of the Fiji Islands* (London, 1933). This volume also contains details of the discoveries mentioned below.

More than a hundred years after Tasman, in 1774, Captain James Cook, during his second voyage to the Pacific, touched at one of the islands, and in his third voyage, in 1777, met some Fijians at Tonga and heard about Fiji from the Tongans. The account of his voyages is given in *Voyage to the Pacific Ocean . . . performed under the direction of Captains Cook, Clerke and Gore, in His Majesty's Ships the 'Resolution' and 'Discovery', in the years 1776, 1777, 1778, 1779, 1780* (London, 1874).

Captain William Bligh, in 1788, during his famous boat voyage after the mutiny in the *Bounty*, sailed through the group, making a rough chart as he went. His own account is given in *Voyage to the South Sea . . . in His Majesty's Ship 'Bounty', commanded by Lieutenant Bligh* (London, 1792). Bligh revisited Fijian waters in 1792 and an account of this is in *Captain Bligh's Second Voyage to the South Sea*, by Mrs. C. S. Marriott (London, 1920).

Captain Edwards discovered Rotuma in 1791, and a tender from his ship, the *Pandora*, stayed at one of the Fiji islands for some weeks. There is no account of the tender's visit, but the discovery of Rotuma is referred to in *Voyage of H.M.S. 'Pandora', despatched to arrest the mutineers of the 'Bounty' in the South seas, 1790–91, being the narratives of Captain Edward Edwards, R.N., the Commander, and George Hamilton, the Surgeon, with introduction and notes by Basil Thomson* (London, 1915). The second part of this volume is a reprint of *A Voyage round the World in His Majesty's Frigate 'Pandora'*, by George Hamilton, Surgeon (London, 1793). Sir Basil Thomson was the author of books mentioned in Group IV.

Captain Barber was at the Yasawa islands in 1794, but no first-hand account of this visit is known. It is referred to at page xxii of *The Journal of William Lockerby*, published by the Hakluyt Society, London, in 1925, and at page lxx of the book next mentioned.

In 1796 the ship *Duff* got among the Fijian reefs and was only saved with difficulty. An account of this is given by her captain, James Wilson, in *A Missionary Voyage to the South Pacific Ocean in the years 1796, 1797, 1798, in the ship 'Duff', compiled from the Journals of the Officers and the Missionaries* (London, 1799).

The last of the discoverers was the Russian, Fabian von Bellingshausen, who called at some of the most southerly of the Fiji islands in 1820. This is described in the second volume of *The Voyage of Captain Bellingshausen to the Antarctic Seas, 1819–1821*, published by the Hakluyt Society (London, 1945).

II EARLY VISITS BY EUROPEANS

The second group of books contains those relating to the early visits of Europeans to Fiji, chiefly in connection with the sandalwood trade, at the beginning of the nineteenth century. Of these the most important is *The Journal of William Lockerby, 1808–09* (Hakluyt Society, London, 1925). In the same volume are *Samuel Patterson's Narrative of the Wreck of the 'Eliza' in 1808*; *A Journal of the Missionaries put ashore on an islet in the Fijian Group in 1809*; and *Captain Richard Siddon's Experiences in Fiji in 1809–1815*.

Peter Dillon's *Narrative of the Discovery of the fate of La Perouse* (London, 1829) gives, like the volume above, a graphic account of the dangers and difficulties of the sandalwood trade.

Another interesting book is *Cannibal Jack, The True Autobiography of a White Man in the South Seas, by William Diapea, printed from the manuscript in the possession of the Reverend James Hadfield, with a foreword by H. de Vere Stacpoole* (London, 1928).

III MISSIONARY LITERATURE

The third group might be called 'The Missionary Literature' as it is confined to the experiences of the early Methodist missionaries.

These books give much interesting information about the traditions and customs of the Fijian people and the first general account of the islands.

They include *Memoir of Mrs. Margaret Cargill, wife of the Reverend David Cargill, by her husband* (London, 1841); *Fiji and the Fijians*, by T. Williams (vol. 1) and J. Calvert (vol. 2), edited by S. Rowe (London, 1860); *Memoir of the Reverend William Cross*, by J. Hunt (London, 1846); *The King and People of Fiji, containing a Life of Thakonbau with notices of the Fijians, their Manners, Customs and Superstitions, previous to the great religious reformation in 1854*, by J. Waterhouse (London, 1866); and *Life of John Hunt*, by G. S. Rowe (London, 1868).

A critical study of these missionary books is contained in Professor G. C. Henderson's *Fiji and the Fijians, 1835–56* (Sydney, 1931).

A small but interesting book is *Joel Bulu: The Autobiography of a Native Minister in the South Seas, translated by a Missionary* (London, 1871).

From the Wesleyan Mission Press at Viwa, Fiji, there were published three books by the Reverend David Hazlewood, *A Compendious Grammar of the Feejeean Language, with examples of Native Idioms* (Vewa, Feejee, 1850); *A Feejeean and English Dictionary* (Vewa, Feejee, 1850); and *A Short English and Feejeean Dictionary* (Vewa, Feejee, 1852). A later edition of the last work was printed in London in 1872. In 1941 there was published in London *A New Fijian Dictionary (based on A Fijian and English Dictionary by David Hazlewood)* by A. C. Capell.

IV BOOKS AND REPORTS WRITTEN ABOUT THE TIME OF CESSION

The fourth group includes books written shortly before or shortly after the Cession of 1874, or by authors who were in Fiji at that period. Most of these contain interesting accounts of the Fijians before their culture had been greatly affected by contact with people of other races.

The most authoritative is that by Lord Stanmore, who as Sir Arthur Gordon was the first Governor of Fiji. The four volumes, printed at Edinburgh for private circulation between 1897 and 1912, contain copies of official despatches and private letters describing the colony and its inhabitants, and the events which followed the Cession. The work is entitled: *Records of Private and Public Life*. Lord Stanmore was also the author of *Letters and Notes written during the Disturbances in the Highlands, known as 'The Devil Country', of Viti Levu, Fiji, 1876*; two vols. (privately printed, Edinburgh, 1879).

Other authors and books in this group are:

BREWSTER, A. B. *The Hill Tribes of Fiji* (London, 1922) and *The King of the Cannibal Isles* (London, 1937). The author was in Fiji before the Cession and later became a civil servant there.

ERSKINE, J. E. *Journal of a Cruise among the Islands of the Pacific including the Feejees . . . in Her Majesty's Ship 'Havannah'* (London, 1853).

BRITTON, J. *Fiji in 1870* (Melbourne, 1870).

FORBES, L. *Two Years in Fiji* (London, 1875).

GORDON-CUMMING, C. F. *At Home in Fiji* (Edinburgh, 1881).

DE RICCI, J. H. *Our New Province in the South Seas* (London, 1875); the author was the first Attorney General of the colony.

SEEMAN, B. *A Mission to Fiji* (London, 1862); Dr. Seeman was a botanist of repute, who was associated with Colonel W. J. Smythe, the Commissioner appointed to report on the first offer of Cession in 1858.

SMYTHE, S. M. *Ten Months in Fiji* (London, 1864); the author was the wife of Colonel W. J. Smythe.

THOMSON, Sir BASIL. *Diversions of a Prime Minister* (London, 1894); *South Sea Yarns* (London, 1894); and *The Fijians, A Study in the Decay of Custom* (London, 1908). Sir Basil served for some years in Fiji.

WILKES, Commodore C. *Narrative of the United States Exploring Expedition* (Philadelphia, 1845); the third of the five volumes of this work refers to Fiji.

Although it was not published until 1946 (3rd edition, Government Press, Suva, 1957), R. A. Derrick's *A History of Fiji* contains an excellent and very readable account of the islands up to the Cession of 1874. The work is shown as Volume 1, but a second volume has not been published. Mr. Derrick was also the author of *The Fiji Islands: A Geographical Handbook* (revised edition, Government Press, Suva, 1957).

In addition to the above books, there are several official reports relating to the same period. These include:

Report on the Proposed Cession of Fiji to Great Britain, by Colonel W. J. Smythe, presented to both Houses of Parliament (1862).

Copies or Extracts of Correspondence and Documents relating to proposals for the annexation of Fiji to Great Britain (C.435, 1871).

Letter of Appointment, Goodenough-Layard Commission, and connected papers (C.983, 1874).

Report of Commodore Goodenough and Mr. Consul Layard on the offer of the Fiji Islands to the British Crown (C.1011, 1875).

Correspondence respecting the Cession of Fiji and the Provisional Arrangements for Administering the Government (C.1114, 1875).

Correspondence respecting the Colony of Fiji (C.1337, 1876).

Further Correspondence respecting the Colony of Fiji (C.1404, 1876).

V LATER PUBLICATIONS

The fifth group contains later publications of general interest, and includes:

ANDREWS, C. F. *India and the Pacific* (London, 1937).

ANDREWS, C. F. and PEARSON, W. W. *Report on Indian Indentured Labour in Fiji* (Delhi, 1916).

COOPER, H. S. *Coral Islands*, 2 vols. (London, 1880).

COULTER, J. W. *Fiji: Little India of the Pacific* (Chicago, 1942).

DES VOEUX, Sir WILLIAM, *My Colonial Service* (London, 1903); Sir William was a former Governor of Fiji.

FISON, L. *Tales from Old Fiji* (London, 1904).

HOWLETT, Lt. R. A. *The History of the Fiji Military Forces, 1939–1945* (London, 1948).

KING, A. G. *Islands Far Away* (London, 1920).

LEGGE, J. D. *Britain in Fiji, 1858–1880* (London, 1958).

LUKE, Sir HARRY. *From a South Seas Diary* (London, 1945). Sir Harry is a former Governor of Fiji.

MORRELL, W. P. *Britain and the Pacific Islands* (Oxford, 1960).

ROTH, C. K. *Fijian Way of Life* (Oxford, 1953); Mr. Roth served for many years in Fiji, where his last post was that of Secretary for Fijian Affairs.

SHEPHARD, Dr. C. Y. *The Sugar Industry of Fiji* (Fiji Council Paper No. 24 of 1944: H.M.S.O., London. Colonial No. 188, 1945).

The Colonial Sugar Refining Company Limited published at Sydney, in 1956, *South Pacific Enterprise*. The fourth chapter of this work refers to the sugar industry in Fiji.

Officially published in London, in 1946, was *Among those Present: The Official Story of the Pacific Islands at War*.

VI RECENT FIJI LEGISLATIVE COUNCIL PAPERS

The sixth group consists of certain official documents published in Fiji as Legislative Council Papers within the last few years:

No. 44 of 1956: *The Pattern of Fiji Economy: The National Income, 1950–53*, by Carleen O'Loughlin.

No. 1 of 1958: *Report on the Census of the Population, 1956*, by Norma McArthur.

No. 13 of 1959: *The Fijian People: Economic Problems and Prospects*, by O. H. K. Spate.

No. 26 of 1959: *Report of the Sugar Board of Inquiry, 1959*, by G. G. Honeyman, P. K. Bhindi, D. M. N. McFarlane, and K. K. T. Mara.

No. 1 of 1960: *Report of the Commission of Enquiry into the Natural Resources and Population Trends of the Colony of Fiji, 1959*, by Alan Burns, T. Y. Watson and A. T. Peacock.

No. 10 of 1960: *Report of the Commission of Inquiry into the Disturbances in Suva, December, 1959,* by A. G. Lowe.

No. 20 of 1961: *Report of the Fiji Sugar Inquiry Commission, 1961,* by Malcolm Trustram Eve, C. J. M. Bennett and I. S. Wheatley.

(The above list is not intended to be a bibliography. It is understood that a *Bibliography of Fiji, Tonga and Rotuma,* by P. A. Snow, will be published shortly by the Royal Anthropological Institute.)

INDEX

Wt. P65203   K5/62   S.O. Code No. 88–472*